Indian English Fiction in the New Millennium

Edited by

R.P. Pradhan

ATLANTIC

PUBLISHERS & DISTRIBUTORS (P) LTD

Published by
ATLANTIC
PUBLISHERS & DISTRIBUTORS (P) LTD

7/22, Ansari Road, Darya Ganj, New Delhi-110002
Phones : +91-11-40775252, 23273880, 23275880, 23280451
Fax : +91-11-23285873
Web : www.atlanticbooks.com
E-mail : orders@atlanticbooks.com

Branch Office
5, Nallathambi Street, Wallajah Road, Chennai-600002
Phones : +91-44-64611085, 32413319
E-mail : chennai@atlanticbooks.com

ISBN: 978-81-269-1928-4

Printed in India at Nice Printing Press, A-33/3A, Site-IV, Industrial Area, Sahibabad, Ghaziabad, U.P.

Dedicated to

My wife
Chandralekha

Acknowledgements

I take this opportunity to thank all those who have directly or indirectly helped me in bringing out this book in such a nice form. I am particularly grateful to all the contributors who have worked hard to present their well-researched papers. I am extremely thankful to Prof. R.N. Rai for his constant encouragement to complete the book. I am deeply indebted to my father, Dr. Ram Prasiddh Pradhan, former Reader & Head, Dept. of English, P.G. College, Ghazipur, who has been a source of great academic inspiration to me. My mother, Smt. Champa Rai's motivation enabled me to accomplish the task. I am grateful to her. I acknowledge with thanks the relentless cooperation of my wife, Chandralekha Rai whose constant encouragement helped me in the process of editing this book. I also appreciate the cooperation of my sons—Yash and Harsh. Special thanks are due to my younger brother, Ravi Prakash Pradhan and his wife Tanu Rai.

R.P. Pradhan

Preface

Indian English fiction in the first decade of the new millennium has won two prestigious Booker Prizes, one for *The Inheritance of Loss* and the other for *The White Tiger*. Other novels, since then, have also been making great strides in reflecting the spirit of the time.

The papers on *The Inheritance of Loss* present multi-dimensional studies. They elucidate contemporary issues of displacement, globalization, ethnicity, migration, marginality, and identity crisis in an effective manner. The sufferings of the people, not only during the period of colonialism, but also in the postcolonial era, have been brought to light. Aspects of immigration and diasporic sensibility refer to migrant situation in which the individual liberty is torn by the oppressive ideas of alienation and estrangement. Contentious issues such as conflict of religion, race and nationalism have been properly presented.

Kiran Desai has probed the psyche of two types of diasporas—first, the migrants of one nation to the other—and second, the migrants of one region to the other, inside their own nation. In the first case, immigrants from third world have gone in the city of New York with the dreams of leading better lives. In the second, people from different places of India have gone to Kalimpong, a small town at the foothills of north-eastern Himalayas. The Gorkhas who inhabit this land and consider it to be their homeland, have engaged themselves in ethnic violence, looting the settlers who do not belong to their communities. Displacement of the individuals from their homeland is, therefore, a prime issue of the novel. The pains of exile for a better and prosperous life in a postcolonial situation have been authentically portrayed. The lives of the cook, Panna Lal and his son, Biju in both the conditions prove illusory.

Papers on *The White Tiger* reveal two different visages of India—one poor, underdeveloped and corrupt—the other, the rich and more corrupt. India has been presented as two countries in one, "an India of Light and an India of Darkness". Balram Halwai, the protagonist, rises from the humble boy-servant in a cheap tea-stall, to a prosperous entrepreneur. He slits the throat of his benefactor and assumes his name Ashok Sharma. Balram's journey from darkness of village life to the light of economic success is utterly amoral, irrelevant, but unforgettable. The novel is an example of the art of magic realism. Under the influence of Marxism, the narrator throws light on the miserable condition of the rickshaw pullers. They remain away from the main areas of the city in order to evade the ugly picture of the country.

Aravind Adiga's *The Last Man in Tower* is a saga of social righteousness. It is a suspense-filled story of money and power, luxury and deprivation. The novel opens up the hearts and minds of the inhabitants of a great city. One of the most important characters of the novel is Masterji, known as Yogesh Murthy, who gives tuition to the children of colonizers. His life is tragic as his wife Purnima died of cancer, and daughter Sandhya had fallen from train. Now he is survived by only son, Gaurav who resides in South Mumbai.

The dominating theme of *Sea of Poppies* exposes "the white man's burden theory". It is a picture of nineteenth century India with its caste-system, feudalism, trade of opium, agricultural economy, migration, and the position of women. The plight of farmers in colonial India has been presented in a vivid manner. The East India Company acquires more and more lands for the growing of poppies and this destroys everyone who is connected with the land. The land can no longer feed those who till it. This suits the imperialists as they can recruit the 'girmitiyas' who are forced to quit their homes and hearths. They are shipped off to distant lands as labourers—to Fiji, to Trinidad and Tobago, and to other parts of West Indies.

Shashi Deshpande's *Ships That Pass* is a story of love and mystery. It is a piece of literature that communicates her moral vision. Stories of crime and mystery have always had a special appeal for her. She has always been keen to revisit a murder mystery. Her writings are inspired by her desire for social reform. In her opinion the core of all great literature is a moral vision. The novel deals with the collapse of family relationship. The wife dies in a mysterious condition and the husband is arrested for murder. Whether the death is a consequence of murder or suicide remains a puzzle and a mystery. A woman's self-realization and self-assertion is the major concern of the novel. Deshpande is a conscious artist with a commitment to humanitarian ideal. Like Jane Austen she chooses her own literary limitations. Her world is self-contained about the lives of ordinary women. Female psychology with a touch of feminist outlook has been aptly shown. The attainment of self-realization on the part of the heroine is her favourite theme. Her moral message rests on the merits of good conduct, good manners, sound reason, and marriage as an admirable social institution.

Remaking a Malgudi reviews the traces of postcolonialism which are still surviving in the 21st century. It illustrates how the mind of the writers, and the readers has shifted from political to economic, and from social to personal and emotional. The novelist expresses the anxiety of the helplessness and restlessness of the depressed. Nowhere in Indian literature is this phenomenon better articulated than in the novels written in English in this century. As far as the thematic pattern is concerned, these novels show a fine warp and woof of subaltern cosmopolitanism, modernity and development; science, reason, and colonization/decolonization see-saw narration; and subaltern histories, and alternative modernity, move from third world narration to first world narrative zest.

In *God's Little Soldier*, the writer points out the need to redefine the way faith is seen in our times. In the conflict between science and religion, the latter is looked upon as a crusade. The moment one starts looking upon faith as a crusade, one is entering dangerous territory. A religious victory means political hold leading to economic clout. Zia is like so many modern intelligent minds who willingly enter the fight for religious supremacy. They are highly ambitious and motivated in power game in the name of religion. The fanatic approach to religion is probably what disturbed Father Augustine and why he felt that there was no hope for Zia to be pulled back into the folds of faith. He thinks that he is devoting his life to God and doing His bidding, but there is no God at the end of the road Zia takes. He is lost on the way, and struggles with claustrophobic darkness.

The paper *Islamic Axe Effect* is an attempt to study various ambiguities and perceptional challenges the novel poses before the readers. Although written against the backdrop of the populist Euro-American *Islamophobia* with the project of essentialising and stereotyping Islam and Muslims through images and visuals, the novel, curiously enough, does not exhibit the cultural clash of two opposite civilizations, but rather makes an effort to engage with and problematize stereotypical representation of Muslims in mass media, which has led to a destructively powerful social epistemology of violence and hate. The paper also brings to the fore the fault lines of secularism in multicultural societies of the West.

In *The Palace of Illusions* there is illustration of the silent aspects of the *Mahabharata*. Issues like feminity, identity, and narrativity are critically explored through the lifelike characters of the *Mahabharata*. Namita Gokhale's novel *Shakuntala: The Play of Memory* is a titillating story of a woman who does not want to walk the path of subjugation laid before her by society. She rather chooses to create a new path for herself, of her own choice, irrespective of the norms and dictates of tradition and society whereupon she progresses with full confidence and strength. She rebels against the rules and codes of society that curb her individuality and right to live her life fully and freely. Shakuntala stands for all that is beautiful in Indian womanhood.

The book will be useful for the students of Indian English literature, particularly Indian English fiction, and researchers in these fields.

R.P. Pradhan

Contents

CHAPTER 1

Globalization, Displacement, Ethnicity and Identity Crisis in *The Inheritance of Loss*

Prakash Chandra Pradhan

I

In the postcolonial scenario, globalization has shortened the world further motivating new kind of entrepreneurship among the dreamy people to explore new possibilities for bettering their lives. Such dreamy madness is often deceptive because migration, that causes displacement, leads to their homelessness and identity crisis resulting often in ethnicity and insurgency. It is not that the migrants in an alien country face such paradoxical situations. Even people leaving their native places for other alien places in their own country are to face the traumatic experiences because of ethnic violence and insurgency. The new home that they establish in the place of migration does not bring any stability for them, nor do they lead a life of peace and security. Such situations dominate the narrative framework of Kiran Desai's Booker Prize winning novel *The Inheritance of Loss*. Jemubhai—the Judge, Sai, the cook, his son—Biju, Gyan, Lola, her sister—Noni and almost all the characters are displaced from their roots, and their identities are deceptive because their acquired existence is founded on loose grounds. In this perspective, it is important to refer to the views of Ania Loomba that critically point to such polarities: "Today's economics, politics, cultures and identities are all better described in terms of transnational networks, regional and international flows and the dissolution of geographic and cultural borders, paradigms which are familiar to postcolonial critics but which are now invoked to suggest a radical break with the narratives of colonization and anti-colonialism" (2007: 213). The hidden and deceptive agenda of the present day empire is to continuously expand its boundary without having any fixed borders. That is why Michael Hardt and Antonio Negri appropriately argue: "Empire manages hybrid identities, flexible hierarchies and plural exchanges through modulating networks of command. The distinct national colour of the imperial map of the world have merged and blended in the imperial global rainbow" (2000: XIII). They argue that contemporary Empire is imperial rather than being imperialist because it does not indulge in collaboration with other powerful nations to invade and subdue it like old powers did, but it rather focused on absorbing the weak nations into a new international framework. The motives of the new Empire are more dangerous because they are not conspicuous:

> ...global networks have not only changed the nature of repression but will in fact facilitate resistance by the global 'multitude' from diverse locations all over the world, resonates in disturbing ways with the claims of globalisation's neo-liberal advocates who argue that the global mobility of capital, industry, workers goods and consumers dissolves earlier hierarchies and inequities, democratises nations and the relations between nations, and creates new opportunities which percolate down in some form or another or every section of society. (216)

Globalization has of course brought many opportunities to some. It has not however lessened the miseries of many migrants as we understand by analyzing the characters in the novel *The Inheritance of Loss*. Kiran Desai, like many post-1980s novelists, believes that one of the most important functions of the novelist is to confront the world—"its authorities, its pieties and settled perceptions" (Andrew Teverson 2010: 12). The fictional artist is therefore to have a sharp pen to turn for "anti-establishmentarianism, iconoclasm and mulish disrespect" (Teverson 12). Desai therefore understands that in the Indian subcontinent the issue of identity is often very crucial. Ethnic origins are perceived as the racial/religious identity with which a person is born. This is therefore necessarily based on notions of continuity and ancestry. A person by belonging to a particular community partakes in its cultural heritage. In course of time, ethnic boundaries turn a particular community to rigid fundamentalists when they perceive that they are threatened economically and culturally by a different community and ethnicity. In a recent paper, Simran Chadha explains the root of ethnic violence perceptively: "As fundamentalist politics takes root, the rallying cry for self-determination finds recourse in violence often euphemized as militancy, insurgency and state suppression" (Jasbir Jain 2009: 182). This paper therefore tries to focus on the issues relating to globalization displacement, migration globalization, ethnicity and identity in the novel *The Inheritance of Loss.*

II

In the contemporary global situations, identity is not a fixed formation; it is constantly evolved due to the continuous displacement of individuals. Racism and ethnicity are also important in the context of home and homeland. Due to large-scale migration in the contemporary world order, identity has become a political issue. Kiran Desai's Booker Prize winning novel *The Inheritance of Loss* inquires into the human predicament of existence in the context of geo-political subjectivities and issues. In the postcolonial scenario during the 1980s, the individual's hopes, dreams and aspirations of leading a better life by getting opportunities through migration seem to be paradoxical. This human aspiration of having a better life is rather illusory. Such aspirations of undertaking journeys by a variety of characters in Desai's novel elucidate complexities of human situations in a new world of globalization and postcolonialism. It is pertinent to refer to the comments made by Tejinder Kaur in her paper on *The Inheritance of Loss* (*CR*, Vol. XVIII, No. 2) in the context of Diasporic journey of the characters of this novel:

> ...by portraying the craze and compulsions of Diasporic journey across the nations and from one region to another within the nation itself which

> entails various travails associated with it, Desai has shown her characters leading the lives of dislocation—physical, psychological, emotional, ancestral and political—both in the alien land and homeland and has also problematized the issues about home, homeland, diaspora and belongingness by treating these from multiple angles. (139)

Desai has explored two important situations by setting the novel in New York city, where innumerable immigrants from Third World countries have gone there with dreams of leading better lives; and at Kalimpong, a politically disturbed small town of the mid-1980s at the foothills of north-eastern Himalayas, where the GNLF (Gorkha National Liberation Front) has launched offensive against civilians who have settled there migrating from other parts of the nation, the displaced identities uprooted from their native homelands. The Gorkhas who live here and consider this part to be their homeland have engaged themselves in a kind of insurgency and ethnic violence looting the settlers who do not belong to their communities, and also terrorizing them.

Desai has probed the psyche of the two types of Diasporas. First, the migrants of one nation to the other (India to America) and the migrants of people of one region to the other (inside their own nation: from different places of India to Kalimpong). Displacement of the individuals from their homelands is therefore a prime issue in this novel. The author has explored the predicament of the individuals due to migration, exile, loss of roots and fluid identities. She therefore inquires into the issues relating to the ideas of home, displacement, ethnicity, identity, migration and globalization in her landmark novel. The pains of exile underlying the ambiguity for a better, prosperous life in a postcolonial/global situation have been authentically portrayed through the dimensions of beautiful situations imagined in the lives of the fictional characters.

It is important for us to consider the lives of the cook Panna Lal and his son Biju, whose native place is Uttar Pradesh. The father has left the sylvan countryside of his homeland for Kalimpong, the disturbed Gorkhaland for prosperity in his life whereas he sent Biju, his son to the dreamland of America for new opportunities and hopes. Probing their miseries in the text we understand that such dreams are entirely illusory, and imaginary "nothingness and fictionalities." The truth is something more complex which is obvious when we refer to the complex ending of the novel when Biju returns from America to his father at Kalimpong, shattering the life-long dreams of the cook:

> "Pitaji?" said the figure, all ruffles and colors. Kanchenjunga appeared above the parting clouds, as it did only very early in the morning during this season.
>
> "Biju?" whispered the cook—
>
> "Biju?" he yelled, demented—
>
> Sai looked out and saw two figures leaping at each other as the gate swung open.
>
> The fine peaks of the Kanchenjunga turned golden with the kind of luminous light that made you feel, if briefly, that truth was apparent. All you needed to do was to reach out and pluck it.

The truth is as high as the Kanchenjunga peak. It is therefore to be understood in the perspective of these displaced, Diasporic, ambiguously dreamy identities in the novel. By going back to the opening page of the novel we understood that Sai, while reading an article about giant squid in an old *National Geographic*, is observing Kanchenjunga's "wizard phosphorescence with a shiver" (*IL* 1). It is not obvious if she has been able to understand the whole truth about the complexities of life reflected in the far peak, Kanchenjunga:

> All day, the colors had been those of dusk, mist moving like a water creature across the great flanks of mountains possessed of ocean shadows and depths. Briefly visible above the vapor, Kanchenjunga was a far peak whittled out of ice, gathering the last of the light, a plume of snow blown high by the storms at its summit. (*IL* 1)

Life has been under the shadows of misty darkness and stormy disturbances despite apparently looking colourful and beautiful in our dreamy aspirations. This complexity of truth about life is also there in the dreams of the cook and his son, the marginalized poor fellows who left their beautiful, sylvan homeland for a stormy life of mists, not visible clearly.

Biju, the cook's son, was the only hope in his life for which he was working in such an old age for the judge at Kalimpong. He therefore expresses in agony: "Terrible... My bones ache so badly, my joints hurt—I may as well be dead. If not Biju..." (*IL* 3). Desai writes about Biju's displacements in a casual tone:

> Biju was his son in America. He worked in Don Pollo—or was it The Hot Tomato? Or Ali Baba's Fried Chicken? His father could not remember or understand or pronounce the names and Biju changed jobs so often, like a fugitive on the run—no papers. (*IL* 3)

Biju is an illegal migrant from the Third World country, India. He is the "fugitive on the run" because of "no papers", and living under perpetual fear of being deported due to the raids of the Immigration Authorities. He is therefore shifting from one job to the other without having any home in his dream land of America. In search of better job prospects and economic prosperity, he left his homeland for the alien land where he would create a "home away from home" by possessing a green card by marrying some materially prosperous "disabled and mentally retarded" green card holder diaspora, of course leading a fake double life. Biju was not the only illegal migrant in such untold miseries. Such is the fake life of many third world Diasporas living in New York City hoping for redemption by marrying the materially prosperous disabled green card holders. Desai vividly brings out the pangs of Diasporic sufferings because of displacement, homelessness and nostalgia for homeland in the transnational land of America. The Diasporic folk, the hopeless and helpless migrant labourers in America, are therefore constantly haunted by a sense of uprootedness, marginalization, identity crisis and cultural conflicts longing for their ideal homeland in their imagination. Salman Rushdie has rightly said that these migrants "struggle two cultures...fall between two stools" (1999: 15). Due to the recent phenomenon of globalization the Diasporic experience has new dimensions in a new economic and political order. That is why the remarks of Robert Cohen are quite appropriate. Although the Diasporic people live in the transnational land, in their imagination they "acknowledge that the old country—a nation often buried deep in language, religion, custom or folklore—always has some claim on their loyalty and emotions" (1997: IX).

Such memories disturb the migrants. As a result, they long for coming back to their native place, and return to their dreamland with fresh memories of homeland. However, that is not possible on the part of the illegal migrants. For a person like Mr. Kakkar, the owner of an Indian restaurant and travel agent, home is not a site for nostalgia. Even his father, who is living in India, persuades him not to come back to his native country, "a shitty place". Moreover Kakkar suggests Biju not to go back to India permanently, but to return to America after finishing his work there. He further tells him that India has no future, and on his return his relations would expect more money from him. Even there is chance of being robbed or hijacked. He also tells him that America is going to buy the whole world. Hence people in their own country are to work for some American company in their homeland. They would however be paid less than they are getting in America. It is therefore not justified to be so much emotional about the homeland. Kakkar's remarks reveal that America is going to be imperialist and neo-colonial ruler to control the whole world. Biju is however too sensitive to lead a fake life in America. Being too much concerned about his father he returns to India with a hope to take care of his father with his saved money. To his misfortune, he is traumatized after being robbed of all his belongings on his return to India. It was a period of terrorist violence and terror spread over by GNLF rebels in Kalimpong.

In the perspective of the pathos in the life of Biju and his father, it is significant to think over their situations after this robbery. The novel ends openly without elaborating their future existence. The question arises if both the father and the son would go back to their homeland in Uttar Pradesh to start their life afresh. It is thought provoking when both of them reconstruct the tranquillity of their original homeland. In the context of Diasporic longing of Biju in America, Desai brings out a living situation wherein we understand how sensitive Biju is:

> While Saeed was collecting shoes, Biju had been cultivating self-pity. Looking at a dead insect in the sack of Basmati that had come all the way from Dehra Dun, he almost wept in sorrow and marvel at its journey, which was tenderness for his own journey. In India almost nobody would be able to afford this rice, and you had to travel around the world to be able to eat such things where they were cheap enough that you could gobble them down without being rich; and when you got home to the place where they grew, you could not afford them anymore.
>
> "Stay there as long as you can," the cook had said. "Stay there. Make money. Don't come back here." (*IL* 191)

Biju's pathetic situation was however more terrible when he was robbed of all his belongings in the forest of Kalimpong:

> Biju sat there in terror of what he'd done, of being alone in the forest, and of the men coming after him again. He couldn't stop thinking of all that he'd bought and lost. Of the money he'd hidden under fake soles in his shoes. Of his wallet. Suddenly, he felt an old throbbing of the knee that he had hurt slipping Harish—Harry's floor. (*IL* 318)

In his distress he thought of America:

> Why had he left? Why had he left? He'd been a fool. He thought of Harish-Harry—"Go for a rest and then return." Mr Kakkar, the travel agent, who had warned him—"My friend, I am telling you, you are making a big mistake."

He thought of Saeed Saeed. (*IL* 318)

Biju's dreams are shattered into pieces. So was the situation of his father after Mutt, the judge's pet dog, was lost, and the cook could not find it despite his best efforts. The judge's anger crossed its limit, and he smacked over the cook's head with his slipper. When Sai, the orphaned granddaughter of the cook intervened, the cook said in utter helplessness and self-resentment:

> Let him. He wants to kill me. Let him kill me. Let him kill me. What is my life? It's nothing Better that it's gone. It's useless to everyone. It's useless to you and me. Kill me! May be that will give you satisfaction. It will give me satisfaction. Go on! (*IL* 320)

The judge was not relenting. He was rather demonic, and went on beating Panna Lal, his cook, quite mercilessly:

> The judge was beating with all the force of his sagging, puckering flesh, flecks of saliva flying from his slack muscled mouth, and his chin wobbled uncontrollably. Yet that arm, from which the flesh hung already dead, came down, bringing the slipper upon the cook's head. (*IL* 321)

Being hopeless, he could not think of his son, Biju, to protect him as he thought he was far away in America. He had his self pity: "The cook did not mention his son…he had none…he'd never one…it was just his hope writing to him…Biju was non-existent" (*IL* 321). The cruelty of the judge was unbearable for Sai who wept about the "filthy" that was going on. The suffering of the cook due to inhumanity of the judge reflects the oppressive measures and cruelty of the colonizers on the natives. The judge is a surrogate colonizer who is insensitive to the miseries of the marginalized folk. That is therefore Desai portrays the thoughts of the judge appropriately: "Give these people a bit and one could find oneself supporting the whole family.... If you let such people get an inch they'd take everything you had" (*IL* 264). Randeep Rana, in the context of the judge's subjugation to the cook has made the following justifiable comments:

> Desai artistically captures the plight and suffering of the marginalized sections and offers a significant awareness. The oppression of these marginalized, rampant in the Indian social system, is evident from the treatment meted out to the poor cook towards the end of the ordeal; in lieu of these services that he rendered for a paltry sum performing all kinds of daily chores, Jemubhai accuses Panna Lal for the disappearance of his dog, Mutt, showing how the British love pets more than the Indians. (*Remarkings*, Vol. II, No. 1, 2012: 54)

The tortures inflicted on Panna Lal reverberate the barbaric treatment of the White Masters to the Negro slaves. The 'colonial mind-set', 'inferiority complex' and 'slavery mentality' have been responsible for which the subaltern cannot speak, and raise his voice against the cruelty and inhumanity. Reflecting upon the situations of the cook in the mid-1980s, it can be argued that the poor, the subservient marginalized folk in India are not free in true sense of the term. Their economic situation makes them suffer perpetually in the hands of the callous rich people like the judge who represents the cruelty, inhumanity and oppression of the European colonizers.

III

In the novel, the locale of New York city is constantly related to the picaresque rural town of Kalimpong where the judge Jemubhai Patel has been living with his dog, Mutt, his cook, Panna Lal and his orphaned granddaughter, Sai, staring at his chess board and reflecting upon his past "burning the memory of his beginnings" (*IL* 61). Ethnic tension and racism are also the central issues in the novel. Jemubhai, the judge has a colonial mindset. He hates the Indians. When he started for Cambridge leaving his native place Piphit in Gujrat, he considered the love of his father and mother to be meaningless. He hates his wife though her dowry had financed his education in England. He had racial hatred towards the Indians: "He did not like his wife's face, searched for his hatred, found beauty, dismissed it. Once it had been a terrifying beckoning thing that had made his heart turn to water. An Indian girl could never be as beautiful as an English one" (*IL* 168). While Jemubhai was pursuing his education in England, he had seen how his friend was facing the "endless racial taunts of classmates" (*IL* 83). After returning from England as an ICS civil servant, Jemubhai hated his wife, his relations and also the Indians in general. He behaved like a colonial monster. Though an Indian he hated the Indians, their culture and emotions. He not only tortured his wife physically and mentally, but also harassed her sexually. In his place of posting in Bonda, he treats his wife in an undignified manner. He did not have any emotional bond with her. His sexual encounters with her are based on brutality, guided by animal impropriety. Referring to his sexual relationship with his wife, Desai writes: "The same blank look of a dog or monkey humping in the bazaar" (*IL* 172). He even hates 'tinkle-tonk' of her bangles and orders to remove them. Once finding her footprints on the toilet seat, he pushes her head in the bowl, which traumatizes her making her invalid. The judge, after a few days, sends his wife back to her father's house where she dies burning herself. It has already been discussed he has been too cruel to the cook, when the dog is not found. The insensitivity of the judge has been described satirically:

> In a place where people died without being given any attention. They died of T.B., hepatitis, leprosy, plain old fever.... And no jobs, no work nothing to it...this commotion over dog! Ha ha, ha. (*IL* 314)

The judge reflects about his own brutality: "Now Jemubhai wondered if he had killed his wife for the sake of false ideas. Stolen her dignity, shamed his family, shamed hers, turned her into the embodiment of their humiliation" (*IL* 308). His degradation is also obvious in his attitude towards his daughter: "He had condemned the girl to convent boarding schools, relieved when she reached a new height of uselessness and absurdity by eloping with a man who had grown-up in an orphanage" (*IL* 308). The judge, being brought up in colonial culture, has no sense of human dignity. He is a monster who is responsible for the death of his wife, misfortune of his daughter, and disgrace of his family. He is rather a curse to his own family and Indian culture. F.A. Inamdar therefore condemns the judge for his colonial temper in a recent paper:

> He also represents the class of bureaucrats who subserve the interest of the British during the colonial rule. In his craze for excellence in colonial rule, he ill-treats his wife, ignores his relatives, indulges in the cynical exercise of power and degrades himself as a human being. (*CR*, Vol. XVIII, No. 2: 142)

The judge can therefore be regarded as evil as the colonial British race who subjugated the Indian race.

Another important racial issue in the novel is related to the Gorkhaland movement spearheaded by GNLF activists. The Nepalese Gorkha and Lepocha local people in the hilly region protested against their negligence, poverty and illiteracy for decades. This movement reverberates in the veins of the novel throughout. Desai remarkably raises the contemporary ethnic violence in the foothills of Himalayas in North Bengal:

> There was a report of new dissatisfaction in the hills, gathering insurgency, men and guns. It was the India Nepalese this time fed up with being treated like the minority. They wanted their own country, or at least their own state in which to manage their own affairs. (*IL* 9)

The uprising in the hills affected the lives of the people of all sections. The Gorkha terrorists ransacked the judge's house Cho Oyu. The beautiful property of Lola and Nona was encroached by the locals who built a slum right in front of their house. Father Booty was to lose all his property because of want of proper documents. Worried over his father's safety, Biju, on his return to India from America, was robbed by the Gorkha terrorists. Such kind of ethnic violence derailed the lives of all communities in the hilly region. The Gorkha militancy is responsible for all these. Desai meticulously presents how the love between Sai and Gyan, her Mathematics tutor, a Gorkha, has also been swept away by the violent waves of the Gorkha ethnic identity movement. Gyan was persuaded by his Gorkha racial friends of his community to rise against the injustice done to their race by the rich people settled there in their homeland, migrating from other parts of the nation:

> It was masculine atmosphere and Gyan felt a moment of shame remembering his tea parties with Sai on the veranda, the cheese toast, queen cakes from the baker, and even worse the small warm space they inhabited together, the nursery talk. It was suddenly against the requirements against his adulthood. He voiced an adamant opinion that the Gorkha movement takes the harshest route possible. (*IL* 161)

The relationship between Sai and Gyan has finally smashed under the wheels of the monstrous racialism and ethnicity which are rather negative perspectives in the context of finer human love, emotions and feelings.

IV

In the perspective of the above discussion, it is obvious that Kiran Desai's *The Inheritance of Loss* is a landmark novel that elucidates the contemporary issues of displacement, globalization, ethnicity, migration, marginality and identity crisis effectively. The reference to colonial ills through the satirical portrayal of the demonic judge is rather nostalgic which highlights the sufferings of the people not only during the period of colonialism, but also thereafter in the postcolonial global perspectives. Kalpana Purohit's comments can be contextualized here appropriately: "This majestic novel which grasps every moment which holds out possibly of hope or betrayal illuminates the consequences of colonialism and global conflicts of religion race and nationality" (*ACR*, Vol. 10, No. 2: 118). She also rightly argues: "From the holistic point of view, Kiran Desai in her novel *The Inheritance of Loss* reveals the pangs of displacement, homelessness, unbelongingness and nostalgia for home and homeland suffered by most of the diaspora in the transnational land" (114). In this context, it is noteworthy to refer to the praise rained by Binnie Kirshenbaum:

> A nation's tragedies, great or small, are revealed through the hopes and dreams, the innocence and the arrogance, the love betrayal and all too human failings of a superbly realized cast of characters. Kiran Desai writes of postcolonial India of its poor as well as its privileged with a cold and warm heart. *The Inheritance of Loss* is exquisite novel mature, significant and a first rate read.... (2006: 2)

However, Kaustav Chakraborty dismisses Desai's novel as a manipulated "live/reality-shows" and the writer lacking the historical sense:

> Rather than documenting the demands of the subjugated class by analyzing the regional issues of ethnicity, cultural minority and socio-economic crisis, Kiran Desai becomes the spokesperson of the lot who represent the domineering elite class. In her pre-occupation to represent every "every contemporary international issue: globalization, economic inequality, fundamentalism and terrorist violence" (*New York Times*). Kiran Desai makes a mess of regional reality; by using a burning socio-political issue of Bengal. Desai must have aimed at projecting herself as the successor of realist/activist documenters like Mahesweta Devi but due to her lack of historical sense/sight she ends up as no better than the script writer of the manipulated "live/reality-shows." (*RC*, Vol. II, 2011: 67)

Considering the aesthetic merits of *The Inheritance of Loss*, these remarks are far from being true. A careful reading of the novel reveals that Desai is very critical of the elite characters portrayed in its framework. The satirical tone in the text paramounts to her sympathy with the marginalized sections of the society. She has however denounced ethnic violence, racial hatred, insurgency and terrorism. That is because she thinks such negative tacts are rather counter-productive, and they are rather anti-social methods which are detrimental to peaceful existence and overall socio-economic progress. In this context, it is pertinent to refer to her views that she expresses in an interview:

> In a world where power imbalance is still intact, a world of huge power imbalance so, sort of went back to my grandfather's time to try to trace his journey. And I wanted to talk about this huge class divide that exists across the world and it's very interesting to see how the same people are poor on both sides of world. I mean when you start drawing the lines between places, it's frightening how closely you can draw the lines. You think of people being poor in a very far away, but when you actually do the work of following the journey, poverty is so close to us. (Kiran Desai's interview CNN.Com)

Desai' views are significant because in today's globalization the economic inequity perpetuates rather than diminishes. To Ania Loomba, in the contemporary globalization, it is true that certain new sections have become prosperous due to wide availability of information and technology: "However the mobility of capital far from fostering ideological openness, has resulted in its own fundamentalism; which then catalyses others in reaction" (218). In this perspective, P. Sainath's remarks are worth quoting: "Market fundamentalism destroys more human lives than any other simply because it cuts across all national, cultural, geographic, religious and other boundaries.... Based on the premise that the market is the solution to all the problems of the human race, it is, too, a very religious fundamentalism" (2001: n.p. quoted in Loomba, 218). The inequities are therefore global rather than local. The neo-imperialism is perpetuating the division between the rich and the poor. However, this phenomenon is quite complex, and the New Empire's hidden agenda is no less dangerous than the past colonialism. The postcolonial societies are being rotten by the deceptive, scheming agenda of apparently progressive globalization. *The Inheritance of Loss* in a complex way probes into these issues in its aesthetic framework.

Abbreviations

ACR: *The Atlantic Critical Review*

CR: *The Commonwealth Review*

IL: *The Inheritance of Loss*

RC: *Research and Criticism*

WORKS CITED

Chadha, Simran. "Ethnic Nationalism and Pluralistic Space of the Nation in the Fiction of Michael Ondaatje". *Crossing Borders: Post 1980 Subcontinental Writing in English*, ed. Jasbir Jain. Jaipur: Rawat Publications, 2009.

Chakraborty, Kaustav. "Kiran Desai's Inheritance of "Documentation Mode" with Loss: Reconsidering the "Reality-show" in the 2006 Booker Prize-winning Novel". *Research and Crititicism*, New Series Vol. II, 2011, 63-69.

Cohen, Robert. *Global Diasporas: An Introduction*. UCI Press, 1997.

Desai, Kiran. *The Inheritance of Loss*. New Delhi: Penguin/Viking, 2006.

Hardt, M. and A., Negri. *Empire*. Cambridge, MA and London: Harvard University Press, 2000.

Inamdar, F.A. "Predominant Issues in Kiran Desai's *The Inheritance of Loss*". *The Commonwealth Review*, Vol. XVIII, No. 2. 141-50.

Kaur, Tejinder. "Problematizing Issues about Home, Homeland, Diaspora and Belongingness in Transnational and National Lands: A Study of Kiran Desai's *The Inheritance of Loss*". *The Commonwealth Review*, Vol. XVIII, No. 2. 129-140.

Kirshenbaum, Binnie. *Praise for Kiran Desai's Novel: The Inheritance of Loss*. New Delhi: Penguin Books Pvt. Ltd., 2006: 2.

Loomba, Ania. *Colonialism/Postcolonialism*, 2nd ed. London and New York: Routledge, 2007.

Purohit, Kalpana. "Impact of Space and Cultural Displacement in *The Inheritance of Loss*". *The Atlantic Critical Review*, Vol. 10, No. 2, 2011, 111-20.

Rana, Ranadeep. "Kiran Desai's *The Inheritace of Loss*: A Postcolonial Perspective". Remarking, Vol. 11, No. 2, 2012, 52-57.

Rushdie, Salman. *Imaginary Homelands*. London: Granta, 1999.

Teverson, Andrew. *Salman Rushdie*. New Delhi, Mumbai, Kolkata and Hyderabad: Viva Books, 2010.

CHAPTER 2

Aspects of Immigration and Diasporic Sensibility in Kiran Desai's *The Inheritance of Loss*

Nazneen Khan

Kiran Desai, a major writer of the Indian Diaspora and the winner of the prestigious Man Booker Prize, 2006 for her second novel, *The Inheritance of Loss* (2006), created literary history by becoming the youngest ever woman to win the prestigious prize at the age of thirty-five. In *The Inheritance of Loss*, Kiran Desai treats with tremendous insight, sensitivity, and often piercing irony, topical issues related to politics and terrorism as well as immigration, globalization, multiculturalism, colonial neurosis, identity-formation and subjectivity, and the nationalist, gender, cultural, ethnic and class differences that inform these processes. From a supremely funny and engaging novel in her joyous debut, *Hullabaloo in the Guava Orchard* (1998), Kiran Desai moved on to write *The Inheritance of Loss* where the prevailing mood is one of implacable bitterness and despair.

The Inheritance of Loss spans two continents and three generations. The story moves between New York and Kalimpong with scenes that contrast the life of illegal immigrants in New York and the growing unrest in Kalimpong. Full of pathos and tenderness, the novel presents its characters as ultimately frail human beings struggling in a search for love and happiness.

Kiran Desai, by setting her narrative in two parallel venues—New York of contemporary America and Kalimpong, a small Indian town at the foothills of Mount Kanchenjunga in the Himalayan ranges—has brought into relief the commonality of problems of the two hub of human insurgency, one tacit and the other vocal and strident. The aptness of the poem by Jorge Luis Borges, *The Boast of Quietness* which Kiran Desai has chosen as the epigraph for *The Inheritance of Loss* adds immeasurably to the impact of the depiction of immigrants in the narrative. These immigrants have lost their homelands and have lost their identity and cannot hope 'to arrive' anywhere:

> . . .
> They speak of homeland.
> My homeland is the rhythm of a guitar,
> a few portraits, an old sword,
> the willow grove's visible prayer as evening falls.
> Time is living me.
> . . .
> My name is someone and anyone.
> I walk slowly, like one who comes from
> So far away he doesn't expect to arrive.
>
> (Epigraph of *The Inheritance of Loss*)

Diaspora can be defined as a community of people who have settled outside their natal country but acknowledge their loyalties towards the ties with the country of their origin by voicing or implying a sense of co-ethnicity with the people of their country back home or as fellow members of their diaspora. Diaspora refers not only to geographical dispersal but also brings in the issues of identity, memory and home which such dispersal causes. There is no denying the fact that migration is a global phenomenon of the contemporary time. Crossing national boundaries has been a recurrent issue of the writers of postmodern literature. In his essay, "The Diaspora in Indian Culture", Amitav Ghosh, the noted writer, has rightly observed:

> The modern Indian diaspora...is not merely one of the most important demographic dislocations of modern times; it now represents important force in world-culture. (Ghosh 243)

Writers of the diaspora often rewrite history and frame new narratives of family, society and nation with a desire to revisit the past. It is here that memory and nostalgia play a very important role. The diasporic writer occupies a kind of space that is one of exile and cultural solitude. While immigrant and expatriate writing are more inclined towards the contemporary experience in the host society, diasporic works are more preoccupied with the idea of the deserted or imagined homeland. Kiran Desai, in *The Inheritance of Loss,* has skillfully blended immigrant and diasporic sensibilities.

Alienation and estrangement are inherent aspects of the migrant situation in which the individual's identity is torn between the old and new worlds of experience and "a major feature of post-colonial literature is the concern with placement and displacement" (Ashcroft 8). Set in 1980s of India, *The Inheritance of Loss* recounts an intensely absorbing story. At its centre, is a family of a retired judge and widower, Jemubhai Patel. In Kalimpong, a hill-station in the Himalayan foothills, the retired judge, who was once a student of the Cambridge University presently lives with his sixteen year-old orphaned granddaughter, Sai. In a painful incident Sai's parents died in an accident in Moscow when she was only five. Jemubhai lives in Cho Oyu, a large dilapidated house built by a Scotsman but now owned by him. Jemu lives in this house with his chatty cook, Nandu, whose only son, Biju, works as an illegal immigrant in a restaurant in New York to fulfil a materialistic longing for prosperity. It is really interesting that while the cook always thinks proudly of his son doing job in New York, a metropolis in America, the son more often sadly remembers his father and childhood days in a village in India. As for Sai, she passionately falls in love with her mathematics tutor, Gyan, a Nepali Gorkha. But then, Gyan gets involved in the violent Nepali insurgency for the autonomy of Gorkhaland and is forced to back out from his commitment to love. After undergoing an agonising experience in New York restaurants as a drab immigrant and embittered with the American dream of success, Biju eventually decides to return to his father in India with the humble dream of buying a taxi and a home of his own. Nonetheless, on his way home from Calcutta, somewhere between Siliguri and Kalimpong, the GNLF (Gorkha National Liberation Front) militants rob him off all his belongings—his savings, wallet, shoes, clothes and belts. Though Biju is united to his father at the end, the novel leaves a deep impact on the reader's mind.

Biju goes to America to fulfil his "lack", to be in the position of power. Fanon has also pointed out that, "the white man is not only the other but also the master, whether real or imaginary" (Fanon 138). Whiteness gets equated with power and he aspires to be *angrez ke tarah* (Desai 105). At the visa counter in the U.S. embassy Biju exclaims: "I'm civilized, sir, ready for the U.S., I'm civilized man" (Desai 99). But in U.S. Biju finds himself possessed of an awe of white people and realizes the snag of being in an alien culture which is not too kindly to him. In America, Biju has to eke out an existence as an undocumented worker. Stumbling from one low-paid restaurant job to another, living in seedy squalor with groups of other immigrant men, spurred by his father, Biju had come to America to realize the American dream, but the reality had something else in store for him. He recognizes that "it's a whole world of basement kitchens" and in exasperation dubs it, "they call this first world ??? *Ekdum bekaar*!" (Desai 300).

Poor and lonely in New York, Biju remembers his village. Lying on the basement shelf in sordid squalor he thinks of his village where he had lived with his grandmother:

> ...Biju and his grandmother with her sari tucked up...on diwali the holy man lit lamps and put them in the branches of the people tree and sent them down the river on rafts with marigolds—how beautiful the sight of those lights bobbing in that young dark...how peaceful our village is. How good the *roti* tastes there ...fresh *roti*, fresh butter, fresh milk. Still warm from buffalo.... (Desai 102-03)

In New York, Biju feels tormented by the crass commercialism, rampant racism and rapacious ruin perpetuated by the neo-colonial exploitation. He eventually comes back to India robbed of his belongings. All his NRI drams of "holding green cards and passports...*dollars me kamaenge, pum pum pum*" (Desai 298) comes to naught. However, the reader finds a quaint satisfaction in the union of father and son in the backdrop of a disturbed Kalimpong. At last Biju feels safe and at peace compared to his lonely life in New York as a waiter moving from one restaurant kitchen to another.

In *The Inheritance of Loss*, Kiran Desai has tried to capture what it means to live between the East and the West and what it means to be an immigrant. The story of *The Inheritance of Loss* predominantly moves between Kalimpong in India and New York in America. The thoughts, actions, aspirations, dreams, memories and sufferings of the two main protagonists, Jemubhai and Biju, as migrants in London and New York respectively, represent the expatriate consciousness. Jemubhai originally belongs to the famous Patel family in Gujarat. He was a brilliant student in school and got scholarship in college. After the completion of his graduation he went to England for higher education. Jemu's father did not have enough money for sending his son to England so he took loan at a high interest rate. In London, Jemu starts living in the house of one Mrs. Rice but feels acutely lonely and sad. In a completely alien West world, he feels hesitant and timid to go out and talk and deal with people comfortably. Jemu actually remains conscious of his brown colour, Indian accents, pronunciation and, above all, the despising as well as discriminatory racial looks of the whites. In Jemu, Kiran Desai has very precisely portrayed the suppressed psyche of a young Indian among the white Britishers:

> For the entire day nobody spoke to him at all, his throat jammed with words unuttered, his heart and mind turned into blunt aching things and elderly ladies, even the hapless—blue-haired, spotted, faces like collapsing pumpkins—moved over when he sat next to them in the bus...the young and beautiful were no kinder; the girls held their noses and giggled, "phew, he stinks of curry!". (Desai 39)

Biju migrates to New York for better opportunities, living standards and wealth. In Biju, Kiran Desai has portrayed the impact of the politics of globalization and postcolonialism on the economic structure of the once colonized nation. When an advertisement appears in the local paper for drudge staffs in America, Biju applies, goes through an interview in Kathmandu, Nepal, and finally gets selected. However, while standing in queue for visa processing at the U.S. embassy, he observes the pitiable conditions of other applicants and undergoes feelings of disgrace and humiliations:

> Standing there, feeling the enormous measure of just how despised he was, he would have to reply in a smart yet humble manner.... In this room it was a fact accepted by all that Indians were willing to undergo any kind of humiliation to get into the States. You could heap rubbish on their heads and yet they would be begging to come crawling.... (Desai 184)

In New York, Biju works in different restaurants as an illegal immigrant and thus encounters unhappy social as well as cultural experiences in the West:

> Biju joined a shifting population of men camping out near the fuse box, behind the boiler, in the cubby holes, and in odd-shaped corners that once were pantries, maid's room, laundry rooms, and storage rooms. (Desai 51-52)

Biju's failure is the failure of the downtrodden in the land of plenty. He goes to New York with all dreams of economic freedom and opportunities but his hopes are belied. Biju epitomizes the plight of the illegal immigrant who has no future in his own country and who must endure deplorable conditions if he is to work illegally in the United States. Always on the run from immigration and often cheated by his employers, Biju suffers furthermore because his father is so proud that his son is doing well in America, and writes to him constantly asking him to help the children of his equally poor friends to find work in the United States. Biju's friend, Saeed from Zanzibar, faces similar pressures from his family, though in his case these young men arrive at his place of work and apartment demanding help and a place to live. His avoidance of these people provides scenes of dark humour. In *The Inheritance of Loss*, Kiran Desai has not only portrayed how Americans look at the people from Third World countries but also how the immigrants view the Americans. Racial situations and reactions have come up at many places in the narrative. Biju has inherited feelings of nationality and hatred for the subjugating white world as such:

> This habit of hate had accompanied Biju, and he found that he possessed an awe of white people, who arguably had done India great harm, and a lack of generosity regarding almost everyone else, who had never done a single harmful thing to India. (Desai 77)

Other minor characters who, in some way, share the sense of "loss" alluded to in the title of the novel include Father Booty (a Swiss priest who runs an unlicensed dairy) and Uncle Potty. Everyone is in some way alienated by their environments and experiences, clinging onto aspects of the colonial past while not belonging entirely to the "old ways" and not filling in with the new.

In *The Inheritance of Loss,* Kiran Desai explores the pain of the immigrants, and the unfairness of a world in which one side travels to be a servant and the other side travels to be treated like a king. India is both the place that Biju, an Indian, dreams of escaping and where Father Booty, who is not an Indian, longs to remain. In New York, Biju is not immune to nostalgia. Longing is perhaps the only thing that the characters in this novel do best—they long for home, love and acceptance, but rarely achieve it. Sai and Gyan inherit the loss, referred to in the title, as do the cook and Biju.

What Kiran Desai ultimately highlights is not just individual experiences, but rather the relations of recognition between immigrants, exile, and foreigners who all grapple with the weight of history. Kiran Desai's realistic portrayal of life on two continents, diasporic on multiple levels, demonstrates a deep concern from the human condition.

WORKS CITED

Ashcroft, Bill. *The Empire Writes Back: Theory and Practice in Post-Colonial Literature*. London: Routledge, 1989.

Desai, Kiran. *The Inheritance of Loss*. London: Penguin Books, 2006.

Fanon, Frantz. *Black Skin, White Masks*. trans. Charles Lam Markmann. New York: Grove Press, 1967.

Ghosh, Amitav. *The Imam and the Indian: Prose Pieces*. Delhi: Ravi Dayal, 2002.

CHAPTER

3

Multi-Locations and Insurgency: A Study of Kiran Desai's *The Inheritance of Loss*

Shikha Singh

Undoubtedly, it is perplexing as well as a point of curiosity that many of the Indian women writers writing in English have consistently and often very categorically refused to be clubbed together as women writers have of and on disowned feminism or their feminist position. To name a mention may be made of Shashi Deshpande, Anita Desai, Arundhati Roy, Jhumpa Lahiri etc. Shashi Deshpande, one can say, as revealed in her works as well as her interviews present somewhat a moderate view of fine 'womanism' placing its origin in the factors or relatedness engulfing women's lives in India. She says, "My writings come out of a consciousness of the conflict between my idea of myself as a human being and the idea that society has of me as a woman" (Bhalla, x). Anita Desai tends to evade questions on her feminism so much that she even identifies the hypothetical writer as 'he'. Desai in an interview with Jasbir Jain says: "I think a writer simply has to be an observant person. If he is not, he is not going to write" (Jain, 9). Anita Desai objects to anyone who tries to categorise her as 'woman writer' and calls it an act which 'herd(s) together women writers as if in a ghetto...' (Desai, 54). Arundhati Roy says her novel *The God of Small Things* examines "the relationship between power and powerlessness" and believes that the inimical reactions were to the book's "explicit treatment of the role of untouchables in the country" (Palmer). Of course there are readers who find other issues and their delineations (of sexuality, gender, caste and women) more attractive. "Perhaps this kind of disowning of women issues/ feminism by these writers is because the concerned writer is not only placed in the category called women writer but also restricts her to write only about women as well as makes it their responsibility to uphold the continuities and traditions of India" (Lal, 151-52).

It would seem that despite the ambiguity about feminism, women's writing from India and India diaspora plays a prominent role in foregrounding themes that are international in their outreach and which significantly relates global feminism with constructions of gender identity in the nation. Women writers like the 'Others' have to negotiate and come to terms with the international themes; be it the diaspora writers negotiation of her identity, by redefining the concept of 'home'. In a specific history and location or be it terrorism or gender related and similar issues. The search for a psychological, social and material locations in which the self is at 'home' has been one of the primary goals of modern literature, particularly in South Asia. Women writers have addressed to and have offered a measure of growing innovations and conscious depictions of gendered viewpoint of most of the important issues, national as well as international: Globalization, economic inequality, partition politics, consequences of colonialism, conflicts of religion, race and nationalism, fundamentalism and terrorist violence and insurgency and related issues. Women writers have dexterously and with some insight not just portrayed these issues in their writings but have often questioned the gendering of these.

Traditionally the critic and the academia has been very dismissive to the literary writings by women as again the representation of the same by the male writers. It is very surprising to accept such reactions in the present scenario when there has been tremendous proliferation in serious writings and studies by women in almost all fields/disciplines not just literatures. Kiran Desai's *The Inheritance of Loss* is one such work which does not limit itself to the women related issues and feminism.

> This majestic novel of our busy grasping times illuminates the consequences of colonialism and global conflicts of race, religion and nationalism.

> Kiran Desai's new novel manages to explore, with intimacy and insight, just about every contemporary international issue: globalization, economic inequality, fundamentalism and terrorist violence. Despite being set in the mid-1980s, it seems the best kind of post 9/11 novel. (*New York Times*)
>
> *The Inheritance of Loss* is written with scintillating assurance and moral rigour. It moves from exotic charm into the darker territory even with horror, as lives are invaded, and nightmare banishes peace of mind for the little people swept up in the larger events which inevitably crush them.

Above are some of the earliest reactions to this spectacular book and one can very clearly understand the wide readerships it has gained. Not only this it amply curves down the narrow-mindedness of such proclamations which categorize women writings as 'feminist' and 'domestic'. Set in the 1980s, in the remote community of Kalimpong in the foothills of Himalayas, the book follows the fortunes of three characters (the Judge, the Cook and Sai) who spend their days alone together in a crumbling villa in the jungle, each logged in his or her own neurosis, obsessions, memories and fears.

The terrifying and terror filed scourge of insurgency has dramatically changed human lives, consciousness throughout the world. While the big powers such as the United States make the world heave and shake in their multipronged war against terrorism and terrorist, quieter battles are also being fought, sometimes in the small, neglected remote corners of this massive world, making a difference in their own way to the existing conditions. For example in Assam where insurgency seems to have found permanent lodgings, women writers have been very vocal in against this phenomenon in recent years. This is not at all surprising, considering that women and children always seem to bear the brunt of insurgency and counter insurgency the most (Borgohian, 121). Kiran Desai takes an unflinching look at the insurgency related issues in her novel *The Inheritance of Loss*. Even though the novel cannot be said to address primarily the issue of insurgency, yet I feel that Desai has dealt with the problem of militancy and politics of terrorism in a sustained and striking way nuanced with a key moral inside and rigour. My paper proposes to analysis, how Desai tackles the problem of violence in a state which has born that burnt of insurgency for many years.

The novel, *The Inheritance of Loss*, takes its historical background from the series of riots between 1986 and 1988.

> In Kalimpong, high in the North Eastern Himalayas where they lived—the retired judge and his cook Sai and Mutt—there was a report of a new dissatisfaction in the hills, gathering insurgency, men and guns. It was the Indian-Nepalese this time, fed up being treated like the minority in a place where they were a majority. They wanted their own country, or at least their own state, in which to manage their own affairs. Here, where India blurred into Bhutan and Sikkim, and the army did pull-ups and push-ups, maintaining their tanks with khaki pants, in case the Chinese grew hungry for more territory and Tibet, it has always been a messy map. The papers sounded resigned. A great amount of warring, betraying, battering had occurred: between Nepal, England, Tibet, India, Sikkim, Bhutan: Darjeeling stolen from here, Kalimpong plugged from there—despite, ah, despite the mist charging down like a dragon, dissolving, undoing, making ridiculous the drawing of borders. (9)

The riots were inspired by demands for a separate state, Gorakhaland, based on ethnic distinctions which eventually became so bitter that the town was virtually besieged, leading to state intervention. The novel opens with the retired judge, Mr. J.P. Patel, and his unwanted, orphaned granddaughter Sai, sitting on the illustrious veranda of their palatial, massive though crumbling and isolated house at the foot of Mt. Kanchenjunga having evening tea. Every now and then Sai looked up "up at Kanchenjunga, observed its wizard phosphorescence with a shiver." The mountain with all the lustre, grand and majestic look is not able to initiate solace in Sai but only a shiver. Kanchenjunga becomes a metaphor in the novel to express the power, the horrors of insurgency which effectively captures the sense of imminent doom to which humanity is destined, its morality, its suffering as well as the irrepressible desire to keep struggling and sustain in the face of every calamity. While the curmudgeonly judge broods over his chessboard, plagued with recollections of his wife he once cruelly drove away, his orphaned granddaughter begulies the long sleep hours with dreams of her earnest impoverished tutor, Gyan, from the slums down the hills. Meanwhile, the Cook pines for letters from his emigrated son, who unbeknownst to him, is facing the bitter side of the immigrant experience in New York City.

So wrap is each in his or her own concerns (dreams, memory) that nobody takes notice of the boys i.e., the insurgents creeping slowly but powerfully the arena of their peaceful existence, disrupting, overturning, destroying, intruding, into the private spaces of each and all. A former judge and a colonial decent is forced to suffer the indignity of serving tea to a gang of unschooled Gorkha boys who drink his wine and rob him of his guns; ('the judge found himself in kitchen where he had never been, not once...the world was upside down an absolutely anything could happen.'). Lives descend into chaos and at every end hierarchies are overturned. Each of them, the cook, Sai and the judge, avert even looking at each other avoiding the other's embarrassment, "it was an awful thing, the drowning of a proud man." The terror of insurgency is thus strikingly mediated through the private space invading and defiling it. Each of them is humiliated and mentally assaulted: even the poor cook inspite of the fact that he 'honed' the same lines repeated through the history of man moving towards civilized living, 'I am a poor man, spare me.' But no one is spared, the Gorkhas exposed their vulnerability, leave shouting their demant: 'Jai Gorkha...Gorkhaland for Gorkhas.'

Exposed and humiliated judge, desperate somehow to save his self respect, sends the cook to the police, only to face more of it. The police visit Cho Oyu, inspecting the downfall of wealth, finding not much to impress them, move on to scrutinize the cook's hut feeling comfortable to unleash their scorn on him; they overturned his bed exposing to the world the very few belongings in a heap.

> The police had exposed the cook's poverty, the fact that he was not looked after, that his dignity has no basis; they ruined the facade and threw it in his face. (18)

The police acts were in fact more humiliating and callous than the insurgents. The traumatic events at the hands of the authorized power holders have invaded and defiled the lives of so many not just the cook. What heightens his pathos is that even hard and humdrum kind of domesticated life to which he was subjected as well as his poor condition could not isolate him from this kind of terror. He had nothing or very little still he had 'lost' so much: "there was age in his temperament, his kettle, his cloths, his kitchen, his voice, his face, in the undisturbed dirt, the undisturbed settled smell of a life time of coking, smoke, and kerosene" (19). The so-called security personals are responsible for the unending nightmare passed on from generation to generation down the ages. The above episode is just a glimpse into the massive and colossal nature of official terror. The state and its repressive machinery is implicated for the devastation of so many lives. Sometimes or often official and authorized terrorism can be a bigger problem. As Sudhir Hindwan points out, "sometimes terrorism can be official or authorized." While the security personals are not to be exonerated, they have intervened the lives of the common, while the misguided boys have chosen the trail of blood. Without doubt the innocent are the victims by compulsion and inevitably the actions of the militants calls a reprisal, which in turn provokes further acts of reprisal. Where and when did it originate? When will it end? To these queries there can be no clear answers. There is a doomed breakdown of all logical explanations and sequentiality, an ironic confusion between one's understanding of what goes before and what comes after. While the insurgence madly pursue a cause belonging to some dim, ill-conceived blue print of the future people such as the Cook, Sai, Gyan grope to make some sense of the cause that has resulted in their too-real terror-filled present. Engrossed in one's petty concerns and the ordinary struggles of life one is oblivious to the bigger issues, to the currents of anger and bitter hatred swirling about the region one occupies until the crusade for a separate state of Gorkhaland literally invades their lives. Yet as the insurgency gathers pace and atrocity is heaped upon atrocity they each struggle to break out of their isolated world and force upon the bonds of affection and understanding that may ultimately save them and perhaps their homeland.

Through the fragmented reveries of the losses in the novel we can piece together the reasons for the turmoil that has gripped the lives of the characters cast in it. Insurgency and counter-insurgency turns the terrain of Kalimpong into a kind of an absurd existence where there are no clear explanations for the horrifying events darkening the lives of ordinary and all. There are stories within stories in the novel depicted in numerous vignettes. It gives a vivid and graphic account of a cross-section of Indian society in the characters like Jemubhai Patel, Sai, Cook, Pannalal who live in the north-east Indian town of Kalimpong. If there is something which is definitely common amongst all these characters is their inheritance of losses and in one way or the other have borne the burnt of insurgency. Sai was sent to the convent even before she was orphaned and after the death of her parents had no one to go to except her grandfather who accepts her but has no love for her. An unwanted intruder, Sai leads a lonely life in Cho Oyu amongst all old men—the judge, the Cook, etc. It was the flowering of a beautiful relationship with Gyan, her maths tutor which bring some kind of light to her shadowy existence which soon ends in the conflicts of views and interests and the boiling insurgency. Her westernized style lacking in Indian-ness and Gyan's misconceived passion for martyrdom for the sake of homeland that is Gorkhaland—puts the romantic love of the two to an end.

> Gyan was twenty and Sai sixteen, and at the beginning they had not paid much attention to the events on the hill side,... "We are stateless," they read. "It is better to die than live as slaves," "We are constitutionally tortured. Return our land from Bengal." Down the way, the slogans persisted and multiplied.... Quite suddenly, everyone was using the word insurgency. (126)

While the post-colonial texts harness the trauma of colonialism the pride of nationalism and the hope for a future, they also give the hint that all is not well in the post colony. The early writers observed indigenous societies moving from colonial corruption to post-colonial decadence. Simultaneously segments of population were marginalized by the native rulers. Post coloniality brought in its wake a new process of exclusion, whereby certain groups/classes dominated by ethnic groups, communities, races and classes, who therefore became disempowered, colonized and marginal (even) in the independent nations (Nayar, 69). The most obvious deviation from the ideal of one nation one state is the presence of minorities, especially ethnic minorities, which are clearly not members of the majority nation. Minorities are constituted along with the nation one offshoot of the zealous nation building process is negative responses to the minorities. Within the nation states ranging from state enforced cultural assimilation, to expulsion, persecution, violence and extermination. Mostly the process and policy of assimilation was state enforced and violence against minorities is always not right; it often occurred due to mob mobilization and violence. History has witnessed the responsibility of the nations state to some of the worst examples of violence against minorities who were not considered part of the nation: "Gyan remembered the stirring stories of when citizens had risen up in their millions and demanded that the British leave. There was the nobility of it, the daring of it, the glorious fire of it—'India for Indians. No taxation without representation....' If a nation had such a climax in its history, its heart, would it not hunger for it again?" Gyan is one of the minorities in the novel *The*

Inheritance of Loss. He belongs to a Nepali family which had migrated to India in the 1800s. His great grandfather had joined the Indian army. He wanted to leave everything behind and fly away to the land of plenty and opportunity like Biju—to America, Britain or Australia. He dreams of a comfortable well settled, secure life in any one of these lands along with Sai

> "Listen Momo" he said to a delighted Sai, "let's go to Australia." Fly away, bye-bye, ta-ta. Free from history. Free from family demands and the buildup debt of centuries. The patriotism was false, he suddenly felt as he marched. (157)

Gyan's is a story of a young man who never wanted to be part of the big questions of nation building and was literally pulled into the currents of insurgency and rebellion: "Without any effort at all, Gyan found himself sliding along the streets of Marwari merchants sitting cross legs on white mattress platform" (156). Gyan is one of the thousand who were just slided and floated into the movement with the weightiness of a "feeling of history being wrought, its wheel churning under him," (157) drawn into the surmounting insurgency. Gyan is an Indian citizen but he and his family are barely on the margins of the middle class. They are treated like minority in the area where they are actually numerically in the majority. A procession of men shouting Jai Gorkha showed him the sense of injustice which the Gorkhas felt: "then he shouted along with the crowed and the very mingling of his voice with largeness and lustiness seem to create, a relevancy, an affirmation he'd never felt before, and he was pulled back into the making of history," (157). In these larger issues Gyan almost forgot his relationship with Sai as well as dreams of an easy life in some foreign land. Just or unjust these dimly lighted causes have destroyed the lives of so many even though the words of the leaders articulating the problem of the Gorkha may seem to be quite convincing. To an extent, it can be acceptable that the negating of the other's affiliations and looking at people singularly leads to growth of insurgency as in the case of the birth of GNLF, Gorkha National Liberation Front. The GNLF demanded the recognition and status for

Indian Nepalese. But for this thousands of young men/women directly/indirectly were sacrificed as thing took a violent turn as the "incidence of horror grew", roads were deserted as there was curfew and Kalimpong was trapped in its own madness. The narrator resides various atrocities like the destroying of government property, etc. A movement which was initiated to create recognition and status for one group leads to the dividing of the others on the basis of state and region making more than obvious that belongingness is not country specific but region specific. The violence that has grown with the movement is not only due to the injustices suffered by the Gorkhas but also due to their ignorance. Neglect is reason enough for resentment but "a sense of encroachment, degradation and humiliation can be even easier to mobilize for rebellion and revolt" (Sen, 144).

Similar to anywhere else, insurgency in Assam is a congeries of myriad motives, factors, compulsions and hidden agendas. It is always not the outcome of the great 'cause'. Lately one thing which surfaces in the region is the growing infiltration of insurgency with criminality. As Sudhir Hindwan points out, 'there is also a growing nexus between terrorist and international organized crime network. Once very separate groups, with a healthy disrespect for each others activities, terrorism and organized crime gangs are now allied.' Desai has unfolded not only the undercurrents of this kind of criminalization through some of the minor characters and their experiences as Lola and Noni but has with some insight dealt into the nature of the social maladies afflicting the state and the nation bringing these problem alive by showing the human drama. The novel has subtly demonstrated the way public issues intrude upon the private and how shock waves created by terrorism are experienced. There is not a soul in the novel, even the minor characters like Father Booty who has not suffered the weathering breath of insurgency and counter insurgency as it has become almost inseparable from gross victimization, violation of privacy, brutality and loss of innocence. Forces unleashed by insurgency have engulfed the land and the lives, even the modest dreams of the people like

Sai, Gyan. Kiran Desai's reactions to the issues in *The Inheritance of Loss* is vivid, immediate and resonant. No matter how religiously one feels attached to these big questions, ultimately life is all about small happiness and modest dreams. The peaks of Kanchenjunga have turned golden with the luminous light, that made this truth of life very apparent to Sai. All she needs is to reach out and decide to embrace it. The concluding message of Sai to Gyan, "I will love u after all" is more than clear to all.

WORKS CITED

Bhalla, Amrita. ed. *Collected Stories of Shashi Deshpande,* Vol. 1, India, Penguin Books, 2003.

Borgohain, Pradipta. "Insurgency and Women Writers of Assam", in Malashri Lal, Sharmistha Panja and Sumanyu Satpathy, eds., *Signifying the Self: Women and Literature.* New Delhi: Macmillan India Ltd., 2004, pp. 121-35.

Desai, Anita. "Indian Women Writers", *The Eye of the Beholder: Indian Writing in English,* ed. Maggi Butcher, London: Commonwealth Institute, 1983.

Desai, Kiran. *The Inheritance of Loss,* Penguine Books, India, 2000.

Hindwan, Sudhir. "Combating Terrorism: Lessons From Around the World", in *Critical Practice Peace Initiatives*, Vol. 1, No. 111, May-June 1997.

Jain, Jasbir. *Stairways to the Attic: The Novels of Anita Desai,* Jaipur: Printwell Publishers, 1999.

Lal, Malashri. "Multilocality: International Themes in Women's Shorts Stories in English", in Malashri Lal, Sharmistha Panja and Sumanyu Satpathy, eds., *Signifying the Self: Women and Literature.* New Delhi: Macmillan India Ltd., 2004, pp. 150-65.

Nayar, Pramod K. *Postcolonial Literature: An Introduction.* New Delhi: Penguin Books, 2006.

Palmer, Judith. *Arundhati Roy: The God of Small Things,* 2003, Independent Digital (UK) Ltd. <www.independent.co.inuk>

Sen, Amartya. *Identity and Violence.* New Delhi: Penguin Books, 2006.

Singh, Smriti. "Texualizing Postcolonial India: Gita Hariharan's *Siege* and Kiran Desai's *The Inheritance of Loss*", *The Criterion: An International Journal in English,* Vol. 111, No. 11.

CHAPTER

4

Discourses on Nation and Nationalism: A Study of Kiran Desai's *The Inheritance of Loss*

Deepak Upadhyay

There is a general consensus among the liberal historians that the formative lessons of nationalism were acquired in the colonial classroom through the teachings of European histories. It is also believed that in its positive aspect nationalism ought to impart its citizen an understanding of the value of international concerns. Some of the thinkers postulated European nation as a universal phenomena, capable of accommodating the rest of the world. This universal ethnocentricism gave birth to colonialism resulting into contradiction between the universal claims of western nationalism and the oppositional development of cultural nationalism in the 'third world'. The awakening of national consciousness is believed to bring rationality and development to the nation state, yet the anti-colonial nationalism in some cases invokes energies which are against the state, for anti-colonial nationalism is born and acquires meaning in terms of struggle which is rooted in shared tradition and culture, and is indigenous. Thus, while some of the thinkers argue that nationness is the most universally legitimate value in modern political life, and at the same time paradoxically, competing or 'separatist appeals' for nationhood are generally condemned as signs of political illegitimacy. This short paper attempts to discuss Kiran Desai's *The Inheritance of Loss* in the light of above contentious issues that surround the concepts of nation and nationalism in contemporary literary theory.

Set against the Gorkha insurgency in North Eastern India in the 1980s, Desai's text juxtaposes three worlds—the colonial world of Judge Jemubhai Patel's youth, the postcolonial India of his retirement, which is also the world of his granddaughter Sai Mistry and her Nepali tutor, Gyan, and finally the globalized world of Biju, the cook's son, an illegal immigrant in U.S. Born in a poor Gujrati family in the remote village of Piphit, Jemubhai's academic brilliance excites the hopes of his father who dreams of sending him to England to train for the Indian Civil Service. To realize the dream, Jemubhai is married at the age of twenty to the daughter of a rich man who pays for the ICS dream. His years in Britain turn Jemubhai into a 'mimic man'—one who learns to act English but does not look English, nor is accepted as such. Jemubhai sees history through colonizer's eyes, learns to eat English food, dress in English clothes and speak with an English accent. Colonial discourse interpolates.

2

Colonial subjects by incorporating them in the system. His stay in England is a constant reminder of his colonised state. He has difficulty in finding lodgings in Cambridge, not surprisingly he is ridiculed by the whites, and at the same time he has been witness to the humiliation and torment of a fellow Indian at the hands of the whites. These memories haunt him all his life. The conflicts warp him and have a deeply damaging effect upon his sense of identity manifested in his use of the impersonal 'one' in referring to himself. Colonial ideology calls him and he begins to consider himself in terms of the racist ideology that informs how others see him. Identity assigns him a role and an identity that he is made to recognize as his own. Though Jemubhai experiences the pain of being represented by others, he also experiences pleasure through a new sense of self-worth derived by complicity with the colonizer. Having internalized colonial ideology, he believes he is participating in the 'progress' of 'civilization'. Jemubhai returns India with a deep disdain for all things Indian, including his wife. The more stubbornly she clings to her culture, silently refusing to learn the English language or adopt the English lifestyle, the more intensely her husband dislikes her. He finds her unfit to play the role of the wife of an Indian Civil Servant who owes allegiance to the British crown. She becomes a major embarrassment to him and he hides her from his official world. His final humiliation comes when she is unwittingly drawn to participate in a ladies' reception for the nationalist Nehru. He sends her back to her home where she delivers a daughter he never sees. She is forced to live on the resentful charity of a married sister, and when she dies of burns under suspicious circumstances, Jemubhai prefers to believe it was an accident.

The rejection of country is symbolized in the rejection of the wife. Jemubhai continues to live as a foreigner in his own country, preferring to forget his nationality. Not surprisingly, when he retires as a judge, he buys a colonial house in Kalimpong from a Scotsman returning home. The only other vestige of colonial glory left in his life is his cook, who helps him play out the pretence of being English. The cook, having internalized colonial discourse with its concomitant sense of inferiority, remains a faithful servant slaving in the antiquated kitchen of Cho Oyu to produce English meals and keep up old pretences. Besides, he believes that it was a comedown for him to be working for an Indian, when his father had served only white men. Like many old servants, he had regretted the Indianization of the ICS, too. He now lives in the hope that his only son Biju would make it in the new white man's land, America.

3

The judge remains cut off from anyone who might point out to him the "lie he had become" (306). He takes in his orphaned granddaughter Sai the hope that "an unacknowledged system of justice was beginning to erase his debts" (308). He is relieved to find that they are two of a kind, for she is as anglicized as he is, having spent most of her seven years in a convent.

The postcolonial world of Sai is circumscribed by the Anglophile Bengali sisters, Lola and Noni, Uncle Potty, an alcoholic from a once affluent Lucknow family and his friend Father Booty, a Swiss Jesuit priest who runs a dairy. Her only link with the native Nepali population is her tutor, Gyan. Her world is not sensitive to the mood of the other world around them, peopled by ethnic Indian-Nepalis.

The novel suggests not only the invention of national borders during the colonial period, but also the internal divisions that have come to the fore after the end of colonization. As Mc Leod rightly puts it

> ...Central to the idea of the nation are notions of collectivity and belonging, a mutual sense of community that a group of individual imagines. These feelings of community are the emotive foundations for the organization, administration and membership of the 'state', the political agency which enforces the social order of the nation. (69)

When the sense of collectivity and community is not shared by all the people living within the nation's territorial boundaries, it can stimulate division and conflict such as the Fiji-ethnic Indian conflict, the ongoing Sri Lanka—LTTE problem or the recent Malaysia-Hindraf confrontation.

Race and ethnicity have been used to set the 'norms and limits' of the nation's imagined community. In West Bengal, the Gorkhas form an ethnic group who feel its interests threatened by the Bengalis. They do not feel they have experienced liberation in the period of formal independence. Their growing sense of continued oppression within the national population culminated in the Gorkha insurgency of the 1980s. The movement announces its arrival with a series of strikes and processions. To Sai's world, it is merely the work of "hooligans in the bazaar". Then new posters appear in the market "referring to old discontents"—"We are stateless", "It is better to die than live as slaves" and "We are constitutionally tortured", "Return our land from Bengal" (126). "LIBERATION" is scrawled across the waterworks. The youth wing of the Gorkha National Liberation Front swears to fight to death for the formation of a homeland, Gorkhaland. Suddenly, there is talk of "insurgency" everywhere.

4

Noni recollects how the Nepalis were thrown out of Assam and Meghalaya and the king of Bhutan had branded them as illegal immigrants. She admits that the Nepalis have cause to be worried. They have been living in the region for several generations and are perhaps justified in demanding Nepali to be taught in schools. Lola's response highlights the internal divisions that have come to the fore in many nations after the end of the colonial period.

As Gyan watches GNLF protest march, stories of nationalism during India's struggle against the British flash through his mind: "India for Indians. No taxation without representation. No help for the wars. Not a man, not a rupee. British Raj Murdabad." A significant thought crosses his mind, "If a nation had such a climax in its history, its heart, would it not hunger for it again?" raising a question about the extent to which all Indians share a "deep horizontal comradeship" (158). Gyan hears fiery speeches not as stories told by others, but live. They are, however, not directed against the British, but against the Indian nation. Gorkha agitators draw attention to the discrimination and marginalization they have suffered in postcolonial India. Their loyal services to the nation have not only gone unrewarded, but they have been denied respect or recognition. The rhetoric continues as the speaker points out how the Nepali makes up eighty per cent of the population; there are ninety tea gardens but none is Nepali-owned. Their children are not taught Nepali in schools; they have no share in the job market.

This view is in sharp contrast to the perception of the sub-divisional officer who remarks to the judge and Sai, "They [the Nepali-Indians] are using the problems of Bhutan, Assam as an excuse to make trouble here. This country of ours is always being torn apart and it's sad for people like us, brought up with national feeling.... These anti-nationals have no respect for anything or anyone.... The whole economy is under threat" (225).

As the insurgency intensifies, there is a realization that there is some justification for it: "It did not come from nothing, even Lola knew, but from an old feeling of anger that couldn't be divorced from Kalimpong. It was a part of every breath. It was in the eyes that waited, attached themselves to you as you approached, rode on your back as you walked on, with a muttered remark you could not catch in the moment of passing" (241).

The colonial world of the judge and the postcolonial world of Kalimpong highlight certain facts. A subjugated society such as that of pre-independence India could, simultaneously, be a subjugating society too. The cook and the judge's wife are examples of subjugation on the basis of class and gender. Further, in postcolonial India, that subjugation could continue, and expand to include in its fold race and ethnicity.

5

Reading the newspapers, Sai reflects that the country appears to be coming apart at the seams with militant activity in Assam, Nagaland, Mizoram and the Punjab. The problematic relation between the nationalist elite and the masses is underscored by a further report that states that the government had unveiled its new financial plan after much secrecy and debate. It had seen fit to reduce taxes on condensed milk and ladies' undergarments, and raise them on wheat, rice and kerosene. As the GNLF bring life to a grinding halt and spread terror in the once-tranquil Himalayan foothills, there is an interrogation of the very concept of 'nation'—the "myth of the nation." A nation is not a natural phenomenon. "What was a country but the idea of it? She thought of India as a concept, a hope and a desire" (236).

The text introduces a third world through Biju—the illegal immigrant's U.S. Kiran Desai, in an interview, remarked "There is such a myth about States being a country where people find their dignity after leaving behind horribly undignified situations. They think of themselves as a benevolent nation. Nations operate like religions. They seduce themselves with their own image and seduce the rest with good advertising" (23). With deep irony, Desai constructs the exploited lives of the Mexicans, Indians, Pakistanis,

Colombians, Tunisians, Ecuadorians, Gambians and Guatemalans slaving in the kitchens of U.S. restaurants, "... perfectly first-world on top, perfectly third-world twenty-two steps below" (23). As he ekes a living, sleeping on dirty kitchens floors, weeping from the cold, saving money in an envelope in his shoes, Biju experiences conflicting emotions. "Biju couldn't help but feel a flash of anger at his father for sending him alone to this country, but he knew he would not have forgiven his father for not trying to send him either" (82). He feels increasingly alienated, despite switching to an Indian restaurant that did not serve beef. Looking down at the Hudson, he thinks that he "possessed no name at all for this black water. It was not his history" (268). Accosted by a Lithuanian Hare Krishna, he thinks, "What was India to these people? How many lived in the fake versions of their country, in fake versions of other people's countries? Did their lives feel as unreal to them as his own did to him?" (268). He begins to wonder if he continued in the U.S., would he too manufacture a fake version of himself, like his Gujarati restaurant owner Harish-Harry. He is filled with nostalgia for his community. He decides to return.

6

Biju has only a very vague idea of the trouble in his hometown. He is shocked to hear comments of his news agent: "They should kick the bastards back to Nepal, Bangladeshis to Bangladesh, Afghans to Afghanistan, all Muslims to Pakistan, Tibetans, and Bhutanese, why are they sitting in our county?" (228). Biju does not know how Father Booty, who had lived for forty-five years in India and had been working for the lot of the local farmers, is suddenly perceived as an "illegal immigrant", and a national threat, who must be forced to leave the country. When Biju returns India, to Kalimpong, to his "imagined community", he is treated as an alien by the GNLF boys who strip him of all his possessions and leave him "without his pride" (317). His father has just been hit by the realization that "instead of foreign enemies, instead of the Chinese, they had been preparing for, building their hatred against, they must fight their own people...." He also realized that "he was not wanted in Kalimpong and he did not belong" (278).

Yet the Sai-Gyan relationship appears to suggest that the nation as an ideal is not completely rejected. The westernized, upper class Sai, despite knowing that Gyan had unwittingly set the GNLF boys on Cho Oyu, still longs for him. Gyan, contemptuous of Sai's convent-educated way, regrets the break in their relationship, and hopes to make amends by finding and returning the missing Mutt.

Perhaps relationships can be built between different people who do not smother differences, nor set "norms and limits", that lead to marginalization and illiberal tendencies.

WORKS CITED

Desai, Kiran. *The Inheritance of Loss*. New Delhi: Penguin Books, 2006. References to the text are from this edition and have been indicated by page numbers in parentheses.

——. Interview with Bageshree S. *The Hindu*, February 6, 2007.

Gandhi, Leela. *Postcolonial Theory*. New Delhi: Oxford University Press, 1998.

Mc Leod, John. *Beginning Postcolonialism*. Manchester and New York: Manchester University Press, 2007.

CHAPTER

5

'Poverty' as 'Property' in Aravind Adiga's *The White Tiger*

Sudhir Kumar Arora

> 'Everyone!' he shouted. 'Take of your shirts! I've got to see a man's nipples before I give him a job!'
>
> He looked at my chest; he squeezed the nipples—slapped my butt—glared into my eyes—and then poked the stick against my thigh: 'Too thin! Fuck off!'
>
> 'Give me a chance, sir—my body is small but there's a lot of fight in it—I'll haul cement for you, I'll—'
>
> He swung his stick; it hit me on the left ear. I fell down, and others rushed to take my place.
>
> I sat on the ground, rubbed my ear, and watched the truck leave in a big cloud of dust. (55)

This is an excerpt from Aravind Adiga's novel *The White Tiger* which demonstrates how 'capital' buys 'labour' with its own choice of the best physique which may be strong enough to work continuously to produce the maximum output. Here, the buyer is a Sikh, a man with blue turban and the labourer is himself a commodity for sale. The buyer examines the commodity before investing. The Sikh also examines physical bodies of the labourers before hiring them or buying their labour. He rejects the hero Balram Halwai on the ground of his thin physical figure despite his continuous requests for hard work for him. This is a visual presentation or a live telecast of the scene of selling or rather marketing the Indian poverty in the Western market to tempt the Western buyers (readers) who enjoy themselves and take pride in being superior to the East which, for them, is simply 'Other'.

Thanks to Aravind Adiga who has done a good job of being a marketing agent who is applauded not only by the West for offering the proofs of India as 'other' but also by the East that swallows the exaggerating exhibition of poverty displayed in the name of "greater process of self-examination" which will transform the dark India into a shining India. No doubt, the Indian landscape is dotted with poverty, bribery, violence, corruption, unemployment and many other dark shades. Is the Western landscape free from the dark shades? Searching wounds for cure is tolerable and acceptable. To exaggerate them as permanent features is not permissible on any ground. This is what Adiga has done for the West without caring for the sentiments of the East. What matters is prize, not the way how it comes. He has skillfully made 'poverty' as his 'property' that makes him earn name and fame across the globe.

The rich cannot live without the poor. The rich always wish for their poverty otherwise who will work for them. As long as the monster capital is there, it will create a gulf and separate the two showing them the two different paths which never meet each other. The novel *The White Tiger* has realistically presented the gulf between the rich and the poor and also what attitude the rich people have towards the poor. The poor people are not better than mere commodities for the rich people who have right over them and consider them as their possessions. The hero is Balram Halwai who calls his life "the autobiography of a Half-baked Indian." He belongs to Laxmangarh which is an ideal village only in papers according to the norms set by the United Nations and other organizations. But the reality is different from what is shown in papers. This is a village where electricity, water, health consciousness, etc., are in papers only while the reality speaks a different story.

> Electricity poles—defunct
>
> Water tap—broken
>
> Children—too lean and short for their age, and with over-sized heads from which vivid eyes shine, like the guilty conscience of the government of India. (20)

This is the true picture of his village where poor people fail to give the proper food to their children. Here, most of the people are unemployed and have no courage to fight against the adverse circumstances. They move from village to the cities in search of employment in the over-packed buses and trains. Their condition is no better than animals. Human beings are seen everywhere in search of employments. They display themselves for selling their labour and unfortunately they do not get even work. Sample the excerpt that clearly reveals the poverty of the people who leave their village in order to earn money in the cities so that they may meet out the basic needs of the families:

> Each year, all the men in the village waited in a big group outside the tea shop. When the buses came, they got on—packing the inside, hanging from the railings, climbing onto the roofs—and went to Gaya; there they went to the station and rushed into the trains—packing the inside, hanging from the railings, climbing onto the roofs—and went to Delhi, Calcutta, and Dhanbad to find work. (26)

A poor man is simply a body without soul and this is his body which makes him earn money which is not sufficient even for his meeting the needs of the families. The novelist also believes that "The story of a poor man's life is written on his body, in a sharp pen" (27). Balram's father does not choose the traditional job (working in the field) which makes man indebted to the landlord. He finds better option in being the rickshaw-puller, but he never thinks to opt it for his son to whom he wants to educate so that he may not be treated like a donkey or the beast of burden.

> My whole life, I have been treated like a donkey. All I want is that one son of mine—at least one—should live like a man. (30)

Balram's father dreams of making his son a man—man with education and, so, sends him to school where he proves himself intelligent enough to get the title of "a white tiger" from the inspector who promises him to send him to a real school with a scholarship. But unfortunately the idea is not translated into action. A big loan is taken for the marriage of his cousin Reena from the Stork who wants all the members of the family to work for him. He works at tea shop where he gets the practical education and enriches himself through listening to other experiences. Adiga uses the river Ganga in the derogatory sense and finds that poverty is best seen along her banks where the human beings, who are better known as human spiders, are found working here and there. Mark the excerpt that displays the condition of the people who work at the places like tea-shop:

> Go to a tea shop anywhere along the Ganga, sir, and look at the men working in that tea shop-men, I say, but better to call them human spiders that go crawling in between and under the tables with rags in their hands, crushed humans in crushed uniforms, sluggish, unshaven, in their thirties or forties or fifties but still 'boys'. (51)

These poor men are tagged as 'boys' in spite of being a man. They pass their life while crushing their dreams. The villages are not the ideal villages or places for romance and peaceful living. Conditions have become bad to worse so much that most of the people remain unemployed and so become hopeless. They have to offer themselves as commodities for sale and even then they do not get any job. Sample the excerpt that displays the scene of tea shops where unemployed people are seen in the frustrated mood:

> Things are different in the Darkness. There, every morning, tens of thousands of young men sit in the tea shops, reading the newspaper, or lie on a charpoy humming a tune, or sit in their rooms talking to a photo of a film actress. They have no job to do today. They know they won't get any job today. They've given up the fight. (54)

Jobs are few; men are many. A truck passes through the way and takes five or six men leaving other men appealing to be taken for work. Balram calls these man "lucky bastards" because of the job that they have got for the day. The people wait for the truck in the hope that they will be employed and taken away to the cities for the work. But, all are not lucky enough to get the job and what remains there is simply 'waiting' and 'crying.'

> Every now and then a truck comes by, and all the men in the field rush to it with their hand outstretched, shouting, 'Take me! Take me!' (55)

People were crushed in the colonial period and after Independence, conditions have not yet improved. Rulers are changed; what is not changed is the poor people's exploitation and subjugation. In old days, caste and class mattered because of their multiplicity and so a kind of hierarchy was in order. After Independence, there are only two castes: "Men with Big Bellies, and men with Small Bellies" and "only two destinies: eat—or get eaten up" (64). The Capitalists develop the big bellies and become the eater while the poor remain poor with small bellies to be gobbled up. The novelist becomes a Marx in his attitude when he presents the case of 'have' and 'have not' and considers the rich responsible for making the poor poorer and hatching a conspiracy so that they may not raise their heads against them. What the rich want is the maximum output from labour out of minimum capital. The Stork who represents the rich class is a fine example of this category as he believes in the exploitation of the labour to the maximum. For him, a man is simply a commodity and so he should be fresh and strong if the maximum output is to be taken. Sample the excerpt that reveals the intention of the rich people who use the poor people as things and take 'good physique' as the priority for the purpose of long time service from them:

> Catch'em young, and you can keep 'em for life. A driver in his forties, you get, what, twenty years of service, then his eyes fail. This fellow will last thirty, thirty-five years. His teeth are solid, he's got his hair, he's in good shape. (66)

What is considered is not the man but his body that will serve for a long time. Man is poor but his body becomes rich for the rich who will exploit it for being richer. Poverty becomes the property for exploitation. Adiga also seems to be a capitalist who exploits the poor class in the name of "greater process of self-examination" while the reality is that the display of poverty makes him rich because the West buys from him this Indian commodity at a higher price along with a certificate of encouragement and appreciation in the form of Booker.

The poor people come out from the darkness to the cities to bring light in their lives but it remains only an illusion throughout their lives. In the cities, they are forced to lead a life of darkness even while living in the light. For the sake of stomach, they are being exploited continuously by the rich people who never show even sympathy to their wretchedness. The novelist attempts to present their pitiable and miserable condition when they have to live under the huge bridges and overpasses. Sample the excerpt:

> Thousands of people live on the sides of the road in Delhi. They have come from the Darkness too—you can tell by their thin bodies, filthy faces, by the animal-like way they live under the huge bridges and overpasses, making fires and washing and taking lice out of their hair while the cars roar past them. These homeless people are a particular problem for drivers. They never wait for a red light—simply dashing across the road on impulse. (119-20)

The novelist Adiga calls these poor people 'bastards' and his presentation is not the way of empathy but possesses the ingredient of snobbery and contempt. He sees the poor homeless people on the pavement and passes the remarks which certainly reveal his insensitiveness. He speaks through his hero Balram Halwai who poses to be uncomfortable while driving in the car as he continues to oscillate between the inside and the outside of the car in his thoughts. Mark the excerpt that reveals what Balram thinks of the poor people:

> These poor bastards had come from the Darkness to Delhi to find some light—but they were still in the darkness. Hundreds of them, there seemed to be, on either side of the traffic, and their life was entirely unaffected by the jam. Were they even aware that there was a jam? We were like two separate cities—

> inside and outside the dark egg. I knew I was in the right city. But my father, if he were alive, would be sitting on that pavement, cooking some rice gruel for dinner, and getting ready to lie down and sleep under a streetlamp, and I couldn't stop thinking of that and recognizing his features in some beggar out there. So I was in some way out of the car too, even while I was driving it. (138-39)

Balram must not forget that he is also one of these bastards. How can he forget that these poor people living in darkness give light to the rich people? For the rich people, they are not human beings but simply commodities which can be purchased at any time, at any cost and at any place. Poor human beings do not matter for them. What matters is their labour. The poor people do not get the proper amount of their labour. A driver is not a driver but a servant who is expected to perform all the activities which are commanded by their masters. These poor people who come to the city do not have roofs to live and so remain devoid of the basic amenities required for the minimum level of living. They prepare roofs for the rich but themselves remain roofless. They build "homes for the rich" but live "in tents covered with blue tarpaulin sheets" (260). They are forced to lead a life of deprivation and humiliation. Slavery is written large on their faces. They are no better than cockroaches which see others being crushed and do nothing because of their helplessness and hopelessness. Light becomes illusion for them. While remaining in the light, they live in the darkness.

It sounds ridiculous that animals are treated as human beings and human beings animals. The rich like to have puppies that are not only treated as human beings but also considered more valuable than the poor bastards. In the Stork's family there are two white Pomeranians that are being treated as human beings. Balram says: "There were two white Pomeranians in the house—Cuddles and Puddles. The rich expect their dogs to be treated like humans, you see—they expect their dogs to be pampered, and walked, and petted, and even washed" (78). When Balram takes them, the Nepali guard asks him not to "pull the chain so hard" because "they are worth more" (78) than he is. The rich make a show of love while the reality is that they exploit the poor and do not give what they deserve.

Balram Halwai is not destined to remain poor and, in the end, succeeds in getting the job of a chauffeur. Even Delhi is two cities—inside and outside. It is car that makes the people safe from pollution while the people on the footpath drink pollution and become the victim of diseases. Balram who drives the car feels himself that he is in the right city. But, at the subconscious level, he imagines his father if had been alive would have been "sitting on that pavement, cooking some rice gruel for dinner, and getting ready to lie and sleep under a streetlamp" (138). He cannot help himself in finding the features of his father in some beggar lying there. Poverty is itself a disease which does not allow a man to enter a mall. The cry: "Am I not a human being too?" (148) seems to be cry of every poor man.

Capital is responsible for creating economic disparities. A man with capital is a human being otherwise his life is no better than an animal. A poor man in sandal is not allowed to enter a mall simply because he is not a human being from capital's angle. Balram is a different man and knows the way to tackle such situation. He makes up his mind to enter the mall but as a driver he cannot enter and so takes a new white T-shirt, wears it and enters the mall through the rear entrance. But, as long as he is there, he tastes "the fugitive life" (152) because of fear of the guards in grey uniform.

Poverty itself becomes a rooster coop that forces a man to lead a life of slavery. But, Balram Halwai is not born to remain in the coop of poverty. He is a white tiger that cannot be confined in the coop and with the passage of time, he breaks it and becomes the master. He reflects over India's past and finds that "The greatest thing to come out of this country in the ten thousand years of its history is the Rooster Coop" (173). He clarifies this term to the Chinese Premier in the letter and states:

> Go to Old Delhi, behind the Jama Masjid, and look at the way they keep chickens there in the market. Hundreds of pale hens and brightly coloured roosters, stuffed tightly into wire-mesh cages, packed as tightly as worms in a belly, pecking each other and shitting on each other, jostling just for breathing space; the whole cage giving off a horrible stench—the stench of terrified, feathered flesh. On the wooden desk above this coop sits a grinning young butcher, showing off the flesh and organs of a recently chopped-up chicken, still oleaginous with a coating of dark blood. The roosters in the coop smell the blood from above. They see the organs of their brothers lying around them. They know they're next. Yet they do not rebel. They do not try to get out of the coop.
>
> The very same thing is done with human beings in this country. (173-74)

This is the picture of the poor people who remain silent and see each other being killed by the butcher capital. The political system also favours the rich people because of corruption at all levels. During election, promises are made to improve the condition of the villages and villagers but as soon as election is over, the direction of the wind changes. Mark the excerpt that reveals the reality of the election, promises and consequences:

> The election shows that the poor will not be ignored. The Darkness will not be silent. There is no water in our taps, and what do you people in Delhi give us? You give us mobile phones. Can a man drink a phone when he is thirsty? Women walk for miles every morning to find a bucket of clean. (269)

Politicians lure the poor people in the name of bringing light through electricity, water-taps and education in the area of darkness. The Great Socialist claims to be "the voice of the poor and the disenfranchised" (269) while the reality is that no one cares for the development of the village. The poor are left to their own miserable condition.

The democratic system also gives liberty to the judicial system in giving the decision in favour of the rich. Balram is to go to jail for the crime that has been committed by Pinky Madam. It seems that the rich masters have the absolute right over the body of their servants. "We have left the villages, but the masters still own us, body, soul, and arse" (170). The poor also dream like the rich but their dreams never clash. It is indeed a paradox that the poor wish to be rich and look like rich while the rich people who have become fat dream of losing weight and looking like the poor. Mark the excerpt that reveals the reality why the dreams of the rich and the poor do not clash:

> The dreams of the rich, and the dreams of the poor—they never overlap, do they?
>
> See, the poor dream all their lives of getting enough to eat and looking like the rich. And what do the rich dream of?
>
> Losing weight and looking like the poor. (225)

The master Mr. Ashok asks Balram Halwai to place an order for a commoners' food as he wishes to eat to his fill with satisfaction. How contradictory it is that the rich man appreciates the food eaten by a commoner while the commoner wishes to eat the delicious food taken by the high class rich men. Mark the excerpt that shows the kind of food taken by the two classes and what opinion they have for each other's food:

> 'Order for us, Balram. Order the commoners' food.'
>
> I ordered okra, cauliflower, radish, spinach, and dhal. Enough to feed a whole family, or one rich man.
>
> He ate and burped and ate some more.
>
> 'This food is fantastic. And just twenty-five rupees! You people eat so well!'
>
> When he was done, I ordered him a *lassi*, and when he took the first sip, he smiled. 'I like eating your kind of food!'

> I smiled and thought, *I like eating your kind of food too.* (238)

The rich people survive because there are poor people. If the poor people become rich, who will give value to the rich? The rich people, knowingly, wish that the poor people may remain poor so that they may exploit and get maximum output out of their labour. Capital and labour are the two identities that never meet at any point at par. Capital has its nature of dominance with its property to buy while labour has its nature of submission with the power to sell. The poor people work because, first of all, they have to satisfy the hunger of the stomach. They pass their lives while struggling for earning money for keeping the body and soul together. They do not have time to see, dream or think of beautiful things. They are not taught to develop the aesthetic sense. The poet Iqbal also thinks that the moment a man recognizes the beautiful, he cannot remain a slave. This aesthetic sense will make him do something that will release him from the fetters of slavery. Hence, this is the conspiracy of the capital to keep the poor away from education so that they may not be so innovative and freedom loving that they may ask for their encroached rights. Balram hints at the idea how the poor can make an end of their poverty.

> Iqbal, that great poet, was right. The moment you recognize what is beautiful in this world, you stop being a slave. To hell with the Naxals and their guns shipped from China. If you taught every poor boy how to paint, that would be the end of the rich in India. (276)

Balram does not wish to marry because he thinks that it will result in children. Today he works as an ass for his master and tomorrow his children will become asses for the rich. He states: "And all I would do, if I had children, was teach them to be asses like me, and carry rubble around for the rich" (193). Asses have no value of their own. They are valuable till they work. He sees the rich people who live in the palaces and big buildings while the poor people have no shelter to live and if they have any, the whole family live together. He recalls the scene of the villages where all the members sleep in one room where they do all activities right from worship to courtship leading to sex. He states: "In the villages there are no separate rooms so they just lie together at night and fuck like that" (190). There is nothing that can free the poor people from all kinds of oppression and exploitation. The novelist towards the end of the novel talks of a revolution that will free the poor people. The world history is simply a record of the clashes between the rich and the poor. He also talks of treating human beings as human beings and animals as animals. But, the reality is that poor people are treated as animals and even worse than animals. "Let animals live like animals; let humans live like humans. That's my whole philosophy" (276) though the novelist himself does not follow what he proposes as his philosophy. The hero who himself belongs to the poor family calls the poor people "bastards" and thinks that they will remain in the rooster coop of poverty.

No doubt, Adiga has presented the picture of 'poverty' which is true to some extent but to consider it as the whole truth will simply be a hoax. The image of poverty and poor people that he paints is incomplete and not authentic. It is painted from the brush of an outsider who has no knowledge of the village roots. He has presented India in such a way that after going through the novel it seems that India is not a place to live in. To present the dark shades of poverty in the name of "the greater process of self-examination" is not justifiable from any angle. What Adiga has done behind the scene is his sincere attempt to offer India as "other" and for this he has given the proofs in the form of presenting the exaggerated picture of poverty. No doubt, poverty is a disease that India suffers from. But, it is not yet cancerous as the novelist has shown. The white man has entered the soul of the white tiger that has taken the burden of betterment of the Indian society and for this he makes 'poverty' as his 'property' and displays it with his dual policy that satisfies India with the plea of transforming her into a better society and the West with the assurance of offering the proofs for selling India as 'other'. 'The Whiteman's burden' has become the white tiger's burden. Poverty, for him, is not a burden but a property that has brought him a name and fame in the form of Booker Prize. The marketing agent has got his commission. The Broker with Booker is satisfied for what he has done for India as well as for the West.

WORK CITED

Adiga, Aravind. *The White Tiger*, New Delhi: Harper Collins, 2008.

CHAPTER 6 A Review of Adiga's Shocked Sensibility in *The White Tiger*

R.P. Pradhan

A review of Adiga's shocked sensibility in his portrayal of India in *The White Tiger* seems inevitable in the present context. The novel has won the prestigious Booker Prize of 2008. The critics have praised it as the most revealing book in Indian English fiction in recent years. A few of them have also given adverse criticism. The situation being thus, it seems imperative to examine whether the novel is a work of art and creative imagination or whether it is the treatise of a commentator. It is further to be discovered whether the writer speaks the total truth about a vast country like India or whether his studies are limited to a particular region showing only partial truth.

The novel in its epistolary form is composed of a series of letters addressed to the Premier of China, Wen Jiabao. The writer of these letters is the protagonist Balram Halwai, the son of a rickshaw puller. He designates himself in the letter pad as *The White Tiger*. One day in school the inspector asked Balram about one of the rarest animals which comes along once in a generation. Balram answered "The White Tiger". From thence on he was called white tiger by his friends, fellows and teachers alike. He began to cherish a dream to be like that and grew ambitious day by day. However, his poor condition could not allow him to become so. He could not complete his school education. He had to work in a tea shop. He broke coal and wiped tables. A dropout in a village school Balram gathered necessary information from several persons. While working in the village tea shop he overheard from others that a driver might earn great amount of money. He took a lesson in driving and after that he went straight to Dhanbad to work in the house of the landlord of the village. The landlord had been forced to leave the village because of naxal threat and he became owner of coal mines in Dhanbad. Balram was engaged as a driver-cum-servant in the family of the landlord. The landlord's son Ashok picked him up and carried him to Delhi and made him his own driver. One day Balram murdered his wealthy master, plundered his money and ran away to Bangalore. He chose the city as his haven because in his opinion it was a city of strangers and outsiders where he could hide his crime and go unnoticed. He took a flat on rent and made a plan to run a taxi. Very soon he became an entrepreneur.

Balram, the protagonist of the novel, is anti-hero. He is a servant, a car driver, an entrepreneur and a murderer rolled into one. He is apparently the villain of the novel but the novelist has aroused the sympathy of the reader for the protagonist pointing to his poverty and deplorable condition. Balram is the mouthpiece of the novelist. Whatever the novelist wants to say, he puts in the mouth of Balram.

The story of the novel shifts from the protagonist's native place Laxmangarh to Dhanbad, again to Bodhgaya and then to Delhi and finally to Bangalore. It ranges over a period of five nights and four mornings. The protagonist writes as many as seven letters to the Chinese Premier on the eve of his state visit. He explains the reason behind his writing letters. It was announced by All India Radio that the Chinese Premier was expected to visit Bangalore to collect information about India's success in business. Balram felt that the Premier must be properly briefed before his arrival. He wanted to acquaint the Premier with "real" India through details of his own life, his own sufferings as a boy in the village tea shop, his own humiliation as a driver in Dhanbad and then in Delhi. In doing so the novel presents a picture of modern India.

Economic disparity in modern India becomes the conspicuous social issue in the novel. The division between the rich and the poor has been presented not only on the Indian level but also on a global scale. The novelist portrays a contrast between the Dark India and the Shining India. The resurgence of modern India from the colonial domination of the west is a great phenomenon in modern age. No doubt, the colonial rule of the past has created so many muddles and puddles in the country but they have been improved in modern age by the enlightened government of the country. The thick population of India does not allow a clean environment and removal of slums and other poor conditions in a quick and speedy manner. The novelist draws the picture of such darker side of India in a naked manner.

The beginning of the novel is full of the note of sarcasm:

> Apparently, Sir, you Chinese are far ahead of us in every respect, except that you don't have entrepreneurs. And our nation, though it has no drinking water, electricity, sewage system, public transportation, sense of hygiene, discipline, courtesy, or punctuality, does have entrepreneurs. (4)

Balram lives in the Dark India, a place where basic necessities are snatched by the capitalist class that live in light. Drivers in Delhi live in rotten basements where spider webs are in every corner. For Balram India is a place of brutal injustice and sordid corruption where the rich only "Feel Good" in "Shining India" and the poor are always tortured by the rich. Balram calls himself "half baked" because he could not complete his education, "Me and thousands of others in this county like me are half-baked because we were not allowed to complete our schooling" (10).

Again and again, Adiga criticizes Indian democratic ideal of equality that is being shattered by the inhuman relationship between master and servant. In India servants are expected to be dedicated like Hanuman but the masters are not governed by a single ideal of Lord Ram:

> At the end of the market is a tall, whitewashed, cone like tower, with black intertwining snakes painted on all its sides—the temple. Inside, you will find an image of a saffron-coloured creature, half man half monkey: this is Hanuman, everyone's favourite god in the Darkness. Do you know about Hanuman, Sir? He was the faithful servant of the god Rama, and we

> worship him in our temples because he is a shining example of how to serve your masters with absolute fidelity, love and devotion. These are the kinds of gods they have foisted on us, Mr. Jiabao. Understand, now, how hard it is for a man to win his freedom in India. (19)

Such sarcastic comments show why Adiga is being accused of belittling India in the eyes of the foreigners. The novelist does not like the lavish life of Indian masters at the cost of Indian servants. The master-servant relationship gives a shocking reflection:

> Every day millions wake up at dawn-stand in dirty, crowded buses-get off at their masters' posh houses—and then clean the floors, wash the dishes, weed the garden, feed their children, press their feet—all for a pittance. I will never envy the rich of America or England, Mr. Jiabao: they have no servants there. They cannot even begin to understand what a good life is. (176)

Balram is forced to take blame of the car accident committed by Pinky madam during her rash driving. He has to sign a paper that contains his confession of the crime. It illustrates the brutal cruelty of Indian masters. Balram is blamed for the elopement of Madam Pinky but it is not true. Like a faithful servant he has followed the instruction of Madam Pinky to drop her at the airport. On the other hand, Mr. Ashok is not at all ready to listen to any explanation from Balram. He blames him for ruining the reputation of his family.

It has been said that the soul of India lives in villages. The villagers are as pure as the water of Holy Ganga. However, the satirical portrayal of villages and villagers is true to some extent:

> Your Excellency, I am proud to inform you that Laxmangarh is your typical Indian village paradise, adequately supplied with electricity, running water, and working telephones; and that the children of my village, raised on a nutritious diet of meat, eggs,

> vegetables and lentils, will be found, when examined with tape measure and scales, to match up to the minimum height and weight standards set by the United Nations and other organizations whose treaties our Prime Minister has signed and whose forums he so regularly and pompously attends. Ha! ... Children—too lean and short for their age, and with oversized heads from which vivid eyes shine, like the guilty conscience of the government of India. (19-20)

The novel is remarkable for minute observation of Adiga from beginning to end. He portrays a contrast between the pathetic life of the poor in Delhi and the luxurious life of the rich entrepreneurs:

> The cars of the rich go like dark eggs down the roads of Delhi. Every now and then an egg will crack open—a woman's hand, dazzling with gold bangles, stretches out of an open window, flings an empty mineral water bottle onto the road—and then the window goes up, and the egg is resealed. (134)

For depicting the miserable condition of subalterns, the novelist uses the imagery of the Rooster coop:

> Go to old Delhi...and look at the way they keep chickens there in the market. Hundreds of pale hens and brightly coloured roosters, stuffed tightly into wire-mesh cages.... They see the organs of their brothers lying around them. They know they're next. Yet they do not rebel. They do not try to get out of the coop. The very same thing is done with human beings in this country. (173-74)

Further, Adiga challenges secular character of India. A Muslim has to change his name as Ram Persad and remain as Hindu because being a Muslim he cannot be employed in the Hindu family, "What a miserable life he's had, having to hide his religion, his name, just to get a job as a driver" (110).

The novelist bitterly criticizes Indian mentality of servitude:

> An Indian revolution? No, Sir, it won't happen. People in this country are still waiting for the war of their freedom to come from somewhere else—from the jungles, from the mountains, from China, from Pakistan. That will never happen. Every man must make his own Benaras. The book of your revolution sits in the pit of your belly, young Indian. Crap it out, and read. Instead of which, they're all sitting in front of colour TVs and watching cricket and shampoo advertisements. (304)

In brief, We may say that the portrayal of Adiga about India appears much exaggerated. Therefore, it haunts our mind whether so standard a novel has deviated from its fundamental fictional trait of being an artistic picture of life through the creative imagination of the writer or whether it becomes a direct and flat commentary and a sermon on Indian poverty. No doubt, Balram becomes the voice of the underclass and feels that such voice cannot be ignored for long. However, the class struggle and the murderous acts cannot offer solution for the removal of poverty.

WORK CITED

Adiga, Aravind. *The White Tiger*, New Delhi: Harper Collins, 2008.

CHAPTER 7

A Tale of Two Indias in *The White Tiger*

Amod Kumar Rai

Aravind Adiga is the last and the youngest in the series of Booker winners from India. He grabbed this award in 2008 for his phenomenal, to some critics "controversial", work *The White Tiger*. Adiga is presently residing in India but he has spent most of his time while studying and learning abroad in Australia, U.S. and U.K. His second and third novels are *Between the Assassinations* (2009) and *Last Man in Tower* (2011). An easily perceptible and recurrent theme of his novels are portrayal of two different dimensions of our country which co-exist with the aid of mercurial and selfish Indian psyche.

To begin with *Last Man in Tower* is justified as it came latest in the hands of readers. The novel starts with a methodical organised detailing of helpless lives of denizens in a metro city like Bombay. The locale is the Vishram society comprising of Tower A and Tower B, typical Mumbai blocks, which are in a state of depletion. Constant neglect and Monsoon lashings would make them collapse at any moment. In the ensemble of middle-class people, unprincipled gatekeeper, Marxist social worker, a precarious internet café owner and a religious but crooked secretary make the community of this society.

In the gallery of different characters, besides, Masterji or last Man, the protagonist, there are more than twenty residents, some more memorable than others committed social worker Georgina Rego, the insecure internet café owner Ibrahim Kudwa, cleaner Mary and strange secretary Ashwin Kuthari. Masterji alias Yogesh Murthy, an unyielding and unbending retired teacher and widower opposes the bait of extravagant money given to the resident to vacate the tower for the construction of new luxury apartments. This cash was offered by the villainous property dealer Dharman Shah through his left hand man Shanmugham. Shah had arrived in Mumbai with just a ten rupees note and his theatrical and remarkable rise has come with a cost. "Like a lizard I went up walls that were not mine to go up." His villainy illustrates what Balram has done in *The White Tiger*. Masterji's civility, decency, community living, sharing, etc. in the long series of efforts are defeated to the pragmatic society. All other except him fall in the trap of extravagant money. The money offered to both the tower—A and B has similar yet delaying response. Unable to comprehend the situation properly they discuss the offer before finally yielding to temptation for a brighter and more secure future. Their typical middle-class mindset surrenders to the bait of being upper class. Masterji's opposition to the rebuilding of the tower somehow represents nihilism, probably his disinterest not only in life but also indifference towards other needs, not a virtuous principle. He is obstinate just for the sake of being resistant, defiant and challenging. He is someone beyond material needs but also one oblivious of other's want of material possessions. His position and disposition raise certain pertinent questions—Is Mrs Puri wrong in desiring better surroundings for her 18 years old son Ramu, a victim of Down's syndrome? Is it too much of desire if secretary Kothari could see flamingoes so that "all the wasted decades in between fell away? Should the eccentricity of one man dissolve and crush the needs and desires of the rest? Still on the ethical grounds, with Masterji's stand, Adiga also questions the requisite and relevance of gentrification and the drive for slum clearance. The theme of "two Indias" runs in this way in the novel but it is more assertive in his magnum opus *The White Tiger*.

His novel *The White Tiger* portrays the life and character of one Balram Halwai who through his rise in life from a simple, non-existent and unremarkable person to an entrepreneur who believes and practices the power of money and blood spilling. The book unfolds two different visages of the country. One is identically poor, undeveloped and corrupt, the second is hidden, the rich and more corrupt. Adiga makes it very clear at the very outset of the novel, "that India is two countries in one: an India of Light and an India of Darkness" (14). Balram's journey from darkness of the village life to the light of entrepreneurial success is utterly amoral, brilliantly irreverent but altogether unforgettable. The writer aims with his writing to unveil the real picture of the country in the wake of post-Raj Indian democratic system and in his journey he discovers that hierarchy and corruption are the rule of the day. Well while it can't be rejected outrightly, yet at the same time it is utterly difficult to accept it wholly. As the majority in this country is still of those who are victim to this system and are far deprived from corrupt practices.

Adiga, nevertheless, appears to be more balanced and justified in his portrayal of the current day India. He explains his intention in an interview given to *The Times of India*, "when India is going through great changes and, with China, is likely to inherit the world from the West, it is important that writers like me try to highlight the brutal injustices of the society." He also hopes that the middle class Indians will also share his concern for the brutal injustices in the society and do something better than offering lip-service. This instance of the writer solicits our sympathy and support. But the jury of Booker award viewed something different while granting the award to this work. One of the member said "In many ways it was the perfect novel. The judges found the decision difficult because the shortlist contained such strong candidates. In the end *The White Tiger* prevailed because the judges felt that it shocked and entertained in equal measure. The novel undertakes the extraordinary difficult task of gaining and holding the reader's sympathy for a thoroughgoing villain. The book gains from dealing with pressing social issues and significant global development with astonishing humour."

It is now apt to review Adiga's work in the context of culture and society as it seems in the book. *The White Tiger* is an epistolary novel where the narrator has written a letter to Wen Jiabao about whose arrival the narrator had heard on All India Radio. He says if Jiabao is coming to visit India, he should meet entrepreneurs. He further says that no one else knew India better than him. He, who has been a driver in various lanes, a murderer and now an entrepreneur, can tell the best things about the place.

The narrator tells about himself, his tender childhood, his honest youth and his corrupt middle-age. He is a fugitive, as per the records of the police, and the poster stuck on the walls around; still he is a free man, free to use the right of franchise, free to have holiday trips, free to hold a business and free to be an entrepreneur. The narrator as a boy was named 'Munna' and later he was dubbed as "the white tiger" by a visiting Inspector to the school who found that Munna got a rare talent. Balram was afraid of lizards which let other boys at school tease him and this made him run back to his place. His father, Vikram Halwai, a brave man, who even revolted against his family business of being a 'Halwai' (a sweet maker) and preferred to run a rickshaw in his village Laxmangarh, went with the narrator in the school to smash the lizard in order to, at least, free his son of the world 'fear' and be bold. While the father tries to catch and crush the animal, the boy screams not to do so.

But the child is taken off the school to work as servant in tea-shop. All others in the family are also taken out of the school to work for the stork, the landlord, as it was he who provided the big loan taken for the lavish wedding of Balram's cousin sister. Here Balram's life is shattered as he is smashing coals, wiping tables and not studying. All other jealous craps of the class poke fun at him. His mother had died in his young age and now the father also dies of tuberculosis. After one month of the cremation of the father, Balram's brother Kishan is married. Later they packed off to Allahabad, with one of his cousin Dilip, where they manage to seek employment at a tea stall. Balram comes up with an urge for becoming a driver of cars and taxis. Here Kishan and Dilip inform him that the Grandmother Kusum has agreed to invest in his driving classes but of course, with a swear that he would sent the entire income to the family back in Laxmangarh; with a swear of 6,40,000 gods of course. He takes the training and proves to be a good student. As an award of being a good recipient, the old man who taught him, takes him to the brothel where for the first time he gets involved in the sexual activity. Then begins the search for a job and he goes on to knock from door to door endlessly, asking for the need of driver. Fortune smiles at him and finally he gets a driver's job at the house of Thakur Rama Deva, the Stork, one of the landlords in Laxmangarh. His son Ashok had recently returned from America and the Stock had bought a new Honda City for him here. Balram is complacent with his position of being the second driver even when the other driver Ram Bahadur never lets him touch the new Honda City. Balram is not only a driver but also a servant to the family where he adjusts himself well. He has to cook at times as he is a 'Halwai' by name, gives massage to the old stork in his legs and serves them honestly.

Ashok one day visits the servant's quarter and melting at the poor condition of the place, promises Balram another room. Balram tells that he is comfortable here as the place is like paradise for him and the masters are like parents. The pleased Ashok asks Balram to drive him to Laxmangarh, the birth-place of Ashok. Balram is at this, pleased with the thought he would look very important while driving his masters to Laxmangarh in front of all the villagers. Ashok and Pinky visit their big palaces and Balram goes to meet his own family. He noticed his cousin Kishan looked more lean and skeleton as he was earning the bread for the entire family, Balram's cunning granny Kusum orders him sweetly to marry a girl of her choice who would bring a handsome amount of dowry. Granny gets this idea from the neighbours. This makes Balram disinterested in the visit. The same fifty lifestyle and the atmosphere he had grown up into is distracting him. He leaves the place immediately. He takes his masters in car and drives past the family members who knew he would not return now. They are back to Dhanbad. While driving Balram bows before the gods in the temple which makes Ashok talk of respect of religion in the Indian culture and is pleased with Balram for doing so.

The fourth night in the letter gives the description of the narrator's further experiences in Delhi. As he is alone here in Bangalore while narrating the story, the narrator called himself a free man to buy as many chandeliers as he wants. He even buys some of them from a country-by. He points out over two usages of the chandelier; one that lizards run off the room and second that if one forgets something, a short but perpetual staring can certainly help in remembering the forgotten. Continuing the story, the narrator says that he was initially confused with the routes of Delhi as all seemed to be the same with no correct order. And for forgetting and being lost in the city routes he was scolded every time by Pinky Madam or by the Mongoose, the brother of Ashok but his master from America Ashok was always calm and quiet and was on Balram's side.

After sometimes Mukesh or the Mongoose returns to Dhanbad but with orders to Balram not to misuse or rather not to use any of the comforts of the A.C. car and suggest Ashok to be careful towards the driver whereas Ashok is extremely careless at this. Mukesh's departure relaxes Pinky and her dresses grow shorter which certainly arouse the excitement among the driver but he avoids the sight of her as he respects her. Here we find the clash of Arcadian values with that of the modern.

Pinky and Ashok had not much good left in their marriage. Ashok is a soft and humble man, unconscious of any evil around him. Pinky requests him to return to America but he has a clear idea of not going back as he has the family here and the comfort of having people at service. This again becomes a reason for the tussle between the two. Although Ashok is a good husband and does everything to please her every time. On their marriage anniversary, Ashok makes Balram look like a Maharaja with a red turban and dark cooling glasses and serving them Pizza in his costume. She laughs but the environment soon grows solemn as they again quarrel and Ashok even slaps Pinky. Later he takes her for a ride to the Connaught Place and both return drunk. On the way back to home, Pinky orders Balram to get down and walk home as she wanted to drive the car on her own. Balram obeys and she drives away leaving Balram to drag himself his way back home. But she returns and takes Balram back into the car although driving herself, that too recklessly. Her drunken driving kills a young child on the road, but without any delay, Balram performs his duty of making Pinky Madam sit back and driving the car himself. Pinky shrieks to help the deceased to the hospital but Ashok chokes her mouth with his hand. Balram washes the car and assures the master that he would be mum about the matter. Ashok pays sincere thanks and Balram puffs up with the thought of saving his master from shame and disgust. When Mukesh returns, he also polishes his speech and thanks him. He then makes him sign a paper which said that Balram was driving recklessly which paved way to the killing of the child on the road. Balram is on his nerves when he comes to know of being imprisoned for committing the crime he had not committed. He is panicked with the thoughts of jail-of its appearance and the tenure he would be in. Meanwhile, he is again summoned in the apartment. But this time no one had any interest in his arrival. He kept waiting when Pinky comes out and shrieks upon the family to at least inform Balram of the happiness in Pinky. And here is the fact disclosed upon him that his help is not required as no one had witnessed the accident. This is a news which lets Balram breathe an air of comfort. The tale moves forward with the details of a 'sweet, innocent, village fool' being corrupted into a citified fellow full of 'debauchery, depravity and wickedness'. The driver is being corrupted day by day and he blames it all to Ashok saying that:

> He returned from America an innocent man but life in Delhi corrupted him and once the master of the Honda City becomes corrupted, how can the driver stay innocent?

Here again we find the binary opposition of Orientalism and Occidentalism. America is being taken as a 'promised land', an 'el-dorado' or a heaven in comparison to the indigenous East. Here we are reminded of the views of Edward Said, when he writes that the people with western mind set find: "The oriental is irrational, depraved (fallen), childlike, 'different'...the European is rational, virtuous, mature, normal." On the statement that "Once the master of the Honda City becomes corrupted, how can the driver stay innocent" (*The White Tiger*, 197)? We are reminded of the statement of Marx with reference to the base and the superstructure:

> In the social production of their life, men enter into definite relations that are indispensable and independent of their will, relations of production which correspond a definite stage of development of their material forces. The sum total of these relation of production constitutes the economics structure of a society, the real foundation, on which rises a definite form of social consciousness. The mode of production of material life condition the social, political and intellectual life process in general. It is not the consciousness of men that determines their being, but on the contrary, their social being that determines consciousness. (Marx, cited by Susan R. Skand in *A Dictionary of Cultural and Critical Theory*, p. 48)

Then came the day when it actually happened. On a rainy day, while driving Ashok from one Bank to another and then to Sheraton Hotel. Balram could see that the red bag is heavy with a weight of seven hundred thousand rupees and the careless Ashok busy with his cell phone. A rainy day and a vacant road acts as a golden opportunity for an insolent driver. His conscience pricks him but his greed reigns over it. He rams a broken glass bottle of liquor into Ashok's skull and then stamps his knees on Ashok's chest. He does not want to take any chance so he even pierces Ashok's neck to lose him completely. The blood is draining from the entire body. He throws the body in the bushes, changes his clothes and rushes all the way to the station. But keeps thinking whether to pick-up his nephew Dharam from the hotel. If he does not to do so, Police would harass the young boy and if he does, it might be that the police caught him in the hotel. Yet he decides to go back to the hotel and save the young Dharam from the would-be-torture of the police. He picks up the boy from the hotel and tells him that they are heading towards South for a holiday. He decides to transfer himself from train to train so that no one can trace him immediately. He is a fugitive now running from one place to another.

While in Hyderabad, a short incident occurs. The police has released Balram's poster. At the station in Hyderabad, when his poster claiming him the murderer is stuck, it is stapled by another poster within seconds which consists of the photographs of two terrorists. An illiterate man enquires about the posters from Balram without recognizing him. Balram calls his poster of a policeman who had arrested the two terrorists. The illiterate man is pleased to know this without recognizing Balram's face in the poster. Balram likes the illiterate man's simplicity and thinks that his father would also have been made fun of by the people because of his being a village-man. The illiterate man says the face in the poster matched his own. At this Balram feels that his is the face which resembles half the men in India. Balram settles in Bangalore and after thinking a lot he plans for the entrepreneurship. He plans to rent cars and to pick up and drop off the people of working class at their desired destination. The reply arrives in negative from every corner until Balram comes up with a plan to bribe the police and disrupt all other taxi-services the working class in Bangalore had. Plan works and provides him a smooth business and Balram is now in the vortex of success. He has a new name now—Ashok Sharma.

He is successful in his business that there held an incident where one of his drives Mohd. Asif hit a boy on bicycle to death, with his Qualis. Asif informs this to Balram, now Ashok Sharma. Ashok orders him to call Police. As he reaches the spot, he tells Asif to take Qualis away and drop the passengers, those are girls, their home, as it is quite late in the night. He talks to the police and the brother of the deceased that he is the owner of the vehicle and suggests that they should settle the dispute at the police station and not on the road. And this was actually an instance of a real chivalry reigning in him. In the police station, the Assistant commissioner of Police, whose palm was greased at times by Ashok, makes the brother of the deceased go back without lodging an F.I.R.

It is an incident giving the surrealistic picture of Indian Police that although stands on the motif—"Paritranaya Sadhunam Vinashaya Cha Dushkritam" for the protection of the gentle folks and for the eradication of evil doers, many such a deeds that check the veracity of the profession and the intention and this is how the world runs. Ashok Sharma promises him his share and leaves victoriously. Later he does the ample humanity to handover some money to the family of the deceased on his own conscience's voice.

An easy inference could be made that Aravind Adiga aims at selling the dirty India to the Western world. He is very cleverly raising the issue of Indian poverty, orthodoxy, child labour and the rivalry among the petty workers. He also focuses at the disdain of the city-born for the Arcadian folk, with the purpose of sheer publicity. I understand that there may be other montage and narrative devices beyond these for making it a narrative of 'surrealistic' social portrayal.

At the end of the discussion, it would be appropriate to stress that Indian literature is certainly the one most resistant to generalizations. Given the high incidence of bilingualism and the high quality of translations from the Indian languages into English, the rubric of Indian English Literature can also now include literature in translation. At the same time, it is becoming increasingly difficult to determine who the Indian writer is, live and work abroad—some are no longer even Indian citizens.... "The domains of Indian English Literature increasingly shifts its boundaries to accommodate global mobility, which has already rendered the 1960s questions about authenticity and relevance rather archaic".

Arvind Adiga's much hyped *The White Tiger* (2008), the Booker Awardee, is the fine example of what Darwadkars' describes as—"the most disorderly of contemporary Indian literature." One more example that is resistant to generalization is Vikash Swarups Q and A. It is not an accident that both not only make use of politics but of poetics of culture and poverty. Some of the writers and actors are critical of

Danny Boyle's Multy-Oscar film *Slumdog Millionaire* based on Swaroop's novel. It is considered a humiliation of the novel. It is claimed that the film does not have even ten per cent of the actual novel in it. The major charge levelled against it is that it exposes Indian poverty to the Western world. Was not this poverty exhibited when some of the rural and Dalit stories and novels were translated into English and specially when the caste based scholarships were a 'reserved' by the American institutions? This is the second phase in which these novelists have lived and worked for a number of years and enjoy more freedom in executing the political agenda also. It would be more interesting to study how "caste conditions Indian fictions and semiotics of the traditional monopolizers of culture determines its content. Adiga, Kiran Desai, Chetan Bhagat and several others belong to this category, albeit it is becoming increasingly difficult to determine who the "Indian" writer is".

This issue has entered the arena of the central Sahitya Akademi. It is reported that Indian authors in English, who are Booker Award winners, are neglected by the Sahitya Akademi. Of course, Kiran Desai's *The Inheritance of Loss* and Arundhati Roy's *The God of Small Things* are intertextually and culturally rich novels. From the literary perspective they are the best 'postmodern' Indian novels, although overshadowed by Marquez, Gunter, and Rushdie. But Adiga's *The White Tiger* meant to entertain the SWZ (Special Economic Zone) readership in the West. Ironically, it can be called an "Indian Tourist" fiction which parades poverty in the international market for the political and financial gain, but subtly incorporates the cultural politics of Bollywood. It is interesting to comment on Adiga's novel as an Indian cultural product which does not subvert European novel but imitates its structures. Why do the elitist comprador upper caste Indian novelists have never resisted the Western aesthetics of fiction?

Arvind Adiga was born in Chennai. He was educated at Magdalen College, Oxford and Columbia University in New York, where he studied English Literature. He is a journalist in English and the journalistic structure of his *Between the Assassinations* (2008) support his attitude. Such an alienated

definition of culture. The American anthropologists defined it as follows:

> Culture consists of patterns, explicit and implicit, of and for behavior acquired and transmitted by symbols, constituting the distinctive achievement of human groups, including their embodiments in artifacts; the essential core of culture consists of traditional (i.e. historically derived and selected) ideas and especially their attached values; culture systems may, on the one hand, be considered as product of action, and on other as conditioning elements of further action. (47)

Since this is a saga of two families, rich and poor, the explicit and implicit patterns of cultural diversity in India, especially in Laxmangarh, in Delhi and in Bangalore, is totally ignored the linguistic diversity of these three settings is neither distinguished nor allowed to enter the text. The patterns of "behaviour acquired and transmitted by symbols" can be traced to the nicknames given to various characters. The essential core of characters in different parts of India consists of traditional historically derived ideas, and especially their attached values. But in this respect Adiga remains at a superficial level. Not a single Kannada words enters into the last section of the novel set in Bangalore. He compares the food and drinks in the North and South without mentioning a single name of the eatables. For example, he simply summarize:

> Lunch was four rupees a plate. The food is good value in the South. It is a strange food, though; vegetables cut up and served in watery curries. Then I went up to my room....
>
> I was eager to try coffee. You see, poor people on the north of this country drink tea, and poor people in the south drink coffee. (296)

It can be argued that this is not a traditional novel. The location of culture is very difficult in it because it is magic realism that makes much difference.

There are some subtle hints showing how 'culture systems' are products of action. Balram looks at the poster of a terrorist, which is his own image. The local person asks him to read it. He admits that he cannot. Balram seems to be Adiga's mouthpiece. He says, "Now I understood why he had come running. It was the desperation of an illiterate man to get the attention of the Literate man. From his accent I knew he was from the darkness too" (134).

It is interesting to note here that accent is the marker of class as well as caste which reminds us of the Greek proverb 'speak out one word, I'll judge you'. However, such cultural markers and culture conditioning symbols are less in this novel than those in *Between the Assassinations*. In the latter caste, creed, religion, caste and other details of their culture conditioned action are displayed in more depth hence it becomes rather difficult to 'affiliations' of *The White Tiger*. Moreover, it seems to be the product of Western culture and imperialism which invokes the exotic colonial images of India as a land of tigers, bears, elephants and snakes. Bharati Mukherjee's *The Tiger's Daughters* capitalizes on the background of Bengal and Assam to please the American readers.

Edward said believes that the pastness of the past is a challenging idea in itself. As a matter of fact, not only the present has got its roots in the past but also the future will be constructed according to the present. Further he observes:

> Appeals to the past are among the commonest of strategies in interpretations of the present. What animates such appeals is not only disagreement about what happened in the past and what the past was, but uncertainly about whether it continues, albeit in different forms, perhaps. This problem animates all sorts of discussion about influence, about blame and judgment, about present actualities and future priorities. (12)

Adiga shows consciousness of past but without any tinge of inter or intra colonialism. Moreover, he ridicules only Thakur's absence of the priestly class which mediates politics more powerfully than the elected members and ministers. This is how he portrays the past and present:

> Now, Mr. Ashok's thinking was smart. Ten years ago, they say, there was nothing in Gurgaon, just water buffaloes and fat Punjabi farmers. Today it's the modernest suburb of Delhi. American Express, Microsoft, all the big American companies have offices here. The main road is full of shopping malls-each mall has a cinema inside! So if Pinky Madam missed America, this was the best place to bring her.

Adiga's agenda seems to appropriate the lower caste/subaltern castes against warrior race in India. Of course, the Western scholars read it not for this cultural politics but for documentation of Indian poverty and also for marketing cultural products. The world politics influence Indian literature in one way or the other. In all dimensions of cultural life, this dominant discourse is a prime agent in creating an essential staging for cultural exchange. Denis Roger, The Director of BWPI (Brooks World Poverty Institute, Manchester) is reported to have said,

> Bestsellers as Indian writer Aravind Adiga's *The White Tiger* and Indian-Canadian Rohinton Mistry's *A Fine Balance*, he said, Convey complex ideas in a most powerful way.... We are not arguing that poets should replace finance Ministers, said BWPI Research Director, But we are stressing that novelists make distinctive and important contribution to the broader store house of knowledge on process, experience and consequences of development. (*The Times of India*, Pune Mirror, 08-11-08, p. 31)

As pointed out earlier modern Indian literatures both in English and translated in English are never recognized as an independent entities. They are called shadow or expansion of Euramerican literature. They are studied as anthropological, socio-economic sources of defining degrees of development award on *The White Tiger* which is the product of alienated as well westernized journalist appropriated by the fundamentalist politicians. Certain varieties of Indian elites are at the best naive information for first world intellectuals interested in the voice of the other. But one must nevertheless insist that the colonized subaltern subject is irretrievably heterogeneous (*emphasis added*).

In *The White Tiger*, Adiga employs the basic technique of first person narration to represent the subaltern Halwai. It is a disguise for the novelist to make the narrator an object of the gaze from above which is much discussed in the film theories. Perhaps this is one of its features, which displays its close affinity to the Oscar Awards winning *Slumdog Millionaire*. A reader of novel confronts a sympathetic fiction where the Dalit subaltern has been represented. Hence, he is a native informant in the postmodern world. He does neither make the empire writes back culturally nor does he describe the Indian stereotypes. But some credit should be given to him for exposing corruption in the area of Darkness to which his protagonist belongs by birth. And his attempt to showcase "two Indias" must be appreciated.

WORKS CITED

Adiga, Aravind. *Between The Assassinations*. Picador. Pan McMillan Ltd. London. 2008.

——. *The White Tiger*. Harper Collins. New Delhi. 2008.

——. *Last Man in Tower*. Harper Collins. New Delhi. 2011.

Calvalaaro, Dani. *Critical and Cultural Theory*. London: The Atlane Press. 2001.

Dhillon, Amrit. "Indians Fear Aravind Adiga's 'The White Tiger' says too much of them". http://www.telegraph.co.uk. 22 December. 2008.

Lutwack, Leonard. *The Role of Place in Literature*. Syracuse University Press. Syracuse. 1984.

Said, Edward. *Orientalism*, in Rivkin, Julie and Ryan, Michael *Literary Theory: An Anthology*. Massachusetts: Blackwell. 1998.

——. *Culture and Imperialism*. London. Chatto and Windus. 1993.

Spivak, Gayatri Chakraborty. "Can The Subaltern Speak" in *Post Colonial Studies: Reader*. London. OUP. 1998.

The Times of India, March 19, 2009.

CHAPTER 8

The White Tiger in Dark India

Sanjay Kumar Swarnkar

A good novelist studies the important issues of his/her time—social, political, economic and philosophical—analyses them and suggests solutions, of course, indirectly or covertly, in his/her novels. He/she never speaks directly. On the other hand, he/she lets his/her views through characters. Sometimes, his/her vision of a new social order is expressed in such a subtle or hidden way that the reader has to study thoroughly to grasp the total meaning.

Aravind Adiga's The Man Booker Prize winning novel *The White Tiger* (2008) deals with the miserable life of the people living in the dark side of India. In the very beginning of the novel, the author divides India into an India of Darkness and an India of Light, the kind of division into Bharat and India in the common parlance.

The novel is the autobiography of Balram, called Munna at home. The White Tiger who is quite different from the other people born in the dark. Endowed with a rare intelligence and the ability to seize every opportunity to ascend the next ladder of opportunity, he rises from the humble boy servant in a cheap tea stall to a prosperous entrepreneur. He does so by kicking and killing all the hurdles on his way and the heinous crime of slitting the throat of his benefactor and assuming his name Ashok Sharma.

The novel is divided into first night, second night, fourth morning, fourth night, fifth night, sixth morning, sixth night, seventh night.

The sixth night changes everything. He sees the white tiger and the spirit of white tiger enters his body.

The novelist has given a clear presentation of the exploitation of the marginalized and weak in the social structure of India. In the novel, we find that India is a land of injustice, dishonesty, subordination, corruption and cruelty. It is symbolic of the baser reality and the sub-culture of the Indian life. The novel moves round the conflict between social classes/categories that clash for capturing economic and political power in the general way. The novelist makes us aware of two interconnected stories, that of Balram and his great desire to be "a big bellied man".

Balram, the son of a rickshaw puller gets his name from his teacher, since his former name is Munna. Thus, the narrator throws light on the miserable condition of low income group Indian couple who are so busy in their daily works of life that they seldom get time even to thinking of an appropriate name for their issue and it is clear: "Now, what kind of place is it where people forget to name their children?" (*The White Tiger*, 14).

When Mr. Ashok, the ex-employer of Balram enquires of him some ordinary questions, he makes the answers in the wrong. Then Mr. Ashok says, "He is half-baked". At this Balram says: "Me, and thousands of others in this country like me, are half-baked, because we were never allowed to complete our schooling" (*The White Tiger*, 10).

The narrator speaks about the unequal distribution of resources and in this connection he says: "...India is two countries in one: an India of Light, and an India of Darkness" (*The White Tiger*, 14). Further, he comments on the political culture of India and says: "One fact about India is that you can take almost anything you hear about the country from the prime minister and turn it upside down and then you will have the truth about that thing" (*The White Tiger*, 15).

The narrator asks Mr. Wen Jiabao not to take a dip in the Ganges that has been a symbol of reverence and sacredness from times immemorial since it is not healthy according to him:

> No!—Mr. Jiabao, I urge you not to dip in the Ganga, unless you want your mouth full of faeces, straw, soggy parts of human bodies, buffalo carrion, and

> seven different kinds of industrial acids. (*The White Tiger*, 15)

While describing the civic basic needs in his village, the narrator seems to be under the impact of surrealism.

> There is one street in the village; a bright strip of sewage splits it into two on either side of the ooze, a market: three more or less identical shops selling more or less identically adulterated and stale items of rice, cooking oil, kerosene, biscuits, cigarettes, and jaggery. (*The White Tiger*, 19)

The narrator also focuses on the problems of sanitation and public health.

> Down the middle of the main road, families of pigs are sniffing through sewage—the upper body of each animal is dry, with long hairs that are matted together into spines; the lower half of the body is peat-black and glistening from sewage. (*The White Tiger*, 20)

The narrator draws our attention towards unhealthy environment prevailing in the villages: "The pigs and stray dogs near the tea shop would scatter, and the smell of dust, and sand, and pig shit would blow into the shop" (*The White Tiger*, 24). The landlords have been very powerful in the village in India for a long time and it is the sad picture of Indian society. Four cruel landlords get their names on the basis of four animals—Buffalo, Stork, Wild Boar and Raven. In this connection the narrator comments: "The Buffalo was one of the landlords in Laxmangarh. There were three others, and each had got his name from the peculiarities of appetite that had been detected in him" (*The White Tiger*, 24).

Under the influence of Marxism, the narrator throws light on the miserable condition of the rickshaw pullers. They remain away from the main areas of cities in order to evade the ugly picture of the country: "Rickshaws are not allowed inside the posh parts of Delhi, where foreigners might see them and gape" (*The White Tiger*, 27). As the father of narrator was a rickshaw puller and in this context he paints the image of a rickshaw puller: "a human beast of burden" (*The White Tiger*, 27).

About the image of schoolteacher the narrator comments: "Now, our schoolteacher was a big paan-and-spit man and his expectorate made a sort of low, red wallpaper on three walls around us" (*The White Tiger*, 29).

The narrator also exposes some bad traditions of Indian society as to spend money recklessly on the occasion of marriages and the mishandling of schools. This is really detrimental to the growth of Indian economy. He writes:

> If the Indian village is a paradise, then the school is a paradise within a paradise. There was supposed to be free food at my school—a government programme gave every boy three *rotis*, yellow *daal* and pickles at lunchtime. But we never ever saw *rotis,* or yellow *daal,* or pickles, and everyone knew why: the schoolteacher had stolen our lunch money. (*The White Tiger*, 32-33)

The narrator focuses on the hydra-headed monster—corruption that is a great hindrance in the improvement of Indian villages despite the government efforts. It is evident:

> There was no doctor in the hospital. The ward boy, after we bribed him ten rupees, said that a doctor might come in the evening. The doors to the hospital's rooms were wide open; the beds had metal springs sticking out of them, and the cat began snarling at us the moment we stepped into the room. (*The White Tiger*, 48)

Balram breaks the feudal principles of mutual faith and individual obligations and in doing so he is involved in the betrayal of the ideals of service, faithfulness and obligation that make one's basic humanity. Further, he does not follow the principles of faithfulness and breaks them in order to make his own way for living in the universe. His philosophy changes into distrust where money has got the sole power and it is clear when Balram murders his master, Mr. Ashok.

Written in the pseudo-epistolary form, the novel follows the tradition of magic realism enunciated by Gabriel Garcia Marquez in his famous novel *One Hundred Years of Solitude*. The other novelists who have employed magic realism as a technique in the continent are Milan Kundera of Czekoslovakia and Italo Calvino of Italy. The great practitioner of magic realism in English is Salman Rushdie. Arvind Adiga has followed Rushdie and Samuel Richardson in *The White Tiger,* more Rushdie and less Richardson.

The novel exposes the falsity of tall claims made by the people in power about India's socio-economic development and their claim that the country is far more developed than China. Munna or Balram is The White Tiger, a rare species, who becomes a multimillionaire by killing his employer Ashok and assumes the name Ashok Sharma. How he develops from the scullery-boy in a tea shop to a millionaire is a fantastic story which is tragic and comic at the same time.

The protagonist of the novel is not an individual, though he has a name, a parentage, a large joint family and a fixed location, his village Laxamangarh; yet he is a type, as Engels would call him, who represents the entire Indian community living in darkness, far away from the bright India centred in the silicon city of Bangalore (now Bengaluru) and the mega city Delhi with its satellite town Gurgaon.

This wide divide between the India of darkness and the India of light is superbly portrayed in the novel. The difference between realism and magic realism is that writers like Flaubert, Zola and Maupassant depict the seamy side of life in the naturalistic way and their focus is always on an individual or a small group of individuals. Marquez and Kundera take an entire group or community. In fact,

> ...magic realism assumes that truth is best viewed as a communal, collaborative construct, rather than as residing in the integrity of individual perceptions, whose authority tends merely to that of caprice and rumour.

The White Tiger, Balram, reaches the top of the ladder, like all entrepreneurs, by foul means. The main principle of capitalism is to amass wealth and control monopoly. This can be done by those entrepreneurs who adopt all kinds of foul means, even murder of their benefactors as Balram does. But entrepreneurship is a bane for society. It divides people into groups, one living in light and the other in darkness. Is there any remedy for this malaise? There is a faint hint on pages:

> Maybe once in a hundred years there is a revolution that frees the poor. I read this in one of those old text-book pages people in tea stalls use to wrap greasy samosas with. See, only four men in history have led successful revolutions to free the slaves and kill their masters, this page said:
>
> Alexander the Great.
>
> Abraham Lincoln of America.
>
> Mao of your country.
>
> And a fourth man. It may have been Hitler, I can't remember. But I don't think a fifth name is getting added to the list anytime soon. (*The White Tiger*, 303-04)

It may be asked: Is the fifth man The White Tiger? Adiga is silent. We do not know what he intends to say. The text is miserably blurred.

The German Rezeption-aesthetik theory says that the meaning of a text suspends between the writer and the reader. Typically German in approach it lays emphasis on the formation of gestalt. Unfortunately, we fail to make a gestalt of the amorphous mass of this text called *The White Tiger*. Lincoln and Hitler are opposites, the first is against all kinds of racism and the other a racist. Similarly, Alexander is an imperialist and Mao anti-imperialist. In addition Barlam's action is inhuman.

We may say that Adiga has a very superficial knowledge of India's socio-economic structure and so he has entangled the threads more and made a criss-cross of the social reality. The novel, at best, is a good example of the art of magic realism. Unfortunately, there is more magic and little reality. In his magic world there is no humanity nor human values that sustain our life.

WORKS CITED

Adiga, Arvind. *The White Tiger*. Noida: Harper Collins, 2008.

Ousby, Ian. ed. *Cambridge Guide to English Literature*. London: Cambridge University Press, 1996.

Sinha, M.P. *Literary Criticism*. Kanpur: Sahitya Ratnalaya, 2007.

CHAPTER

9

Nativity Among the Natives: *Sea of Poppies*

Sarvajit Mukerji

Quitting their ancestral villages in the Indo-Gangetic plains, the marginalized and the dispossessed march towards the Indian Ocean under the grim supervision of the henchmen of the British. These are the indentured labourers, a new species of slaves, uprooted from their native soil to be transplanted and survive if they can, in alien climes—in Mauritius, in Fiji, in the West Indies. Turning the clock back, Amitav Ghosh focuses on this group—the unsung first of the Indian Diaspora.

Paradoxically, it is in the cradles of such rejects that the messiahs of mankind are born—a Christ, a Kabir. In *Sea of Poppies* too, a saint is fashioned from unlikely materials—the gomasta , Baboo Nabo Kissen. Traditionally, it is in the hour of darkness that the saviour is born—a Krishna, a Christ. Metaphorically, the darkness is the darkness of oppression. Clearly then, *Sea of Poppies* is based on myths which lie buried deep within our racial memories, to tell a tale that is also radically new.

The first novel of the *Ibis* trilogy, Amitav Ghosh's *Sea of Poppies* tells the tale of the 'girmitiyas', a forgotten first of the Indian diaspora, that was marginalized and dispossessed, of labourers who quit their homes and hearth and were flung to remote outposts of the Raj to work as virtual slaves of the Empire. The second novel of the series, *River of Smoke* is just out. Quitting their ancestral villages in the Indo-Gangetic plains, the marginalized *Sea of Poppies* is the first novel of a trilogy, focusing on the 'girmitiyas' or indentured and the dispossessed, the cheated and the hounded, march towards the Bay of Bengal, under the grim supervision of the 'dafadars'.

The novel flows along like a river in spate, gathering unto itself many streams, many stories of broken, disrupted lives, of people forced into the margins by the forces of history. The chief cause of this calamity is the opium trade with China. The East India Company acquires more and more land for the growing of poppies and this destroys everyone connected to it, both peasants like Diti and landowners like Raja Neel Rattan Haldar. Local economies are destroyed as the land can no longer feed those who till it. It has been rendered as inhospitable as the sea—only it is a sea of poppies. This suits the British who can recruit the 'girmitiyas' from this ever growing host of people marginalized by the bitter fact of losing their land, and ship them off to distant lands as labourers—to Fiji, to the West Indies, to Trinidad and Tobago and to Mauritius.

Baboo Nob Kissen Pander is introduced rather late in the novel. He is the gomasta of Burnham & Co., a firm involved in the opium trade as well as in the supply of indentured workers to remote corners of the Empire, and as such not a figure for whom the reader feels any immediate liking or sympathy. In fact, he is instrumental in the fraudulent acquisition of the Rashkhali zamindari by Burnham & Co. which leads to Raja Neel Rattan imprisonment and deportation to Mauritius. He is also a comic figure.

> The gomusta was a man of middle age, with cheeks that hung down as if weighted with melancholy; he was stout in girth, with dark shapeless ears that stuck out from his huge head like outgrowths of fungus on a mossy rock. Although he still had a full head of hair, his brow was shaven clean, while the locks at the back of his head were braided into a long, priestly tikki. (*TSP*, 132)

The risible impression is enhanced every time he uses the English language, which is 'baboo English' at its best or worst. His employer Burnham always addresses him as 'Baboon' in private. In fact, Baboo Nob Kissen Pander teeters on the edge of caricature. Surprisingly, the first reviewers of *Sea of Poppies*, while detailing the stories of the human cargo on the *Ibis* are silent on Baboo Nob Kissen. Obviously, they do not know what to make of him. Yet, though he is a puzzling figure, Baboo Nob Kissen does have a story.

Baboo Nob Kissen belongs to a Vaishnav family of Nabadwip, in Bengal. In his unlikely veins flows eleven generations of bhakti—his ancestor, eleven generations ago, was initiated into the love of Krishna by Chaitanya Mahaprabhu himself. Nob Kissen too was educated with the view of taking on priestly duties after the demise of his uncle. But destiny intervenes in the form of Taramoni, his aunt and an ardent devotee of Krishna. Nob Kissen becomes the first disciple of this saintly woman and earnestly desires to devote himself to the ascetic life. Unfortunately, his spiritual life is put in abeyance by his guru, Taramoni. Like another famous Guru and disciple duo, Ramakrishna Paramhans and Vivekanand, Taramoni requires Nob Kissen to go back to the world and collect resources for a grand temple whose location she would reveal to him in due course. Is Nob Kissen on the margins? By considerations of caste and wealth, definitely not. Professionally, he is on the fringes of the mercantile establishment of Calcutta, the throbbing centre of the opium trade with China and of coolies with other parts of the Empire. Both these are incidental to Baboo Nob Kissen's character. For essentially, he is mad man of God. And in the realm of the spirit, there is no centre, and there are no margins. The meditating consciousness seeks to ever widen its limits in an effort to comprehend the entire universe. Like a stone dropped into a still pool of water which sends out wider and wider ripples till at last it merges with the margins of the pool.

This perhaps is the reason that it is in cradles of the marginalized and rejected that the great visionaries of mankind—the avatars, the seers and the sages—are born. Where was Christ born? Who were Kabir's parents? While the minds of lesser beings grapple with concepts of centre and margin, figures such as these establish a kingdom of the spirit which serenely transcends these categories. In fact many madmen and women of God, born in the so-called centre, opt for the life ascetic, renounce the centre as it were and opt for the margin. Is that not the way of the Buddha? Of Mira? Can we understand the character of Baboo Nob Kissen from this perspective?

The development of Baboo Nob Kissen's character is interesting. His development from a young 'bramhachari' preparing himself rigorously for the life of a Vaishnavite priest, to a 'gomasta' in Burnham and Co. has already been mentioned. He shows great acumen in business including sharp business practices, he lends money to those in financial distress, he is loyal to a fault to his British bosses, but characteristically none of this is done for personal gain or enrichment. His aim is to realize his guru, Taramoni's dream. By the time we meet him in the novel, he is already tired of waiting for the sign that she had promised him at the time of her death. He was to expect a sign, and seek it in the most unlikely places. Then she would reveal to him the location of the temple of their dreams. Also, he would not be alone in his struggle, for the Taramoni would be with him in spirit, indeed, her spirit would pour into him and she would come to inhabit his body. Baboo Nob Kissen' search leads him to the unlikeliest of persons, to Zachary Reid, the 'malum' of the *Ibis*. Baboo Nob Kissen's growing conviction that it is through Zachary Reid that his dream will be realized is finally sealed when he reads the word 'black' written next to Zachary's name in the ships papers. The fact is that Zachary is a mulatto, but for Nob Kissen it is proof that this is the 'cloud dark lord' that he is seeking. However ridiculous this may appear, it is in keeping with Ghosh's non-eurocentric vision. While the West may be obsessed with whiteness, for Nob Kissen the very word 'black' is holy. He is sure his long wait is now over and the Dark One has manifested himself. Nob Kissen's way is now clear. It is to Mauritius he must go, and build his temple there. His long exile in the mercantile world is now over, and he sheds the personality he had acquired there effortlessly. His attire now is the 'alkhalla' the androgynous habit of the saint. He now wears his hair long, having opened out his shikha and alarmingly becomes increasingly feminine and motherly. This is confusing. What is happening here?

And here I must recount a personal anecdote. Many years ago, during an informal chat with my late father, a monk of Ramakrishna Mission had recounted a strange detail. He mentioned that Ramakrishna Paramhans worshipped God in many ways. Not only did he worship the Creator as Muslim and Christian, he also sought the Divine as friend, devotee and beloved. During this last form, he thought and lived as a woman. Surprisingly, his body too underwent certain changes, to the extent that many people failed to recognize him. I cannot quote the chapter and verse for this and as I say this is anecdotal. But may be this holds the key to this later phase of Nob Kissen's character.

This apart, is it possible to totally divorce the feminine component from the men of God? Compassion and caring, love and charity—qualities assigned to women by patriarchy are also the qualities of the saints and sages. Who can divorce the personality of the Buddha from compassion, that of Jesus from love and forgiveness, and that of Kabir from tolerance? Do these supposed 'androgynous' characteristics push them to the margins or are these values that will ever endure in the core of human civilization? Does the movement from margin to centre also involve bringing to the centre everything that has been condemned and rejected by those who have sought to take human civilization to the next level?

Perhaps Ghosh has romanticized the voyage out of the *Ibis*. Certainly the 'dabusa' or the hold of the ship where the 'girmitiyas' and the 'quoddies' huddle together is imagined as little world where people liberated from the shackles of caste and region of their native land, live, love and relate to one another. They are now 'jahaj bhais' and there is death and childbirth and marriage in the little world under the feet of the white lords of the ship. Atwood describes a similar journey to America in *Alias Grace* that seems much more authentic. On the deck, there are the lusts and jealousies of the white men in charge of the ship. Here, among the maisteries and *silahdars*, the malums and the *subedars*, it is Nob Kissen who represents the incursion of the feminine in the male bastion of the *Ibis*.

> Nowhere was this transformation more evident than in himself, for the presence of Taramony was so palpable within him now that his outer body felt increasingly like the spent wrappings of a cocoon, destined soon to fall away from the new being that was gestating within. Every day offered some fresh sign of the growing fullness of the womanly presence inside him. (423)

As the novel races towards its climax, the microcosm that the *Ibis* has come to represent is wracked with calamity. A furious tempest rages, tossing the ship on the turbulent seas. The powerful white masters mock and humiliate the two convicts, Neel and Ah Faat, Diti and Munia are threatened with violation, Jodu stripped and flogged, and Kalua is to be executed. The relatively stable world of the 'dabusa' is threatened with dire calamity. In times of trouble, the myths of nations remind us, when evil seems supremely triumphant it is only the intervention of the Divine that can redeem the situation. And the Divine, in the guise of Nob Kissen intervenes to help oppressed escape from the dire circumstances. The escape of Ah Faat, Neel, Kalua, Jodu and Serang Ali is facilitated by Nob Kissen, the enigmatic and eccentric man of God. The myths of nations abound in such stories. When the powers of evil are at their most triumphant, the Redeemer is born in the huts and homes of the marginalized and the dispossesed. So deep does Ghosh reach into the collective racial unconscious to sweep *Sea of Poppies* to a close.

WORKS CITED

Atwood, Margaret. *Alias Grace*, Virago, London, 1996.

Ghosh, Amitav. *Sea of Poppies*, Penguin/Viking, New Delhi, 2008.

CHAPTER 10

Sea of Poppies as Historical Fiction

Prabin Sinha

Several important themes emerge from Amitabh Ghosh's novel *Sea of Poppies*. Caste-system, feudalism, trade of opium, agricultural economy of India, migration and the position of women in nineteenth century India are important themes, and in the progression of the plot, all these themes are adroitly handled to create a veritable nineteenth century India. While the novel handles different aspects of Indian life, the central and dominating theme of the novel is the "White man's burden". In effect the dynamo of the plot is the "altruism" of the White man in all its hideousness.

Opium and its trade with China are central to British altruism in the *Sea of Poppies*. Mr. Burnham, who along with Justice Kendalbushe is the representative of the British ruling class in India, argues that British rule in India could not have been sustained without the revenues generated by opium and all the blessings and benefits conferred by British rule on India would not have been possible. Opium is therefore the greatest blessing of India. British merchants and members of the ruling class are orchestrating a plan to impose war on China where they are being denied their so-called "right" to free trade by its Manchu ruler. The argument is that the benefits and blessings of British rule and missionary help will accrue to the Chinese people only if the British are allowed free trade in opium to meet the costs incurred in civilizing China. Mr. Burnham is clear on this issue, "If it is God's will that opium be used as an instrument to open China to his teachings, then so be it..." (116). If the Chinese Emperor proves obstinate and is adamant in his attitude towards the trade in opium, he would be made to see reason by force. However, British avarice is dressed in the garb of freedom as Mr. Burnham explains to the simple Raja of Rakshali, Neel Rattan—"The war, when it comes, will not be for opium. It will be for a principle: for freedom—for the freedom of trade and for the freedom of the Chinese people..." (115). The world has not changed much since the nineteenth century. Freedom, democracy, justice, civilization and other such related words have been summoned by the dominant race to mask their motives which have not always been altruistic.

The acquisition of the Rakshali estate was a breach of trust by Mr. Benjamin Burnham. There had been a mute understanding between the old Raja of Rakshali and Benjamin Burnham that the Raja could sign hundees in the name of the latter. When Mr. Burnham thought of acquiring the Rakshali estate after the rumours that the East India Company was to relinquish its control on opium production and only merchants with their own tract of land would stand to prosper in the trade of opium, he had no qualms in indicting the son of the old Raja of Rakshali as a forgerer who had signed forged hundees in his name. In the name of Justice, Judge Kendalbushe orders the forfeiture of the Rakshali estate and the transportation of Neel Rattan Halder to Mauritius. Apart from the sentence, the import of Justice Kendalbushe's long-winding sentence is that just as a parent who fails to chasten a child is guilty of shirking the duty of guardianship, so in the affairs of men, those people who are entrusted by God Almighty with the task of spreading his word and civilization among the races who are "still in their infancy of civilization" will be considered guilty of neglecting their sacred trust if they were "insufficiently rigorous in the chastisement of such peoples as were incapable of the proper conduct of their own affairs" (115). Therefore, we have the exemplary punishment of the unsuspecting, young and certainly inexperienced Raja of Rakshali.

The condescending attitude of the British can be seen everywhere in the novel. Mr. Burnham calls Baboo Nob Kissen, his *gomasta*, a respectable, man in his own right, by the name of "baboon". The captain of the ship *Ibis*, Mr. Doughty cannot stand hearing English from the lips of an Indian and says that hearing Neel Rattan speak in English seems like a "bandar" reading aloud from *The Times*. The Indians of even the higher strata of the traditional Indian society are equated with monkeys and apes.

The case of the second mate of *Ibis*, Zachary Reid, is fascinating. He has been transformed from a mulatto freedman to a European and the change in attitude and the treatment he receives astonishes him. When finally, he is discovered by Mr. Crowle, the first mate of Ibis, he feels that he has been unburdened of a very huge load of pretence. While on the other hand Mr. Crowle thinks that he has got a powerful tool to blackmail Zachary Reid. Paulette Lambert, an orphaned French girl is one of the important characters in the novel. Ghosh chooses her as the heroine of the amorous love affair with Zachary Reid. She is the exact opposite of Zachary Reid—while he is a mulatto American freedman taken to be a White man by accident, Paulette Lambert is a free-spirited European orphan who has been raised by an Indian woman and has imbibed more of the Indian culture than the European. Paulette, in the views of people like Mr. Burnham and Justice Kendalbushe, needs acculturation in European ways and therefore, the philanthropist Mr. Burnham takes her in his tutelage.

Paulette is in some ways comparable to India. Both have been provided with undesired tutelage. Paulette has to be cultured in European ways so that she does not cut a sorry figure in the eyes of the natives. Similarly, India has to be civilized and brought at par with civilized peoples through administrative and missionary civilizing projects. The White Man has taken it as his duty and burden sanctioned by providence. Paulette is given shelter in Mr. Burnham's house and is provided for by his generosity and philanthropy. Mr. Burnham's philanthropy, as later on revealed by Paulette, is because of some refined sexual practices that he has with Paulette. Paulette is instructed in her religious studies by Mr. Burnham himself. He instructs her in the Bible in a closed room after his wife has gone to sleep with her daily dose of laudanum. In the process of her instruction, he asks her whether she has known chastisement because chastisement is essential to true penitence. When she admits her ignorance of chastisement, he asks her if she would not like to know it as it is an essential part of religious instruction. Paulette fears being chastised by such a large and strong man but she steels her nerves for her lesson in chastisement. However, she is taken by surprise when Mr. Burnham presents himself as the object on which she would learn her lesson in chastisement. Mr. Burnham then assumed a most singular posture with his face at her feet and his derriere raised high where Paulette was to aim her chastisement. He bade her to strike on his derriere with all her strength. This practice continued till Mr. Burnham thought of the improvisation of using a sweeper's broom for his chastisement. Mr. Burnham bade Paulette to strike with all her strength and with each stroke squirmed and squealed in agony. Finally, he went slack on the floor. There was a wet strain on the floor where Mr. Burnham had squirmed like "some creature of the soil". It was only when a *khidmatgar* told her that the mark on the floor "was not made by a serpent of the jungle" but by "the snake that lives in man" (115). Did she understand after thinking hard and long that she had been sexually abused by her benefactor? This whole episode of Mr. Burnham and a Paulette suggests that the philanthropy of Mr. Burnham was the mask for hiding the ugly face of illicit sexual indulgence. The chastisement that Mr. Burnham suffers at the hands of his beneficiary is not chastisement but a refinement of sexual indulgence. Paulette is there for the appeasement of Mr. Burnham's sexual appetite and philanthropy and fellow feeling for a European is just a ruse for hiding this ugly aspect of his personality. As we understand later on in the novel, the presence of Paulette in Mr. Burnham's household is not a burden on him but on Paulette. Similarly the burden that the White man suffers in the case of civilizing the people of India is a ruse for hiding his avarice. The high-sounding and sonorous words of civilization are a means to deflect attention from the exploitation of the resources of India. It is easy to ascertain who the benefactor is and who the beneficiary in the case of

Paulette and Mr. Burnham as well as in the case of India and the British ruling class.

Consider the case of British rule in India. Amitabh Ghosh suggests that British rule in India was sustained to a great extent by revenues generated by opium. It is not a mere coincidence that only after about twenty years after the trade in opium was stopped, the British rule in India came to an end. British and even Indian history glosses over this fact. The empire in which the sun did not set was built on the foundation of the income from trade in opium. India under British rule was the greatest producer and exporter of opium in the world. The cost that this dubious distinction entailed in terms of human and material resources is staggering in proportion. Indian peasants suffered as they were forced to grow poppies in their fields and sell them at low determined prices to British opium factories. The peasants were forced to borrow money from native moneylenders who were themselves indebted to British buccaneers. The peasants were deep in the mire of debt which increased with each passing year until it became unbearable. It would have been really unbearable for small peasants because something really drastic could force traditional Indian people to abandon their ancestral land, sever ties with their motherland and cross the "black-waters" to work as indentured labour in foreign fields.

Opium yielded one seventh of the total revenue of British India in the nineteenth century. The trade in opium was essential to the prosperity of the British empire. Michael Greenburg says, "Opium was-no-hole-in-the-corner petty smuggling trade, but probably the largest commerce of the time in any single commodity" (104). With so much at stake, it was imperative that the British look into the matter aggressively and if negotiations fail, explore military options. Considering the wide discrepancy between British and Chinese military technology, it is not surprising that the British merchants were clamouring for war, the result of which was a foregone conclusion. Mr. Burnham informs his British friends, "Mr. Jardine has written to say that he has prevailed on the Prime Minister at last" (260). This Mr. Jardine in the novel *Sea of*

Poppies is the historical figure at the vanguard of technological and commercial ventures, William Jardine of the trading firm Jardine Matheson and Co. who wrote anonymously to the China Repository in 1834:

> Nor indeed our valuable commerce and revenue both in India and Great Britain be permitted to remain subject to a caprice, which a few gunboats laid alongside this city would overrule by the discharge of a few mortars.... The result of a war with the Chinese could not be doubted. (Pannikar, 97)

Jardine was the first person to breach Chinese law in sending a steamer upstream the Pearl river between Canton and Macao in defiance of the official decree and was forced to retreat after the Chinese bombarded his steamer.

The general opinion regarding opium trade and the obduracy of the Chinese government veered towards the inevitability of a war. The British Prime Minister Lord Palmerston also considered it a prudent step to wage war with China for safeguarding British commercial interests. What Chinese officials considered law enforcement against smuggling and narcotics, the traders saw as unjustified interference with free enterprise. In such a state of affairs, a broad consensus emerged between the British ruling class, merchants and the military establishment about the inevitability of war.

This is what Edward Said has called *cultural consensus* about the empire and overseas dominions of Europe in the metropolitan centres. By the end of the nineteenth century England's empire was preeminent in the world and the cultural argument for empire was triumphing. The period with which the novel *Sea of Poppies* is concerned coincides with the scramble for Africa between the European powers. Cultural documents of this period like the novel of frank exoticism and confident empire, travel narratives, works of colonial exploration and scholarship, memoirs, all evince a spirit of exhilaration and triumph at the fact of empire. Almost without exception, these narratives, far from casting doubt on the colonial enterprise, serve to confirm and celebrate its success. The public opinion in metropolitan Europe was in favour of empire and one only has to see the writings of philosophers and political theorists like Carlyle, Ruskin, Mill and the like to have a good overview of the cultural phenomenon of support of overseas dominion in England. It is with regard to this aspect of metropolitan English culture that I find the character of captain Chillingworth as going against the current of the culture which he has inherited as an Englishman.

Since the novel, *Sea of Poppies* is based and steeped in history, it is expected that it conforms to historical verities to sound convincing. Captain Chillingworth, the captain entrusted with the ship ibis transporting the coolies, seems to be unconvincing in his skepticism towards the colonial enterprise as he questions the unquestionable premise in the colonial mission of spreading the light of civilization to hitherto unilluminated portions of the globe. He does not support the war against China and seems to think on the lines of class interests when he says, "I am sure it will do a great deal of good for some of us. But I doubt I'll be of that number, or that many china men will" (262).

Conrad whose *Heart of Darkness* has been interpreted and analyzed in depth as a narrative of skepticism towards the colonial enterprise has the narrator Marlowe say in the novel, "The conquest of the earth, which mostly means the taking it away from those who have a different complexion or slightly flatter noses than ourselves, is not a pretty thing when you look into the matter too much. What redeems it is the idea only. An idea at the back of it; and an unselfish belief in the idea—something you can set up, and bow down before and offer a sacrifice to..." (Conrad, 10). Captain Chillingworth says about the war with China, "The truth is, sir, that men do what their power permits them to do. We are no different from the pharaohs or the Mongols: the difference is only that when we kill people we feel compelled to pretend that it is for some higher cause. It is this pretence of virtue, I promise you, that will never be forgiven by history" (262).

In saying this, the character of the captain seems unconvincing. What he says is against the conventional wisdom of the ruling race and, in fact, it was unthought-of in the period of the scramble for any and every piece of land in Asia and Africa. Conrad, himself a Polish émigré and victim of Russian imperialism, writing in the beginning of the twentieth century, could not break the cultural and ideological barrier and commended colonialism and condoned its excesses in the name of "idea", the idea of regenerating and civilizing degenerate peoples. Existing in the novel in the 1830s, captain Chillingworth can look through the hypocrisies and pretence of the colonizers and that too when he is reaping the benefits of the colonial enterprise is highly improbable. Moreover, it seems highly incongruent that a person serving the colonialists and traders and whose livelihood depends on the colonial enterprises could look at the issue in such a light.

Though Amitabh Ghosh has created a veritable nineteenth century India, sometimes, it seems that he has projected thoughts and actions on characters which are incongruous to the grain of the character. Captain Chillingworth's thoughts are an example as is the action of one of the main characters, Kalua. The character of Kalua may be attractive but there are some blatant inconsistencies in the character. He first imposes himself on the reader as a huge and heavily built man but placed at the bottom of the Indian social hierarchy. He is humiliated and tortured to the extreme of physical endurance by three scions of the local landlord and he only pleads for mercy before going senseless. The same Kalua is seen to wield the unwieldy bamboo platform of his ox-cart to ward off a mob of religious fanatics assembled to witness the gruesome spectacle of *sati*. He emerges without any rhyme or reason to save Deeti from the clutches of an imminent gruesome death and carries her off to safety. The man who did not have courage enough to protect himself from three juvenile youths in the face of extreme torture and humiliation could muster courage to intervene in a religious rite of the magnitude of *sati* and that too to protect a woman with whom he has no apparent relation is untenable as a realistic character. As captain Chillingworth has been given thoughts that would be more acceptable in a character of the late twentieth century, the character of Kalua has been given thoughts that hardly suit him as an uneducated pariah in the early eighteenth century. The same captain Chillingworth who spoke against the colonial warfare and seemed ahead of his time can be seen in a different light in the ship transporting the *girmitiyas* where he takes the side of subedar Bhairo Singh in his insistence on taking revenge on Kalua for having shamed his family honour by carrying away Deeti from the funeral pyre of her husband. He says to the second mate Reid, "...What would you, or I, or any of us, do with a darkie who'd had his way with our wives or sisters? Why should we expect the subedar and his men to feel any less strongly than we would ourselves? And what right do we have to deny them the vengeance that we would certainly claim as our due?" (482) The captain here emerges as a shrewd and calculating colonialist who understands the social dynamics of the colony and also understands the value of the support of the castes and classes which serve as the props of the colonial empire. He says, "For this you should know, gentlemen, that there is an unspoken pact between the white man and the natives who sustain his power in Hindoostan—it is that in matters of marriage and procreation, like must be with like, and each must keep to their own. The day the natives lose faith in us, as the guarantor of castes—that will be the day, gentlemen, that will doom our rule" (482). He continues, "This is the inviolable *principle* on which our authority is based—it is what makes our rule different from that of degenerate and decayed peoples as the Spanish and Portuguese. Why, sir, if you wish to see what comes of miscegenation and mongrelism, you need only visit their possessions..." (482).

The "idea" of Marlowe in Conrad's *Heart of Darkness* is not much different from captain Chillingworth's "principle" in the valorization of the rule of their people over the rule of other colonial powers. It is hard to come to grips with the fact that in the novel captain Chillingworth could speak on both sides of the scale. In the novel, captain Chillingworth is both the critic of colonialism and its observant and shrewd apologist. Similarly the character of Kalua shows the extremes of cowardice and courage that does not rhyme. Moreover,

Amitabh Ghosh has projected contemporary Dalit consciousness on a character of the eighteenth century which does not seem a probable character seen in the historical perspective. The episodes relating the dissent of captain Chillingworth on the issue of the colonial mission and that of Kalua's humiliation could have been discarded from the novel and it would have been more realistic, belonging as it is to the genre of historical fiction dealing with colonized India of the nineteenth century.

WORKS CITED

Conrad, Joseph. *Heart of Darkness,* Harmondsworth, Penguin, 1973.

Ghosh, Amitabh. *Sea of Poppies,* New Delhi: Penguin, 2008.

Greenburg, Michael. *British Trade and the Opening of China, 1800-42,* Cambridge, 1951.

Pannikar, K.M. *Asia and Western Dominance,* New York, 1969.

CHAPTER

11 Kiran Nagarkar's "God of Small Things" as a Quest for Faith

Jaya Kapoor

Kabir says at one point in the novel to his followers—"Nothing can be more dangerous than to be too sure of yourself—to be too certain about the rightness of your own cause. That paves the way for intolerance towards others."

This approach which Kabir is referring to, where there is no room for any ambivalence or doubt and with a professional no nonsense approach reminds of the way the modern age looks at life in general and religion in particular. There is a clinical precision to everything including human relationships and no scope for a second chance. Like in a corporate culture, there is always a target and a deadline to be met. If there are ambiguities, doubts or uncertainties, then your performance is not optimum and you will be flushed out of the system. The sheer simplicity of a God as a father, as a comforter, as a protector is lost to the corporatization of religion. Human history shows that religion does become militant when it comes into an existential conflict with another religion or any other subversive authority. But when religion is distances God from man and builds Him up as one who is happy to see his children sacrifice and suffer just to show their love for him, things become a little more difficult. Especially as Kabir puts it in the book, when sin is so attractive and Satan always at leisure and always available while God is always a little preoccupied and we need to strive hard to catch his attention. Such an image does the institution of religion a lot of good in giving it authority and power, but takes away from God the easy accessibility as a father, a friend always there when needed and always a source of strength. The paper is an attempt to understand how I see Nagarkar's book exploring the idea of faith and religion as shaped up in the last few years.

There has been a change in the way people relate to religion in the last few decades of the twentieth century. There are several aspects to this perception of religion which go beyond any particular religion. First there is a rise in violence which is attributed to religious beliefs but which somehow defies the fundamental idea of religion where man tries to establish a relationship with God. The second aspect is in fact a lot of beliefs that are taken as a way of worshipping God but which in fact are not including self torture for going against the dictates of God and the belief that one's religion is pure and the only true faith. There had come a time when it had seemed that such ideas are of little or no consequence in the modern world. But suddenly like a genie let out of the bottle, they seem to be everywhere. I see Nagarkar exploring both these aspects and also the reason thereof in the book. As I see it, it is not a story of a terrorist but rather of a man who is trying to discover faith in God through religion when God lies somewhere within us. In a discussion on globalization and faith, eminent political scientist Prof. Doughlas Rae explores this distinct course in the growth of religion which can help us understand this change. He observes that while there has been a steady growth of religion as an institution, there has been a sharp rise in the way polarization has occurred across the world along the fault lines of faith. He further observes about two kinds of religions—Acute religion and Chronic religion. He talks about several criterion for acute religion—it demands to subordinate other forms of knowledge to religion/doctrine/dogma, when combined with certain external circumstances, it is the most dangerous (factors include poverty, isolation, undemocratic authoritarian and wholly inapt forms of government, illiteracy, early stages in world demographic transitions, i.e. disproportionally large number of young people in a population and low expectation of life span). He points out and says that commerce is a good thing since it leads to greater exposure to people with different beliefs leading to greater tolerance and more open attitude. Chronic religion is more porous, more penetrable by other ideas and leads to a more tolerant attitude. He is not referring to any particular religion here but every religion evolves into the two variants over a period of time.

Nagarkar's protagonist Zia is such a man who grew up with the belief that he will become a voice of God and an agent of the will of God, but gets lost on the way. On the other hand are people like Zafar and Amanat who are family but who think differently. Their liberal view of religion is matched by the deeply introspective religious minds of Father Paul and Father Augustine. As a result, so that even though their religious identities differ, they can identify with each other, something that neither can claim to share with Zia though they share the same religious identity with him at different points. Amidst all this runs the thread of the voice of Kabir who advocates irreverence as the only way to understand God. Nagarkar sets the voice of Kabir as a contrast to the way Zia thinks so that each time the former makes a move to prove his religious belief, the latter appears with an alternate course almost in an attempt to pull him back.

Nagarkar's protagonist can be considered a classic believer in acute religion. But he fulfils none of the criterion of acute religion observed by Prof. Rae. He comes from an affluent liberal educated Muslim family which lives in a metropolitan city in a democratic society. The remarkable thing is that Zia is living in open liberal societies and getting the best available education. The secular politics and democratic institutions thrive in a social setup where the religion is not subversive. So why should Zia become the person that he does? When Nietzsche talked about death of God he is probably referring not just to God but to a world where faith bound the socio-cultural set up. And so when such a faith is no more, there is attempt by other forces to replace the vacuum thus created. There are two ways of moving henceforth. The first is to try to revive the institutions that symbolized faith and God, the second is to exist in a state of ambiguity and doubt. The first leads to the acute religion that Prof. Rae was referring to while the second will lead to the Chronic religion. Zia's journey can be seen as an attempt to understand this crisis of faith. Doubt is a part of growing into faith in most religions. And if the doubt is not converted to faith at some stage, the doubt can be taken as an attack on religion. And Zia as a self-appointed protector of the sacrosanct religion feels the compulsion to set things right. He cannot doubt and he cannot bear the doubting mind. Both Father Paul and Brother Jonathan-Christophe reveal the world of ambivalence and doubt where he felt there was no place for either. Both feel the urge to love Christ stronger than the need for sexual life. But both have to constantly pull back. Each pulling back is an assertion of faith and not a moment of failure. This is an understanding that deludes Zia. He has an amazing understanding of the most complex puzzles and can master the probabilities of the market but simple deludes and confounds him. At one point in Amanat's novel Kabir asks his followers to show irreverence to the guru and to all and sundry and most of all to one's own solemnities. He explains that if God is all powerful then evil also a creation of God. He also says at another place that if given a choice between a God and beautiful woman or a beautiful sunset or a song he would choose the woman, the song or the sunset because God is eternal while the other things would pass. That is probably what Father Augustine had also meant when he called Brother Jonathan-Christophe and Father Paul as lucky cross and pull them back into the fold of God each time they slipped away. That could be the reason why though Zia is Amanat's brother, it is Father Augustine who appreciates the voice of Kabir in Amanat's book. Zafar and Amanat do not follow Islam very rigorously but do have a deep understanding of the human values. Father Augustine, although he is a devout Christian feels an affinity with Zafar and Amanat and can understand Amanat's Kabir talking about irreverence as a way of realizing God. So while Father Augustine never lost his faith in Father Paul knowing that the latter had to struggle between his colourful past life and love for God, Zafar always accepted the going away and coming back home of Shagufta. He never gave up on Shagufta right up to the end of his life and his will is a proof of it. This is not an example of any tolerance but sheer simple faith. Tolerance involves a stand and a breach thereof vis-à-vis tolerance is shown. Theirs is a far deeper understanding borne of love where you realize things are not very complicated. That could be why Zafar's finest creation is a Trappist monastery. And the figures he carves for the entrance of the church, though unconventional, are appreciated by Father Augustine.

Zia was all through living with people whose source of faith ran far deeper than Zia's making it ironic that he should take up religion in the fundamentalist way that he did. The only exposure to religion he had as a child is through his aunt. But even her idea of religion is not the corporate religion which he adopted. He became almost a stranger to her as he trudged along the path of self torture, bloodshed. She had wanted to create an oasis of faith in the Khan household where the liberal life could not initiate the children into what she saw as tradition of faith. She could never have fathomed that she was creating a monster. Zia was like a man possessed who wants to be at the top of his profession and possibly thereon turn into a business tycoon whose achievements set the bar. His participation in the Muharram procession was the first step he took in what was to be a long and disturbing journey. He was studying in a Christian institution but was holding his religious ideas in a cocoon where nothing could dilute them. The journey to Oxford only intensified his search for a proper platform to display his faith and himself to be the *walee* Zubaida Khala had led him to believe he was. His attempt to assassinate Rushdie is not only his first test of faith but also the initiation into the world of politicized religion. He fails in proving himself a *walee* by assassinating Rushdie but then raises his bar and decides that he can do it by killing become one by joining the battle of the jehadis in Afghanistan. He refuses to accept the political game behind the entire movement. Even when converts to Christianity, he feels the compulsion to take the toughest test of endurance and enters the Trappist monastery as a statement of his faith. In his mind there is no place for doubt or weakness. And then when his past comes up before him in the figure of Nawaz Irfan, the entire unholy nexus religious forces is revealed as an attempt to gather more power. Zia enters into arms trade to finance his religious mission in nexus with Shakta Muni, a powerful Hindu tantrik who is a already an arms dealer and wants to use Zia's financial wizardry to occupy a bigger market. And the chunk of the supply goes to terrorist groups and rogue states—both sources of political clout for governments that depend on arms industry for survival. Zia can see and understand all this but he had already set his agenda and nothing can change his chosen course. Even when he starts the movement to get abortion declared illegal in U.S., he does it not for the children, but because it has been declared wrong in the scriptures. Even when his close ally in the cause finds herself with an unwanted pregnancy, he does not see the logic behind the law. He is focused on the cause and not bothered about the wherefor's and whatfor's of the issue. If he has to resort to unfair and immoral practices to achieve his target he does it without a second thought. He can follow the scriptures to the word and still not understand the spirit behind the scriptures. He cannot understand the logic behind the deep love and high regard that the priests of the monastery have for Zafar. He also cannot understand the deep love and understanding that Zafar had of the turmoil in his own soul which led Zafar to show the reflection of Zia in Judas carved on the church entrance and show him being almost forgiven by Mary.

Nagarkar says he is unable to identify with Zia, but is ambivalent about him. Zia's intolerance makes Nagarkar examine his own prejudices and reflect. When Zia enters the realm of religious belief, he enters with the conviction about an absolute rightness of his own cause. And in each attempt he makes to underline his faith, he is also simultaneously trying to create a scale himself for measuring the level of faith and displaying the highest levels of faith by his understanding. People like Yunus, Dawn Gold and even Antonia who work by his side are not quite as highly intelligent as Zia but that probably keeps them sane while Zia crumbles under the weight of his brilliance and faith. He breaks down, and pulls back but Zia only adds one more weight to his turmoiled conscience.

Even after he converts, he has to be able to display highest faith. His beating and punishing himself is not approved by Father Augustine but Zia cannot stop himself from bleeding out his guilt and pain. It is probably because of this uncalled for self torture as a mark of faith that Father Paul thinks Zia is Father Augustine's lucky cross. Father Augustine realizes that Zia is no lucky cross and he is proved right. Zia gets so blinded by his ambition to make his movement a success that he does not hesitate in converting yet again into a Hindu at the behest of Shakta Muni. He allows the tantrik to control his mind so he can get his genius with markets back. He agrees to even entering the world of arms trade and supplying nuclear weapons to rogue states and terrorist groups in order to succeed. He reminds of Faustus who sells his soul to the devil to fulfil his aspiration. This is not the path of any religion and certainly not of any faith.

The amazing thing in *God's Little Soldier* is that the conditions mentioned by Prof. Rae are not applicable to Zia. And yet he goes to amazing levels of religious extremism. When he dabbles with the market he succeeds making profits against all odds, when he jots down points for a good terrorist attack, it becomes a handbook of sorts on the subject. He was not of mediocre intelligence, not prey to be indoctrinated along the path of religious extremism, lives in comfort, gets the best possible education, comes from a liberal background. He chooses his path willingly each time after much painstaking research. Whether, it is the plan to exterminate Rushdie or the attempt to get abortion banned in U.S. or have a shot at arms trade, he knows what he is getting into and what he will gain out of it. People who lead him into these narrow bylanes of faith or those who accompany him there fall by along the way as he keeps moving ahead on his frightening and lonely journey. Zubieda Khala, Vivian, Antonia, Roy, even those who fought the battles by his side like Yunus and Dawn Gold. They are not exceptional minds with amazing capacity to be highly motivated in the face of impossible situations like Zia, and that is probably their saving grace because it saves them the deep troubles that a mind like Zia faces. Roy is able to see through most of the things that Zia gets swayed by cautions him against dabbling in the Markets and also against going under the guidance of Shakta Muni. Yunus is a terrorist as well but cannot see the young child being massacred in the name of faith. Zia's intelligence, his exceptional talent and sharp mind place him at a position different from others. Normally such a mind should be able to argue and see where his fanaticism could lead him to by the basic arguments of morality but for Zia, morality and religion are not the same thing. Religion becomes an obsession where morality does not come in at all. It is a task that must be completed at any cost. So although the subject is religious violence at one level of the narrative, the novelist is not talking about terrorism or religious violence. He sees religious extremism as a symptom of a graver disease of the human civilization.

What Nagarkar is trying to do in *God's Little Soldier* is to point out the need to redefine the way faith is seen in our times and the turbulence it causes. In the conflict between science and religion, the casualty was faith. He is not talking about a terrorist but about a modern mind which looks upon religion as a crusade, a mission with a set target. The moment we start looking at faith as a crusade, we are entering dangerous territory. There is no telling where we will be led. And ultimately the fight in the name of religion is only a fight for political and economic clout. The world is more prosperous than at any other time in human history. Although the disparities of prosperity have increased and the poor are poorer than ever before, yet the rich are richer than ever before. A religious victory means political hold leading to economic clout—as Zia tells Irfan Nawaz. Alister McGrath a well-known an atheist converted to apologist in his book on the history of the rise of atheism tried to understand the reason why religion lost to atheism in the last two centuries. He says in his book "The 20th century gave rise to one of the greatest and most distressing paradoxes of human history: that the greatest intolerance and violence of that century were practiced by those who believed that religion caused intolerance and violence." What he is trying to say here is also probably what

Nagarkar is also trying to understand in the novel. It is not like the believers are all fanatics, in fact, Zia is almost an exception—and one which is increasingly turning to religion for the wrong reasons. He has closed approach to religion where God is not the friend but the corporate boss who demands the target of performance for each period to be met as a mark of excellence.

Zia is like so many modern highly qualified and highly intelligent minds who willingly enter the fight for religious supremacy. They are highly ambitious and motivated though it is doubtful how much any indoctrination could have contributed to their shaping up. They could easily see through the entire façade of the power game in the name of religion. But like Zia they refuse to doubt. This refusal to see through the entire game, to sit back and undergo a moment of doubt, to challenge the scriptures and to test them through basic human values has disastrous repercussions as Zia's journey shows. As a Muslim it made Zia a terrorist, as a Christian it got him into a struggle between religious scriptures and basic human dignity that bordered on unlawful and definitely inhuman. And finally as a Hindu he is moving into the dark and murky world of tantriks who ruthlessly use their powers to manipulate lives and gather power and influence. This fanatic approach to religion is probably what disturbed Father Augustine and why he felt that there is no hope for Zia to be pulled back into the folds of faith. He thinks he is devoting his life to God, communicating with Him and doing His bidding. But there is no God at the end of the road Zia takes. He is lost on the way and Zia struggles with claustrophobic darkness. At any point had Zia begun to doubt or shown irreverence, he might have questioned his actions, but he is so sure of himself that he cannot accept even Zafar or Amanat's liberal doubting mind and even Zafar's acceptance of Shagufta's unconventional behaviour. He cannot understand why Zafar accepts Shagufta each time she comes back though he has seen the love his father has for her all his life. How can he understand that God does not reprimand when you do what might be wrong. He cannot understand the simplicity of love for he could never open his heart to love.

When we take a look at the journey of Zia, we get a feeling that probably if he had been left alone as his father had advised to choose the faith of his choice, probably he might have come to a better understanding of faith. At least he might have come to a better understanding of his own mind. He might have lived a simpler life and thereby understood the beauty of life.

Nagarkar says in an interview to Lewis Gropp "there is only one God and her name is Life. She is the only one worthy of worship. All else is irrelevant." So Nagarkar also places the voices of sanity in this cacophony. The voice of Kabir returns again and again to underline the need for going back and taking a fresh look at the very idea of God. When Kabir talks about the simpleminded ironsmith who inspired him to leave his life as a hermit sage and come back into the fold of life of a family man and weaver, I see him trying to emphasize upon this very idea.

His echoes are found quite predominantly in the figures of Amanat, Zafar, Father Paul and Father Augustine. What Nagarkar seems to be doing here is to highlight something very basic about religion or rather faith. The difference in the two terms is the difference that Nagarkar is trying to bring out. The idea of any religion should basically be to bring the individual close to the supreme power which is the source and strength of life. Problems start coming up when the path of faith is narrowed so that it becomes a one way street where there is no way for the individual to speak to Him and He can only be heard through the parapets of the scriptures.

WORKS CITED

Lewis Gropp's Interview of Nagarkar dt 20/04/2007 at www.quantara.de.com also said by Kabir in *God's Little Soldier*, p. 180.

Magrath, Alister. *The Twilight of Atheism*, the Doubleday Religious Publishing Group, 2005.

Nagarkar, Kiran. *God's Little Soldier*, Harper Collins, New Delhi, 2006, 2012.

This is a classroom lecture in the Yale University on "Violence in the Name of Faith", uploaded on www.Youtube.com on 23 Nov. 2009. Also refer to another lecture on the same day by Prof. Rae "Historical Forces in Faith and Globalization".

CHAPTER 12

Re-Imagining Draupadi: Chitra Banerjee Divakaruni's *The Palace of Illusions*

Gourhari Behera

The *Ramayana* and the *Mahabharata* are culturally foundational texts and continue to hold sway over the minds of millions of Indians even in the twenty-first century. These grand narratives have inspired a plethora of writers for centuries and one can easily identify not only references to these texts but also complete rewritings of them from contemporary perspectives. For instance there exists the *Chandrabati Ramayana* written in the sixteenth century Bengal that narrates the *Ramayana* from Sita's perspective. In recent years Samhita Arni's *Sita's Ramayana* (2011) is a retelling of the *Ramayana* from Sita's point of view. Similarly, Arshia Sattar's *Lost Loves* (2011) and Navaneeta Dev Sen's *Site Theke Suru* (1996) are attempts at rewriting the *Ramayana* from contemporary perspectives.

The *Mahabharata* too has been retold from various perspectives by Indian writers. Shashi Tharoor's *The Great Indian Novel* (1989), Sethu's *Pandavapuram* (1982), Shashi Deshpande's *The Stone Women and Other Stories* (2000), Mahasweta Devi's *After Kurukshetra* (2005) are some of the significant works that re-render the *Mahabharata* from contemporary perspectives.

Of all characters in the *Mahabharata* the one that have fascinated the contemporary Indian writers the most is Draupadi. Numerous mutations of the character of Draupadi can be seen in works like Bachint Kaur's *Draupadi* (1990), Surendra Verma's *Yudhistir and Draupadi*, Mahasweta Devi's *Draupadi* (1997), Pratibha Ray's *Yajnaseni* (1995), P.K.

Balakrishnan's *And Now Let Me Sleep* (1973) and Meena Alexander's *Manhattan Music* (1997). One can classify the representation of Draupadi in contemporary literature into two categories. Whereas in works like Mahasweta Devi's *Draupadi*, Kaur's *Draupadi*, Sethu's *Pandavapuram*, the character of Draupadi is transplanted from classical context to the contemporary one, in works like Ray's *Yajnaseni*, Balakrishnan's *And Now Let Me Sleep* and Deshpande's *The Stone Women and Other Stories* the context and setting of the epic era are retained. Chitra Banerjee Divakaruni's *The Palace of Illusions* (2008) is one of the recent attempts at rewriting the *Mahabharata* from the perspective of Draupadi by retaining its classical context.

Chitra Banerjee Divakaruni, an Indo-American novelist and poet, has the distinction of writing more than seventeen novels and many collections of poetry. She has been a Professor of writing at the University of Houston Creative Writing Programme and has received prestigious awards like the American Book Award and the Crawford Award. Born in Kolkata in 1957, she studied at the University of Calcutta, Wright State University and University of California. She is known for her works like *The Mistress of Spices, Sister of My Heart* and *Arranged Marriage*. Much of her writing revolves around the experience of South Asian immigrants, especially women. In *The Palace of Illusions*, Divakaruni takes a different turn by attempting to rewrite the *Mahabharata* from the point-of-view of its most important and enigmatic woman character, Draupadi.

Divakaruni expresses her fascination with the grand Indian epic, the *Mahabharata* in the 'Author's Note':

> ...the epic weaves myth, history, religion, science, philosophy, superstition, and statecraft into its innumerable stories-within-stories to create a rich and teeming world filled with psychological complexity. (13)

She further comments on the genesis of the novel:

> I was left unsatisfied by the portrayals of the women [in the *Mahabharata*]...they remained shadowy

> figures, their thoughts and motives mysterious, their emotions portrayed only when they affected the lives of the male heroes, their roles ultimately subservient to those of their fathers or husbands, brothers or sons. (14)

Her creative engagement with the *Mahabharata,* she says, 'would uncover the story that lay invisible between the lines of the men's exploits' (15). This leads her to rewrite the grand epic with Draupadi or Panchaali at the centre:

> It is her life, her voice, her questions, and her vision that I invite you into in *The Palace of Illusions.* (15)

At the outset, thus, the reader is initiated into a feminist version of the *Mahabharata.* What is interesting about Divakaruni's novel is that it makes the reader identify the various facets of the *Mahabharata* because of its close resemblance to its various popular versions. Yet her version is original in the sense that it reverses the perspective by making the reader gain access to the mind of Draupadi. Thus, the novel is partly psychological. Also it can be read as a bildungsroman too because it charts the growth of Draupadi from her birth through her youth to her final demise. In the process, she is shown to have gained knowledge about her 'self' and the world.

Divakaruni provides interesting twists in the 'original' narrative making it a kind of counter discourse. Simultaneously many of the much celebrated incidents and characters of the *Mahabharata* are downplayed or are presented in such a manner that the reader is left with doubt about the authenticity of such over-hyped representations in the popular versions. Although the novel has Draupadi as the chief narrator, Divakaruni also incorporates into it other narrators like Vyasa, the narrator of the 'original' *Mahabharata* and Dhri, Draupadi's brother in order to project the difference in perspectives.

In this feminist rewriting of the *Mahabharata* Divakaruni attempts to fill many gaps in the *Mahabharata.* For instance she again and again highlights incidents and situations like Draupadi's obsessive infatuation with Karna, her intimate friendship with Krishna and her direct experiencing of the Mahabharata War through the special vision granted to her by Vyasa. Also sensitive issues like the plight of the widows after the war and her attempt at alleviating them find prominence in Divakaruni's version.

The feminist strain in the novel can be identified right in the beginning of the novel. Draupadi emphasizes again and again how her birth from the sacrificial fire was incidental, being born 'uninvited' to king Drupad. Her naming as Draupadi, daughter of Drupad, is in stark contrast to her brother's naming as Dhristadyumna, 'destroyer of enemies'. Thus, Divakaruni is able to problematize the 'important relation between names, gender and identity' (Hoydis). Despite the prophecy that 'she will change the course of history' she is given a raw deal in terms of her upbringing and choices.

Divakaruni also highlights the difference in the kind of education that Draupadi receives with that of her brother. Draupadi comments on the restrictions placed on her education:

> At first, no matter how much I begged, King Drupad had balked at the thought of me studying with my brother. A girl being taught what a boy was supposed to learn? Such a thing had never been heard of in the royal family of Panchaal! (23)

Draupadi rebels against the education she receives—lessons in sewing, painting, poetry—which she considers useless and she longs for lessons on justice, power royal rule and so on. We see throughout the novel Draupadi's uneasiness with the 'roles' assigned to her sex. But she slowly learns to manipulate her 'femininity' from the lessons she receives from Dhai Ma and the Sorceress. She realizes that "I was a woman. I had to use my power differently" (99).

One of the highpoints of Divakaruni's novel is that unlike other novels that represent Draupadi as a victim, here she is portrayed as a woman who questions not only patriarchal norms of social behaviour and propriety but also her own previous representations. The palace that she desires and acquires becomes 'my domain' and is symbolic of her alternative existence as against the claustrophobic life she leads in her father's palace and at Hastinapur after marriage.

Divakaruni's Draupadi emerges as a figure of immense strength and agency in Divakaruni's novel. Despite repeated humiliation and victimization the reader is full of admiration for her because of her power to challenge patriarchal order. In the infamous disrobing episode she emerges much more powerful than all other male characters present in the Kuru sabha. Her humiliation at the hands of Duhsasana, Duryodhana, Karna and the entire 'elders' along with her 'helpless' husbands leads her to her famous curse and vow that she 'will not comb it [hair] until the day I bathe it in the Kaurava blood' (194). The reader is convinced that Divakaruni's Draupadi is destined to 'change the course of history'.

Julia Hoydis in her essay "A Palace of Her Own: Feminine Identity in the Great Indian Story" has shown how Divakaruni's Draupadi is 'far from a univocal representation of the ideal Indian female, always torn between devoted wife and independent outspoken critical woman'. Draupadi is presented in Divakaruni's version as an ambivalent character in the entire novel torn between conflicting emotions, desires and choices. Divakaruni does not attempt at projecting her protagonist as an ideal and points out her flaws and mistakes. This makes her Draupadi more credible. Moreover, by giving Draupadi agency Divakaruni, in the words of L. Kavitha Nair, 'recovers the voice of womanhood' (130-37).

The Palace of Illusions not only throws light on the silent aspects of the *Mahabharata* but also explores issues that are highly contemporary. Issues like femininity, identity, narrativity and agency are critically explored through the life-like characters of the *Mahabharata*. In Divakaruni's novel gender becomes an important trope by which she is able to reorient the *Mahabharata* so as to make the contemporary readers critical of age old intuitions like patriarchy. And also by recovering the past the novel succeeds in forging a critical relationship between the past and the present, between myth and reality.

WORKS CITED

Divakaruni, Chitra Banerjee. *The Palace of Illusions*. London: Picador, 2008.

Hoydis, Julia. "A Palace of Her Own: Feminine Identity in the Great Indian Story". *Gender Forum: An Internet Journal of Gender Studies* 38, 2012. /http://www.genderforum.org/issues/passages-to-india/a-palace-of-her-own/. 9 Nov 2012.

Nair, L. Kavitha. 'Panchaali as the "Sutradhari" in Chitra Banerjee Divakaruni's *The Palace of Illusions*,' *JSL*, Autumn 2010: 130-37.

CHAPTER

13 Female from Object to Subject: Namita Gokhale's *Shakuntala: The Play of Memory*

Neeru Tandon

> A woman is never anything but a woman, an interchangeable object with no other characteristic than her femininity, whose fundamental characteristic is belonging to the class of women.—Guillamin, Colette. (1995: 178)

Colette Guillamin is a French feminist who writes about the discrimination of women on the basis of gender and ideology. She feels that women are doomed to belong to the class of women and they cannot escape this categorization in a male dominated society. Guillamin believes that the specific nature of the oppression of women is caused by the appropriation of the class of women by the class of men, thus reducing women to the state of material objects. It's high time to ponder how women may come to understand them as speaking subjects located within historically specific, discursive social structures, to question those structures aloud, and to seek to change them. Writers like Namita Gokhale constructs a double story of coming to writing and coming to feminism, in order to explore the formation of a writing subject and show the critical importance of the connections between subjectivity and oppositional imagining, and to highlight the need to find ways of producing knowledge which do not rely on the notion of the detached observer.

Psychologists are of the view that people of both genders view 'men as people but women as objects.' Psychologists believe that the two sexes mainly have biological, social and psychological differences. The study, conducted by Philippe

Bernard, Sarah J. Gervais, Jill Allen, Sophie Campomizzi and Olivier Klein, is based on a fairly simple idea: we can recognize objects easily when we see them upside down, but not people. "For a man, erotic pleasure is objectified; so it is simple and the desire gets directed towards another person. Hence, he becomes the subject, as opposed to object(s) he conceptualizes and through feminine prey he accomplishes his desires. A woman's eroticism, on the other hand, is much complex and reflects the complexity of the feminine situation. So if sexualized women are viewed as objects and sexualized men are viewed as persons, then sexualized female bodies will be recognized equally well when inverted as when upright (object-like recognition), whereas sexualized male bodies will be recognized better when upright than when inverted (person-like recognition)" (Rosenberg, 1).

The concept of sexual objectification and, in particular, the objectification of women, is an important idea in feminist theory and psychological theories derived from feminism. Many feminists regard sexual objectification as objectionable and as playing an important role in gender inequality. Some social commentators, however, argue that some modern women objectify themselves as an expression of their empowerment over men, while others argue that increased sexual freedom for women, gay, and bisexual men has led to an increase of the objectification of men. The idea of sexual objectification has also been an important area of discussion and debate in the area of sexual ethics and the philosophy of sex. Feminists argue that women have historically been valued mainly for their physical attributes. Some feminists and psychologists argue that such objectification can lead to negative psychological effects including depression and hopelessness, and can give women negative self-images because of the belief that their intelligence and competence are currently not being, or will never be, acknowledged by society. Some would argue that the feminist movement itself has contributed to the problem of the sexual objectification of women.

In Laura Mulvey's groundbreaking essay *Visual Pleasure and Narrative Cinema* she uses Sigmund Freud and psychoanalysis to explain and criticize female objectification in film. Women are on display for the pleasure of the male viewer and thereby turned into objects of desire. Laura Mulvey suggests that "the sexualisation and objectification of women is not simply for the purposes or eroticism; from a psychoanalytic point of view, it is designed to annihilate the threat that woman poses." A woman is turned into an object due to many reasons; one of which being the silenced, inferior and passive female with the threatening genital organ (lack of phallus), to that of the contrasting active omnipotent agent of the male (with phallus). Mulvey further suggests: "Instead of acknowledging this evidence of castration they set up a fetish which substitutes for the missing phallus of the woman, but in doing this fetishists have their cake and eat it: they both recognize that women are castrated and deny it, so the fetish is treated with affection and hostility, it represents the *absence* of the phallus and in itself, by its very existence, asserts the presence of it" (Mulvey, 361-73).

In this connection I will like to refer Simone de Beauvoir's statement in the chapter 'Dreams, Fears, Idols'. She says, "Appearing as the Other, woman appears at the same time as an abundance of being in contrast to that existence the nothingness of which man senses in himself; the Other being regarded as the object in the eyes of the subject, is regarded as en soi; therefore as a being" (de Beauvoir, 173).

She further elaborates, "women do not set themselves up as subject and hence have erected no virile myth in which their projects are reflected, they have no religion or poetry of their own: they still dream through the dreams of men. A female is thus turned into an object when she is there solely to give pleasure to the male gaze. Conversely a female is treated as a subject when she is a fully-formed, three-dimensional character that is an active and vital participant in the story or image. In a single image a female can be turned into an object or treated as a subject" (de Beauvoir, 173).

In voicing various viewpoints about the realities of Indian life for women, contemporary Indian English writers also addressed changes in relationship dynamics and promoted liberated sexuality as viable avenues for personal discovery and growth. Namita Gokhale's experiences in life, beginning from her early marriage, her academic let down, her brush with death and her husband's death had perhaps left her emotionally and mentally drained. By her own admission she "had a very eventful life" (Gokhale, 2006: 1). These events in her life could have led to her philosophical bent of mind where she tends to view everything philosophically. Talking of her grandmother Shakuntala Pande, she says that she (her grandmother), got married when she was just thirteen years old. She had been a tomboy, cycling through Nainital in her sari, and a rebel, speaking her mind in a progressive family. Gokhale says that she learnt "the value of doing your own thing, unashamedly" from her grandmother (Gokhale, 2007(a): 1). Perhaps her grandmother's rebellion and independent streak of mind rubbed on to her which is also seen in her female characters Shakuntala, and Ammi. Gokhale's characters are thus a reflection of her own independent and rebellious streak of mind which emerges in her creativity also. A psychoanalytical analysis of the authors enhances our in-depth understanding of the text, apart from getting closer to the writer's mind. It also enables us to bring out the uniqueness possessed by a writer as compared to another due to the varied experiences lived out by them.

Before I start analyzing *Shakuntala* by Namita Gokhale, I will like to remind my readers about her another novel *Gods, Graves and Grandmother*. The novel, by and large, is dominated by the female characters who use their power (of either attachment and bonding or sexuality) to create a space for their existence. The grandmother (Ammi) and granddaughter (Gudiya) are thrown out of house to suffer in the male-dominated society. But they make it a point to turn themselves from object to subject. Novel begins with Gudiya, the narrator who tells us about her illustrious, fearless, creative and dominant grandmother, known as Ammi who refused to become an object. The narrator describes the circumstances when Ammi, who belongs to the family of singing prostitutes, was thrown out of her house, she instead of becoming a parasite or object for someone decides to stand on her own. She comes to reside in a jhuggi near a construction site. She had the courage to build a makeshift temple under the peepal tree behind her jhuggi. Although Ammi was a muslim yet she takes up the role of a pujarin of the temple to earn her livelihood. She used to sing bhajans in her melodious voice, which causes the increase in the number of devotees. By and by she could become the power centre of the temple and control the temple like a true subject. I quote, "There were those who, presuming upon grandmother's otherworldliness, tried to fiddle with the accounts or take home an offertory of ghee or sweetmeats. They were always rudely surprised by the range and vigour of her vocabulary as she rebuked them for their misdemeanours" (*GGG*, 30).

Another example of refusing to be treated as an object is visible in the case of marital relationship between Phoolwati and Sundar Pahalwan. Here, it's Phoolwati who dominates her husband and he too respects her talent as well as the efforts put forth by her. When Sundar Pahalwan proposes marriage to Phoolwati, she keeps certain conditions. Firstly, she asks him to build a pucca house for her—which she would own. Secondly, she wants his approval of her businesses, and, thirdly, she asks him to adopt Gudiya as their daughter.

Sundar is referred to as—"...a most indulgent husband, and no cost or effort was spared to make Phoolwati happy" (*GGG*). He is always full of praise for his wife's intelligence and boldness.

'I tell you, Gudiya', he said fondly, 'no one in the whole of India can match my Phoolwati for brains. M.A., B.A., PhD.—she is cleverer than all that' (*GGG*).

Though it cannot be denied that Namita Gokhale tried her level best to inspire women to behave like a subject and not a mere object in the hands of another gender, yet she also presents the second side of the coin by showing the case of Gudiya and her husband, who treats her like a possession.

Gokhale's novel *Shakuntala: The Play of Memory* is a titillating story of a woman who does not want to walk the path of subjugation laid before her by society. She rather chooses to create a new path for herself, of her own choice irrespective of the norms and dictates of tradition and society where upon she progresses with full confidence and strength. She rebels against the rules and codes of society that curbs her individuality and right to live her life fully and freely. She does not allow her dreams and desires to be crushed under the heels of male dominance and undertakes a journey to fulfil and realize her desires and aspirations. Shakuntala stands for all that is beautiful in Indian womanhood. She would risk her honour as a woman for the love of a man, and yet she would not take one harsh word that goes against her dignity from that man. She has the softness of the softest flower and yet she is as fierce as fire itself. She has strength that knows how to bend. She is the courage to trust. She is silence that knows how to be eloquent when the need arises.

Shakuntala, the heroine of the novel is a provincial girl born into a poor 'vanvasi' family, hill people who live near the forests of the mountainous areas in India. She grows up roaming the woods, and spends her time watching clouds and birds. Shakuntala's brother Govinda is predicted to be a great rishi, a descendent of a great line of sages. Their mother gives all her attention to his education and care, neglecting her. Once deeply hurt by the mother, Shakuntala runs away from home and meets a rock-demoness who gives her shelter. She teaches Shakuntala about the many faces of the mother-goddess who takes many forms, but is always "Swamini, mistress of herself."

She is a carefree and very spirited girl, eager and restless to see the world. However, Shakuntala's life is dictated by the conventions and norms of a patriarchal society that are ingrained into the feminine psyche. According to her mother her life is meant only to be a wife and mother. Shakuntala is denied of basic happiness and space, which she yearns for but fails to achieve. She is forced to lead a life that denies her any freedom. She is portrayed as a simple girl cherishing the desire to lead a life that fascinates her. She lives in a family that neglects and ignores her as human being. The very ground for becoming a successful female is denied to her on the ground of gender discrimination between her and her brother by her mother.

On the slightest mistake of Shakuntala, her mother cries, "You wicked, heartless girl!" and says, "were you born only to trouble and torment me?" (*SPM*, 6). Shakuntala's mother showers all her love upon her son Govinda. For the entire day, things are planned and done only for Govinda in a proper manner by the mother. She provides good food and education for her son and also appoints a teacher for his studies. But when Shakuntala asks her mother for her education, she is chided by her mother who says, "the scriptures" are "forbidden to women" (*SPM*, 11). Being a male child Govinda is entitled to better facilities for his career but Shakuntala is denied the same on the name of tradition. The mother is only concerned for her son's future and considers Shakuntala to be a burden on their life.

On several occasions Shakuntala is dominated by her mother for being a female child. On reaching puberty when Shakuntala's menstruation starts, she is treated scornfully by her mother who is driven by orthodox beliefs and rituals. When her mother sees the blood trickling down the legs of Shakuntala who is in the kitchen at the time, she cries out, "Have you no modesty, girl!" (*SPM*, 31). During menstruation, restrictions are laid upon the movements of women especially from the view of rituals related to notions of purity and defilement. A woman is considered impure and is not allowed to come out of their seclusion, touch or even show her face to others, or touch cooked food during the period of her menstruation. The idea of purity is forced on women by religious beliefs and values in the various communities in India. Shakuntala is dragged to the low stoop beside the cowshed by her mother. Full of anguish and pain Shakuntala asks herself, "What had I done wrong?" (*SPM*, 31).

Bitter experiences of her childhood lead Shakuntala to spend her time in loneliness. She hates everything about her mother. Sometimes she reacts against the discrimination of her mother, "with an anger so violent that it surprised" (*SPM*, 27). Shakuntala's 'self' fully develops into a rebel in a system in which everything needs to be opposed and fought against.

When the mother compares Govinda as a "reflection of some divinity" (*SPM*, 19), Shakuntala dissolves into a jealous rage, plucks all the marigolds in the garden and stomps on them till they are interred in the damp earth. Her rage is symbolic of her rebellion against the male-female child discrimination. Shakuntala feels burdened up by the oppressive dominance of her mother who always insisted on her confirming to the traditional way of life. Shakuntala decides to free herself from the bondage of her mother. So she says, "I was eager to be married, for I saw it as an escape from the bondage of my situation" (*SPM*, 22).

The institution of marriage is of unrivalled significance in the life of a young person. In the life of an Indian woman it marks a point of maturity and signifies the flowering of life. But for Shakuntala it is a way to rebel and release herself from the clutches of her mother. Shakuntala's mother settles her marriage with Srijan, chief of fourteen villages and a widower; Shakuntala is his third wife, the earlier wives having died during childbirth. Marriage provides Shakuntala with a rare degree of freedom like to swim in the river, climb the trees in the forest and rest in the grassy meadows. Though Shakuntala resents the role assigned to a wife in our country who is called upon to stay at home, keep out of the rest of the world and look after the babies, yet it is the only way of rebellion at hand. She greedily laps up the opportunity as a way to revolt and free herself from the dictates of her mother.

Shakuntala's aspired freedom and joy is however illusory and short-lived. Srijan brings a beautiful handmaiden called Kamalini from one of his foreign journeys. The exotic beauty of Kamalini makes Shakuntala jealous and insecure of her authority and position in Srijan's life and house. She becomes anxious of her future and is apprehensive of her possible replacement by Kamalini. Shakuntala feels betrayed and frustrated by Kamalini's presence in the house and says:

> I was not angry with Srijan—he was a man, men were allowed many women, it was the way of the world as I knew it. But the hurt and betrayal, the prickling of thorns under the sheath of my skin—I had never known or anticipated these feelings, just as I had never expected my husband to return from his journey to the east with an exotically beautiful woman with cold and mocking eyes. (*SPM*, 58)

Besides, Kamalini hardly behaved like a maid. This sets off a kind of rebellion in Shakuntala. Shakuntala finds herself unable to handle her unspoken jealousies. She decided to adopt a simpler way and walks out of the relationship. Shakuntala decides to leave her husband's house as she feels insecure of her future there. Arrival of Kamalini and Shakuntala instinctual and eternal desire "to wander with the freedom of birds and clouds" (*SPM*, 8-9), are two motives that triggers off a transformation of the very course of her life.

The rebel and seeker in her revels in the new found freedom and independence, and she does not even hesitate to form a sexual relationship with Nearchus. Shakuntala is aware of the fact that Nearchus is a Yavana, a melachha, a foreigner who is considered impure and unclean. His presence is considered to be a polluting influence on the high castes but still Shakuntala dares to run away with him. In her rebellion, Shakuntala rebels not only against the patriarchal norms and constraints but also against social and religious codes and dogmas.

Another significant dimension of Shakuntala's personality is her desire to shed all her memories associated with her old identity that was more of an imposed identity than her own. In her endeavour to break away from her earlier life she tries to carve out and create a new identity by discarding her old name and adopting a new name. She assumes the name of Yaduri, 'the uninhibited', the fallen one. Through Shakuntala's calculated attempts to acquire a new name and thereby a new identity, the novelist makes its explicit that women need to redefine themselves. *Shakuntala: The Play of Memory* is a reinterpretation of the Shakuntala myth. A woman is shown as rediscovering herself—fighting against patriarchy helped by her own efforts; not by a man. In the temple, for instance, Shakuntala talks to the Goddess. Jacques Lacan's theory of 'mirror image' gets reflected in this particular episode in the novel. Moreover, the novelist reflects both the sides of the same coin. One is that of a girl who chooses to get married so that her pathetic condition gets better so that she too enjoys the freedom of a married woman; to explore the world. The other side of the coin deals with the constant endeavour of the girl, to prove her worth and get noticed and appreciated. She would often think—

> She glows with marital happiness and love. The lady of the household she cherishes her new found freedom, and enjoys her walks to the forest and her swims in the streams. However her freedom is bound to her duties as a wife. As a part of the after marriage rituals, Srijan had taken her outside to view the night sky and guide her sight towards, "...the star Arundhati." (*SPM*, 42)

Gokhale uses notions like *karma* and the birth cycle but there are times when it seems overdone. Again the meeting with a mysterious woman in a cave, who introduces the teenage girl to the worship of the mother-goddess, seems clichéd. The novel's climatic sequences also seem overly descriptive. However Gokhale's description of the ancient Kashi is lyrical and lingering. While the book starts off on a high note, somewhere along the way Gokhale goes off track with a mixture of exotica and erotica. Shakuntala's quest to live life on her own terms is reduced to her being an equal sexual partner. Surely there's more to life than just sex.

The escape of Shakuntala from the comfortable confines of her home and her role as a wife happens not of its own accord but through the agency of an individual whom she chances upon while returning from her visit to the Shiva shrine. The stranger whom she encounters is a Yavana, a Greek traveller and merchant who is enticed by her beauty. The intimacy and exhilaration in his embrace, and the charm and attraction of the strange unknown world he embodies; a world for which she had always craved to know and experience engenders a strange feeling of abandonment in Shakuntala. She leaves him only to return later. Once the priest had explained to her the symbolism of her anklets; "Your anklets weigh down your feet to keep you rooted in your home and family" (*SPM*, 103), and so when Shakuntala abandons her home and her husband to flee with the Yavana, Nearchus, she abandons them too. "Taking off my silver anklets, I flung them into the water and ran towards him" (*SPM*, 115). With Nearchus she redefines her identity as Yaduri, a name that broke the taboos like she did for it stood in slang as a word that "...signified a yoni, a woman's private part" (*SPM*, 119). The free spirit that she was born with, Shakuntala flies from her nest, abandoning and breaking the codes of society and culture. Her actions negate any attempts at comprehension at a superficial, practical and materialistic level. Giving in to her sensual instincts with a wild abandon, she embodies the free flowing spirit of nature that breaks all bounds and barriers constructed to obstruct and control her way. She is the life force itself, wanton and free willed losing her way in the maze of sensory pleasures in her unquenchable thirst for an identity of her own; free and liberated. She is a knowledge seeker to become a subject. She admits, "I was hungry for knowledge, as a bear for honey. The Yavana did not scorn my curiosity, he did not think it inappropriate of me to ask so many questions. I could have listened forever, even if were lying.—I listened spellbound as he talked knowledgeably of ginger and cinnamon-bark, of camphor leaves and cardamom, cloves and sesame" (*SPM*, 135). It is not strange that Shakuntala wanted to know more about the world. Strange is the reaction of Nearchus.

He admits, 'Nearchus was amused by my hunger for the smallest scrap of knowledge or information.' 'You are a peculiar woman,' he said. 'You find more pleasure in my tongue than in my kisses! Do you really want to know more about trade and commerce?'

> 'Although I am neither a merchant nor a tax collector, I want to know everything I possibly can,' I replied. I was not attempting to be humourous, but

> Nearchus broke into uproarious laughter, crinkling up his eyes and throwing back his head until those long curls touched his shoulders. (136)

"Society, being codified by man, decrees that woman is inferior; she can do away with this inferiority only by destroying the male's superiority" (Beauvoir). Shakuntala destroys the rules and codes of patriarchy by forging her own path, breaking the taboos that kept her safely reigned in within the honour and decorum of socially sanctified relationships and roles. She travels with Nearchus across the country, eagerly absorbing all the details and experiences of his travels and knowledge of the world. His passionate and wild love excites and arouses Shakuntala, who devours as much as she herself is devoured. She had loved Sirjan and carried his child within her, yet she is also attached dearly with Nearchus. Their arrival at Kashi, the holy and mysterious city of redemption, renunciation and salvation touches her soul with an awareness of her own self. Stranded on the left bank of the city meant for outsiders, Shakuntala is reminded of her fall from grace. She becomes deeply conscious of her growing detachment from the body that indulges in sensual pleasures with Nearchus. Her thirst for travel and experiences satiated, she does not want to wander any longer and one night leaves Nearchus to journey across the river to the other side. Shakuntala's wanderings on the streets of Kashi and finally her death re-assert the sanctity and inevitability of the codes that define honour and morality for a woman. Fallen from grace and dignity, a woman's transgression can only be met with human or divine retribution. Shakuntala meandered in her path to find her own 'self' but even in her death she declared, "I had not wasted my life" (*SPM*, 208).

Over and again, Gokhale's Shakuntala stresses on the fact that having been named Shakuntala, after Kalidasa's heroine, she carried within herself the samskaras of abandonment. So we meet a woman who has always seen herself aloof from her life. As a girl, she is 'restless to see the world, to wander with the freedom of birds and clouds' and 'saw no error in disorder, it seemed to be the natural condition of life. Shakuntala grows up and is wed to a man who is much older than her. That little Shakuntala, tortured by her mother who could be found hovering by the door seeking to glean knowledge as her brother is being taught the rules of grammar' turns into a wife who does not belong to her man in any sense, resulting in a somewhat face of a whore who is ruled by shame. Eventually Shakuntala seeks redemption.

In the *Mahabharata* her story is told by Vaishampayana in response to a question by King Janamejaya about his remote ancestors. The protagonist Shakuntala of Namita Gokhale's *Shakuntala: The Play of Memory* is named after the fifth century dramatist Kalidasa's heroine Shakuntala. While the original Shakuntala is a helpless nymph who is deserted by her husband King Dushyanta and needs her mother Menaka, 'the celestial apsara,' to put things right for her, Gokhale's mortal Shakuntala is bold and restless at a time when women are confined to the household. Shakuntala questions the rules and customs of society, and when the opportunity arrives, she goes out into the unknown to satisfy her adventurous spirit.

In the novel, Gokhale's language flows easily, and has a wistful edge to it, which serves as a reminder of the many precious things Shakuntala has lost in her lifetime. The tone of the novel is quiet and a bit haunting, because of the supernatural and the mystic that have a constant presence in the background of the story. Perhaps this is enhanced by the knowledge that Shakuntala is already dead at the beginning of the novel, and the story is a flashback recounted by her spirit. It took Gokhale five years to write Shakuntala, and in her own words, it is 'her most painstaking work.' She finally conveyed her message through Shakuntala's love of freedom. When Nearchus commented upon Shakuntala's insatiable desire of knowledge by saying that probably she is not a female at all, because she never complains while travelling and she takes interest in the most unusual things. Shakuntala expresses her innermost feelings, "I was intoxicated by this utter and absolute freedom, the constant movement, and I was ready to go and on, until the end of the world if necessary" (136).

It can be argued, and rarely contested, that Namita Gokhale as a female writer has strived to create a space for female agency in Indian society, with the belief that gender can be used as a vehicle for challenging and attempting to change ideas and values engrained in patriarchal society and thus the values and ideas portrayed through dominant practices. However, they reminded us through their use of characterization that this process must be seen as ongoing and there is still a lot to be done and a long way to go before these stereotypes can be once and for all dispelled from modern society. Through the direct and indirect feminist discourse in her work of fiction she constantly tries her level best to present women as subject and not as mere objects to be used or decorated.

WORKS CITED

Gokhale, Namita. *Gods, Graves and Grandmother*. Penguin Books: New Delhi (1994). 182.

——. *Shakuntala: The Play of Memory*. New Delhi: Penguin Books, 2005.

——. 2006. "Nawab, Kebab and Behenji". Interview with Smita Khanna. *The Times of India*. 24 July. <http://www.timesofindia.com> p. 1

—— 2007. "A Good Partnership". Interview with Mita Kapur. 10 February. http://www.hindu.com/mag/2008/02/20/stories/2008021050140500.htm. pp. 1-2

Guillamin, Colette. *Racism, Sexism, Power, and Ideology*, Routledge, 1995.

Parshley, H.M. and Simone de Beauvoir. *The Second Sex*, Vintage, London, 1997.

Juliet, Mitchell, *Psychoanalysis and Feminism,* Harmondsworth: Penguin, 1975.

Mulvey, Laura. "Visual Pleasure and Narrative Cinema." *Art After Modernism: Rethinking Representation*. Ed. Brian Wallis. New York: The New Museum of Contemporary Art, 1999. 361-73.

Rosenberg, Alyssa. *Study: Women are Objects, Men are People Study* submitted on May 25, 2012 at 10:55 am (www.google.com).

Williams, Linda. "Film Bodies: Gender, Genre, and Excess", Robert Stam and Toby Miller (eds.) *Film and Theory: An Anthology*, Malden, Mass: Blackwell, 2000, p. 215.

CHAPTER 14

Remaking of a "Malgudi": Indian Novel in English in Twenty-First Century

R.P. Singh

The present time has brought many avenues before human race, and a human being is almost baffled in making a choice. In the same tone, in the twenty-first century India the creative tension of Indian novelists in English leads them to accept a 'glocalised' situation where they get allured to the international charm but feel tortured by many a transcultural and commercial forces in the smooth sail of their vision. This juxtaposition results in creating an alternative sub-cultural landscape which gets cemented in a neo-Indianness which on the one hand claims certain association with the icons like Che Guevara, Pentagon, and Hollywood, and on the other keeps a root intact in re-making a 'Malgudi' of their own. Many a times the literary aesthetics slips into a tone of social document. Literature, in the contemporary times, is rather a product of market forces and socio-economic pushes. In the case of new literatures in English, and specially that of the Indian writing in English, this trend has an old root which can be understood in the words of L.W. Pye:

> From the 1950s, the US designated modernity as a complex imbrications of industrial, economic, social, cultural and political development, towards which all peoples of the world were progressively headed. The founders and husbands of this discourse were political scientists and economists, mostly associated with US universities, research institutes, foundations, corporations, and international organizations. Among the premises of this modernity were nationalist fellow

> feeling and individual/state sovereignty as habits of thought.... Development necessitated displacement of 'the particularistic norms' of tradition by 'more individualistic' blends of the modern to help create 'achievement—oriented' societies. (Pye, 19)

The traces of Post-colonialism are still surviving, in the 21st century, on the mindset of the writers and readers both but the focus has been shifted from political to economic, and from social to personal and emotional. The unidentified and liquid anxiety of helplessness, the depressive restlessness, claustrophobia, and rivalry for the apex are setting the core of Indian novel in English in the twenty-first century, which tries to manifest it fresh directions under gradually strengthening trend of globalisation and its influence on Indian literature in English. The present phase of cultural confluence, across the globe, has claimed major shifts in the patterns of human behaviour and its socio-cultural manifestation. Be it the representation through literatures or other performative arts, the changing geo-political contours of the world are clearly visible. In the movement of skilled human resources and resulting cultural configuration never has there been such shuffling of people and shifting of boundaries, intertwining of histories and overlapping of cultures as observed during the transition of the twentieth and the twenty-first century. The causes are, for this, too many to be enumerated ranging from the emergence of a cyber world, emergence of India as a strong global force and a big market, increasing trends in power equation and sinister forms of economic colonialism to the satellite networking, and super expanding of world trade. Consequently the trajectories of the 'culture' has broken down and a panorama of hybridity, heterogeneity and unmonolithic vision comes a board. If any culture retains something of its own identity, its own flavour, its distinctness, it's seen only in sub-cultural practices. It is within this context that a remapping of cultural cartography has been at work for quite recent time to reproduce something worthy to be called glocalization. Nowhere in Indian literature is this phenomenon better articulated than in the novels written in English in twenty-first century. As far as the thematic pattern is concerned, these novels show a fine warp and woof of subaltern cosmopolitanism, modernity and development, science, reason, colonization/decolonization see-saw, narration and nation, roots and routes, submerged and subaltern histories, alternative modernity, move from third world narration to first world narrative zest.

Popular culture and literature is exceedingly significant for a milieu like this or for that matter for any society where cultural plurality is the real determinant of a healthy existence of citizens. If the search for national identity or the quest for the self or unity in diversity is to be an accomplished fact and not merely a ritualistic slogan, we have to take cognizance of the voices coming from the national culture, subculture, and co culture, altogether. To appease the demands and flairs of the masses, and to serve something palpable and authentic to the busy and perturbed brain, there emerges a need of something light and easily fascinating. Here comes surrealism and fantasy. Literary fantasy is no longer a lightweight thing. It may be considered as an overlapping discourse. For a longer time in cultural history, it was associated only with the marginal; but in the postmodernist plurality by virtue of its de-doxifying nature, it is looming large over the set patterns of 'grand', 'authoritative' and 'canonical'. One of the significant features of these discourses is that, it is not only counter-hegemonic, anti-establishment, anti-foundationist, anti-authoritarian, but it also provides us with an alternate mode of looking at things.

This new trend starts with the vigour of Salman Rushdie when his *Midnight Children* proved a faction on Indian History. Vikram Seth visualized a new India of aristocratic values and Amitav Ghosh presents a postcolonial kaleidoscope. Arundhati Roy, Jhumpa Lahiri, Shobha De, V.S. Naipaul, Shashi Tharoor, etc. have given Indian English novel a rainbow colour bringing into its scope different patterns of fact and fiction, and bringing it to the next door events and day-to-day problems. Women writers have pointed out many a feminist patterns and different forms of exploitations, at large.

In the first decade of the twenty-first century, Chetan Bhagat with his novels like *One Night @ the Call Center, Five Point Someone, 2 States* and *The 3 Mistakes of My Life*, has just reshaped the tenor of Indian English novels. Although he is still struggling in academia for acceptance as a serious writer, and his literature falls more under the category of popular literature, his mass appeal cannot be ignored. In the postmodernist pattern, he has really written a new chapter in the history of Indian English novel. Some less known novelists are also doing well. Among these Amish Tripathi's *The Immortals of Meluha*, is based on the origin of Lord Shiva, and reflects a relook at mythology in the 21st century. He is preparing a trilogy, with *Secret of the Nagas* as the second premiere. *Secret of the Nagas* deals with the origin of the Nagas and their encounter with Lord Shiva. *The Oath of the Vayuputras*, the third novel of this trilogy, is still to be published. His use of myth is quite facinating, and finds itself agreeing with the statement of Michael Bell that "by the end of the twentieth century, whether in literature or in anthropology, myth had become a less numinous and more workaday category. The metaphysical and universalistic claims were replaced by cultural historical specificity, in which it is both an object and a means of investigation" (Bell, 128).

Rashmi Bansal's *I Have A Dream* and D.D. Bruno's *Bollywood Extras* are the other important literary products. Sharath Komarraju's *Murder In Amaravati* (2012) and *Banquet on the Dead* (2012), Rukmani Anandani's *A Mysterious Death at Sainik Farms* (2012) have created a shift paradigm by introducing many a subcultural, postmodernist, and uncanny devices into fore. When we look at the total oeuvre of Indian writing in English, specially under the genre of novel, we find the trends like more than average sensibility, enchanting visual appeal, literature as social document, and polyphony of the texts and narrations coming to front.

The complexity of life in the modern phase has settled down in its *sui generis* form in the atmosphere or lot which has come to face, and the continuous practicing in that complex human environment has smothered the exigency, in a way as the continuous flow smoothens the rough edges of an uncut stone. But the urge for the ideal never extinguishes, it may be cornered into background. The same happens over here. Many a young writers seem to be struggling with the 'Bazzar' and their own ideals and call of the locale. While reading the excerpts from the best novels of the year in every December from the last 12 years, I have got myself reminded of the opening lines of Canadian poet Earle Birney's "Bushed" to apprehend this situation in Indian writing in English. The poem brings the imagery of the narrator. Let's see the lines, "He invented a rainbow but lightning struck it/ shattered it into the lake-lap of a mountain/ so big his mind slowed when he looked at it/ Yet he built a shack on the shore/ learned to roast porcupine belly and/ wore the quills on his hatband" (Bushed, *Madness and Exorcism of Poetry*, 1974).

In this situation, the Indian novelist, many a times, finds himself in the boots of a cultural hero, and wants to add something to the perennial endeavour of humanity for making this planet a better place to live in. It works as chalking out a circle where more than average sensibilities take a leap. We can say Aravind Adiga's *The White Tiger* to be such an attempt to magnify the "good" and the "bad" features of Indian social construct, and various trajectories of culture as well. Market has propelled the creativity of most of the Indian novelists, who have undertaken a project to excavate the uncovered, the unseen, the taboo, and the things having the prefixes 'un' and 'non', for it can make them 'especial' in the alien landscape of behaviour. Deconstruction of almost everything in human sensibility and perception has sometimes negated even the good. Good cannot be good for everybody. One's right can be wrong for the other, and weakness, in the same way, can be the strength. Reader, today, has become a consumer, and more so (please mind the sovereignty of consumer) in the developed economies like India where the nation has shrugged out the tag of the third world. Although ironically some academicians and critics hesitate to accept the fact. Their training in, and related allegiance with the so-called "foreign-heaven" does not allow them to shed out this branding. Once they would stand in the common Indian academic lot, which most of the times exposes greater perception and exposure. So this cocooning and shielding also levies different 'should be done'/'must do' type mental set-up and pre-conceived notions for the nation and culture. The other side of the picture which relates themselves to the root that an ordinary reader like me better explains to himself in a phrase "Ezekiel's Tribe" narrate with an agenda of conformity to the local and national. Naipaulian School of writers, sometimes who do not hesitate to sketch poverty porn, always engage their sensibility to show the hole in the landscape.

As postmodernist artistic representation, the novelists in the twenty-first century India are more inclined to bring enchanting visual appeal for readers. Literature under such spectacle has attracted the attention of cinema and television also. There are many a cinematic reappropriation and presentations of literary texts. Aravind Adiga's *The White Tiger* is a good specimen for this. The following description from the novel is remarkable:

> At the end of the market is a tall, whitewashed, conelike tower, with black inter-twining snakes painted on all its sides—the temple. Inside, you will find an image of a saffron—coloured creature, half man half monkey: this is Hanuman, everyone's favourite god in the Darkness. Do you know about Hanuman, Sir? He was the faithful servant of the god Rama, and we worship him in our temples because he is a shining example of how to serve your masters with absolute fidelity, love, and devotion. These are the kinds of gods they have foisted on us. (*WT*, 19)

The White Tiger has become a realistic faction. The following detail is quite moving:

> There is one street in the village; a bright strip of sewage splits it into two. On either side of the ooze, a market: three more or less identical shops selling more or less identically adulterated and stale items of rice, cooking oil, kerosene, biscuits, cigarettes and jaggery.... I am proud to inform you...that the

> children...when examined with tape measure and scales, to match up to the minimum height and weight standards set by the United Nations and other organisations whose treaties our prime minister has signed and whose forums he so regularly and pompously attends. (*WT*, 19)

The description presented by Aravind Adiga is not simply an imagination but the reality in the most parts of the rural India even today. It may be proved by the statement of Hon'ble Justice V.R. Krishna Iyer and O Chinnappa Reddy in the case of Municipal Council Ratlam vs. Shri Vardichan and others; where the Hon'ble judges have commented on the issue:

> The circumstances of the case are typical and overflow the particular municipality and the solutions to the questions emerging from the matrix of facts are capable of universal application, especially in the Third world human space of silent subjection of groups of people to squalor and of callous public bodies habituated to deleterious inaction. The Ratlam Municipal town, like many Indian urban centres is populous with human and sub-human species, is punctuated with affluence and indigence in contrasting co-existence, and keeps public sanitation a low priority item, what with cesspools and filth menacing public health. Ratlam town in an area where prosperity and poverty live as strange bedfellows. The rich have bungalows and toilets, the poor live on pavements and litter the streets with human excreta because they use roadsides as latrines in the absence of public facilities. (164 (1980) 4 SCC)

We find, thus, a literature showing the hardcore social reality. Jeet Thayil's novel *Narcopolis* has been nominated for the Man Booker Prize. Speaking with Srijana Mitra Das, Thayil has discussed drugs, poetry, criticism. He has also questioned whether India has a literary culture. On being asked, 'In *Narcopolis*, why do you choose a series of drugs to depict political history?' He says,

> By choosing to tell an opiated socio-political history, I was able to look at a city over three decades and track its unraveling, from the open-minded cosmopolitan Bombay of the 1960s, 70s and 80s to the divided right-wing McMumbai of today. The period coincided with a change in the drugs that roiled the city's underclasses. The slow poetic world of opium was replaced by the quick brutal degradation of heroin. (*The Times of India*, 28 Sep. 2012)

Further as the answer to the question, "Writing badly will make you ill", one of your poems says. Yet, we see the Indian scene flooded with best-selling bad writing, better books often ignored. What does this indicate about literary culture here? He says, "Because of court patronage which is insidious and widespread, the lack of a critical tradition and a market economy that controls the book trade, Indian writers are not encouraged to take risks or be experimental. They are encouraged to stay with the tried and tested, the commercial and cliched. Excellent novelists and poets toil in obscurity" (*The Times of India*, 28 Sep. 2012).

This statement is not completely valid but such a situation clearly evinces the encroachment of market into the thinking lines of the novelists. Vikram Kapur in his essay "Escapist Fantasy" sums up a new trend of Indian novel in English today:

> We inhabit times where we are constantly bombarded by reality. It comes at us in the form of 24 × 7 news channels, websites that are updated by the minute, mobile update that are more persistent than a pest.... All that on the top of the crummy lives that most of us lead. In such an age, would anyone want to pick up a novel for how faithfully it depicts real life? Some would, I am sure. But for most people losing themselves in a novel is tantamount to escaping the daily ordinariness of their lives. They wish to immerse themselves in new worlds, to be dazzled by the force

> of imagination, to experience breathtaking adventures. (*The Hindu,* October 6, 2012)

Amitav Ghosh has set a new tone of Indianization. His *Sea of Poppies* and *River of Smoke* have brought many indigenous trends into the main course. In *Sea of Poppies*, he has freely used the non-English expressions like *thug, pukka, sahib, serang, mali, lathi, dekko and punkah-wallah shanbaff dhoti, alliballie kurta, jooties and nayansukh, dasturi, sirdar, maharir, serishtas, burkundaz*, and many more freely and frequently. The *Kirkus' Review* finds the *Sea of Poppies* to be a true historical document.

> A historical novel crammed almost to the bursting point with incidents and characters, but Ghosh (*The Hungry Tide*, 2005, etc.) deftly keeps everything under control. It's 1838, and Britain is set on maintaining the opium trade between India and China as a buttress of its economic, political and cultural power. Ghosh orchestrates his polyphonic saga with a composer's fine touch. He lays out multiple narrative lines, initially separate, that eventually conjoin on the Ibis, a schooner bound from Calcutta to China across the much-feared "Black Water." Neel, the sophisticated raja of Raskhali, is convicted of a trumped-up forgery charge. Kalua, a prodigiously strong member of the lower caste, rescues the higher-caste Deeti from ritual burning on the death of her egregious husband. Paulette, a feisty French orphan, stows away on the Ibis to escape the restricted life of a white woman in India. It also might have something to do with the attractions of Zachary Reid, the ship's mixed-race second mate from Baltimore. He's commanded by brutal first mate Jack Crowle, who has no sympathy for anyone of any color, and by Captain Chillingworth, who warns passengers and crew, "at sea there is another law, and...on this vessel I am its sole maker." (reviewed on September 1, 2008)

Amitav Ghosh in *Sea of Poppies* presents the historical account of the plight of farmers in the colonial India through Deeti, a subaltern voice:

> ...the factory's appetite for opium seemed never to be sated. Come the cold weather, the English sahibs would allow little else to be planted; their agents would go from home to home, forcing cash advances on the farmers, making them sigh asami contracts. It was impossible to say no to them: if you refused they would leave their silver hidden in your house, or throw it through a window. It was no use telling the white magistrate that you hadn't accepted the money and your thumbprint was forged: he earned commissions on the opium and would never let you off. And, at the end of it, your earnings would come to no more than three-and-a-half sicca rupees, just enough to pay off your advance. (*Sea of Poppies*, 30)

Amitav Ghosh has created social documents. In an interview with Michelle Caswell (Asia Source September 6, 2004) he has accepted, "For me, the value of the novel, as a form, is that it is able to incorporate elements of every aspect of life-history, natural history, rhetoric, politics, beliefs, religion, family, love, sexuality. As I see it the novel is a meta—form that transcends the boundaries that circumscribe other kinds of writings, rendering meaningless the usual work a day distinction between historian, journalist, anthropologist, etc."

With the advances of India towards being a developed nation, flattening divide between Metro India and rural India, seepage of liquid nationality and many more factors, we find that Indian novel in English is set out find new terrains to settle down a fresh.

WORKS CITED

Adiga, Aravind. *The White Tiger*, Noida: Harper Collins, 2008.

Bell, Michael. "Anthropology, Myth and Modern Criticism" in *Literary Theory and Criticism* (ed.) Patricia Waugh. New Delhi: Oxford University Press, 2006.

Birney, Earle. "Bushed" in Bennett, Donna, Brown, Russell. Eds. *A New Anthology of Canadian Literature*. Oxford University Press, 2002.

Ghosh, Amitav. *Sea of Poppies*, Oxford: Viking: Penguin (India), 2008.

——. *River of Smoke*. New Delhi: Penguin, 2011.

Kapur, Vikram. "Escapist Fantasy", *The Hindu*. October 7, 2012.

Pye, L.W. "Introduction: Political Culture and Political Development" in L.W. Pye and S. Verba (Eds.) *Political Culture and Political Development* (pp. 3-26). Princeton, NJ: Princeton University Press.

Supreme Court Cases 162, Municipal Corporation Ratlam Vs. Shri Vardichan and others Special Leave Petition (Criminal) No. 2856 of 1997.

The Times of India, 28 September, 2012

www.http://www.kirkusreviews.com/book-reviews/amitav-ghosh/sea-of-poppies/#review,visited on December 3, 2012

CHAPTER 15

"Islamic Axe Effect": Fault Lines of Secularism in Tabish Khair's *How to Fight Islamist Terror from the Missionary Position*

Rahul Chaturvedi

Tabish Khair is an established Indian English poet, novelist and critic. He has published two poetry collections *Where Parallel Lines Meet* (2000), *Man of Glass: Poems* (2010); five novels, *An Angel in Pyjamas* (1996), *The Bus Stopped* (2004), *Filming: A Love Story* (2007), *A Thing About Thugs* (2010), and *How to Fight Islamist Terror from the Missionary Position* (2012); and widely acclaimed critical works, *Babu Fictions: Alienation in Indian English Novels* (2001), and *The Gothic, Postcolonialism and Otherness: Ghosts from Elsewhere* (2009). Born and educated in a small town of Bihar, Khair now lives in Denmark and teaches at University of Arhus. His poetry collections and novels have been shortlisted for several prizes including the Encore Award, the Crossword Prize, the Hindu Best Fiction Prize and the Man Asian Literary Prize etc.

Khair's first two novels *An Angel in Pyjamas,* and *The Bus Stopped*—which narrated the incident of a Bus journey on a particular day with a wide assortment of characters and is about the death of a child of a tribal woman who had boarded the bus—claimed moderately well response. Set in Bihar and telling multiple stories, *The Bus Stopped* offers a quintessential insight into Indian subcontinent—its backwardness and poverty, but never with contempt and derision but with a witty seriousness and satirical self-reflexivity. His next novel *Filming* was set in pre-partitioned India and wove together major historical events like the partition of India, the assassination of Gandhi, the rise of photography and the rise of Bombay film industry, the development of barbed wire which serve as the backdrop to unfold the personal everyday moments and make up the main fabric of its character's lives. It tells multiple stories as the narrator of this story tells us in the very beginning that the "strands of this story are entangled like the spool of a film slipping from its reel, like lengths of curling barbed wire" (*Filming* 68). *Filming* did not confront the partition directly rather obliquely used it as a larger monstrous shadow which devoured the existence of its characters. Moving between India and England and written in an ironic, satirical and hilarious mode with the purpose of evoking seedier side of colonialism, his fourth novel *A Thing About Thugs* is a fictional and engaging critique of colonial construction of *thugee* in India. His most recent novel *How to Fight Islamist Terror from the Missionary Position* which is the subject of analysis of this paper is another subversive, satirical and wittily humorous foray into speaking about/against *Islamophobia.* Contrary to its provoking and propagandist title *How to Fight Islamist Terror from the Missionary Position,* the novel is not about a clash of two civilizations, that is Islam and Christianity. It doesn't evoke one Mr. Huntington who wrote a theoretical tale of an inevitable clash of two essentially opposed civilizations rather, like every great work of fiction, this novel is about individual human failings born out of social and cultural conditionings which lead to, at times, catastrophic sufferings of individuals or communities.

How to Fight Islamist Terror from the Missionary Position tells the story of three persons—an anonymous 'atheist' Muslim narrator who teaches English Literature in the University of Arhus in Denmark; Ravi, a 'liberal' Indian Hindu who is pursuing his Ph.D. in that very University; and Karim, a 'religious' Muslim and a taxi driver from India, and in whose flat they live together with all the 'differences' never felt till Karim is implicated of being linked to a terrorist organization. Written retrospectively, the novel comes as a reminiscence of the unnamed Muslim narrator who tries to link religiosity of Karim with fundamentalism which makes him suspect Karim's integrity and friendship after he is implicated in an event called

'Islamic Axe Plot' in the novel. This 'Islamic Axe Plot' is about a Somalian Muslim living in Denmark who is arrested for the attempted murder of an Old Danish cartoonist with 'an axe'. This man, as it turns out, was a regular visitor at the Quranic sessions at Karim's apartment wherein Ravi too often formed a part. This implants the doubt in the mind of the unnamed Muslim narrator, who perceives himself to be a 'secular' person and an atheist, that Karim must be linked to this terrorist act as he used to be mysteriously missing, had been in 'Egypt,' and above all was 'too religious.' He persuasively tries to convince Ravi that better they go to police and intimate what they had felt and known about Karim before the police comes looking for them. The otherwise reluctant and 'liberal' Ravi too hesitatingly follows him to the police station and they speak about Karim and his Quranic sessions which leads to the arrest and detention of Karim. Fortunately, Karim is set free by the police as he is not found guilty of the attack on the cartoonist. But this has changed their lives and everything else.

As it is very much obvious that the plot of the novel is apparently based on Danish cartoon controversy of 2005. In 2005, a Danish newspaper *Jyllands-Posten* published 12 editorial cartoons—the most controversial cartoon of the series was one which sketched holy Prophet wearing a bomb in his turban drawn by Kurt Westergaard. These cartoons were reprinted in Austria next year, and later in a number of European newspapers in France, Germany, Italy and Spain which led to a major fallout of protests and violence which included the bombing and burning of the Danish embassies in Pakistan, Syria, Lebanon and Iran, storming of European buildings and burning of Danish, Norwegian and French Flags over middle-east Islamic nations. Islamic extremists placed a $1 million price on the cartoonist's head for his act of mockery of Islam and, a Somalian Muslim was subsequently shot and wounded by the police for an attempt of murder on Westergaard in 2010. He had entered his house with 'an axe and knife' and shouted slogans of Revenge and Blood, as claimed by the cartoonist, and tried to break down the door after the cartoonist has closed himself in a room. This same incident has been fictively described in the chapter 'Islamic Axe Plot' in the novel.

Islamophobia: The Unfounded Fear of Muslim Immigration

This cartoon controversy poses some paradoxically complex questions supplemented by several other such incidents of negative stereotyping, stigmatization, religious hatred and denigration of Muslims, their religion, their Prophet, Holy Book and symbols which can be best understood if seen in the historical backdrop of *Islamophobia*, a new myth of multicultural European societies. As a matter of fact, there is no denial that this *Islamophobia* is necessary linked to the issue of demographic compositions of post-globalized and post-capitalist western nations. It would be more appropriate if we analyze this issue with reference to Denmark where the novel is set as it would lead to some interesting observations. Denmark was a remarkably homogeneous and insular society. However, she underwent a rapid change over a period of time when workers, mostly Muslims, started emigrating there from Turkey, Pakistan, Somalia and other neighbouring countries. This sudden and rapid growth in the population of Muslims in Denmark let native populations see Muslims as threats which was further exploited by right-wing political parties like Danish People's Party, a far-right, anti-immigrant group for their political benefits. In today's Denmark, Muslims constitute approximately 3 per cent of the population and form the country's second largest religious community and largest minority religion. Thus, we can argue that the substantial emigration to Western countries which inevitably leads to what the west call multicultural society has led to a new kind of problem wherein two culturally and religiously diverse communities are perhaps failing to co-exist peacefully. It is this radical cultural encounter which has created in the mind of the native population a new myth of *Islamisation* of Europe which has conditioned cartoonists like Westergaard, politicians like Geert Wilders and film makers like that of *Innocence of Muslims* (2012) make their own image of Islam in the name of combating *Islamisation* of Europe.

Beyond Secularism

But this is merely one aspect of the story. Now the question is: what this *Islamophobia* points out? This certainly brings one to the issue of the relationship between the secular Western societies and Islam. It certainly connotes a moment of crisis for Western secularism. Secularism can be broadly defined as a political ideology which holds that there is no place, and if there is it is very limited, for religion in politics. There are at least two major ways of defining secularism—one is to define it along the lines of the idea of the separation of church and state, and the other presupposes that the state maintains a neutral equidistance from different religions coexisting in a multicultural society. However, there has been an overemphasis on the former with obvious agenda of 'secularization' of religious communities which has, curiously enough, led to a religious resurgence of almost global dimensions in the last few decades. Historical and economical changes and visible religious conflicts have now made us think that the importance of religion has not waned in our societies posing a kind of serious challenge to this grand-narrative of modernity which believed that modernization would necessarily lead to secularization. In fact after 9/11, religious resurgence has become a major challenge in Western secular societies leading to several cultural conflicts between what Habermas would call the conflict between radical multiculturalism and militant secularism. Habermas opines that in a post-secular society like that of west

> the party of the multiculturalists appeal to the protection of collective identities and accuses the other side of representing a "fundamentalism of the Enlightenment," whereas the secularists insist on the uncompromising inclusion of minorities in the existing political framework and accuse their opponents of a "multiculturalist betrayal" of the core values of the Enlightenment. (*Notes on Post-Secular Society: New Perspectives*)

Habermas further argues that multiculturalists define secularism as a militant ideology, a "fundamentalism of the

Enlightenment and warns against the enforced assimilation of cultural minorities and claims for the claims of preserving the intrinsic characteristics of minority cultures" (*Notes*). On the other hand, secularists, Habermas writes, criticize multiculturalism as "anti-racist racism" and points out the dangerous consequences of the politics of identity which would lead to "small, self-isolated social groups, each of which adheres to a different norm" and leading to almost parallel societies in a given territory (*Notes*). Habermas points out the flaws of both viewpoints—secularism is communitarian and egalitarian and multiculturalism is divisive wherein each culture is a "semantically sealed whole, cut off from dialogues with other cultures" (*Notes*).

Read in the wake of the crisis as suggested by Habermas, *How to Fight Islamist Terror from the Missionary Position* foregrounds this continuing and ever-transforming nature of religion and secularism in today's world. It implicitly evokes the most urgent and compelling question of the place of religion in contemporary secular societies. It generates a debate on our post-secular multicultural societies, whether religion should have a place in social scientific thinking about the world or be rejected as a pre-modern, unscientific and uncivilized belief. In the novel, the unnamed Muslim narrator and Ravi represent these two conflicting viewpoints. Ravi is a 'radical multiculturalist' who believes that "Muslim immigrants cannot be integrated into Western society in defiance of their religion but only with it" (*Notes*). He seems to advocate collective cultural rights of immigrant ethnic groups in the pluralist and democratic Danish society. The unnamed Muslim narrator, although his stance is never so obvious and cannot be clearly pointed out whether forced or coerced, seems to be that of a 'militant secularist' who pines for a policy of abstract integration of cultural minorities subjecting them to the norms and beliefs of the majority culture. The conversation between the unnamed Muslim narrator and Ravi can be a case in point:

> It had by now become clear to us that we had underestimated Karim Bhai's religiosity. His flat was

a hub for informal Quranic studies every Friday evening, when young men, mostly bearded, and women mostly shrouded, would descend on for long discussions over coffee, tea, *nimki* and other snacks that Karim diligently stocked. These ended up at nine sharp, when Karim went off to ply his taxi, unwilling to let religion deprive him of the lucrative Friday-night custom.

'You underestimate them, bastard,' he replied. 'They are far more pertinent and political than almost all the academic seminars that I have attended. They discuss matter of significance and do it honestly: how to make sense of the world, how to make it a better world. They still have a conscience, these young men and women, not just like a bank account like the rest of these people.'

He waved his hand at the young people drinking and dancing in the Irish pub we were in.

'I know all about the politics,' I retorted. 'I grew up with politics beating down on me. Basically, it all boils down to three points: the Quran is the final hand-autographed word of God; the West is fucking us; the Jews are fucking us via the West.'

. . . 'Listen to yourself, yaar. You sound like a Danish tabloid. What do you think they are? The secret Arhus cell of Al Quaeda?'

'Who knows?'

'Karim Bhai, a terrorist! Really, have you ever come across a person with more seriousness of purpose, more consideration for other people's space, you fanatic? He lets us drink in his flat, and you know what alcohol means to people like him.'

'Perhaps he needs the money more than he hates alcohol.'

'Oh yes, perhaps he is the main funder of Al Qaeda? That's why he needs the money so badly!' (29-31)

This very casual conversation between Ravi and the narrator problematizes the ideals of both secularism and multiculturalism foregrounding a general public debate between the two. There is need not only for the liberty of worship, the equality of different faiths in political sphere, but also that of religion in state policy-making—to disregard religion as a dead, non-scientific and pre-modern ideology is also questionable. However, there is also a simultaneous need for identifying common societal goals in any multi-religious society towards which all the citizens of the state should strive to achieve despite religious differences among them. There is the importance of a society allowing the democratic participation of all religious voices in shaping commitments of its polity. And there is also the need to turn one's focus away from just religion to acknowledging and respecting wider forms of cultural integration.

Images of Muslims: Stereotypes, Media and Mis-Representation

Many popular images of Muslims are stereotypical, distorted, inaccurate, and mostly fallacious. When individuals of one community are confronted by a continual exposure to such distorted repeated images about the other community, these images often congeal to construct stereotypes or generalizations which individuals use to understand and define the other community, interpret its ways of life and cultural practices. These stereotypical (mis)representation fictively construct an 'imagined community' which is homogenous, stagnant, changeless, and deny the dynamic cultural heterogeneity of the other community or its culture.

Although stereotyping is a natural and very common form of social discourse, these stereotyped images and misrepresentations are internalized, later cause epistemic violence, and can be a highly polemical and politicized act of (mis)representation. As suggested above, stereotyping is often an exclusionary cultural production which produces a set of false assumptions about a group of people which is often uncritically populist judgement based on biasedness of several kinds, caste, class, creed, religion and so on. It can be defined as an act of people generalizing people—an attempt of defining a group of people with limited prejudiced perceptions which is often disapproving and mostly connotes a sense of dislike. Thus, stereotyping can be defined as a systematic process of generating negative, simplified and reductionist false consciousness towards the other which can be purposefully used to organize our perceptions to achieve ethnocentric, cultural and political control. Stereotyping works mainly on following three principles:

(a) It essentialises an idea.
(b) It expels 'difference' among individuals of stereotyped community and extols differences of stereotyped community from the one which stereotypes.
(c) It thoroughly negates the otherness of other.

Thus, stereotyping is a homogenizing project which proscribes and delegitimizes 'difference', imposing one's own cultural agenda on other groups. This is vividly portrayed in the novel suggesting how deeply stereotyping has invaded our worldview and determines the way we look at individuals and communities. All through its narrative, the novel tries to critique such stereotypes. Its very title is ironical and attempts to critique deeply embedded stereotype that Muslims are terrorists. There is no attempt anywhere in the novel to take sides or justify any kind of violence in the name of religion, be it any kind of religious fundamentalism. What the novel seems to foreground is that Islam, Islamic fundamentalism and terrorism need to be viewed separately—Al Qaeda is not Islam; Egyptian Brotherhood does not speak for all Muslims of the world. It emphatically asserts that Muslims are not groups but also individuals. It profusely debunks and challenges stereotypical rhetoric of clash of civilizations which is founded on the idea that the 'Islam' and the 'West' are distinct and separate entities that can never meet. It questions this imaginary idea that Islamic civilization is a homogeneous civilization based on the concept of pan-Islamic brotherhood which is in an outright opposition to secular Western civilization. The twain can never be compatible as these two civilizations are dialectically opposed to each other—if the west is secular and democratic, the Islam is conservative and feudal. Karim's story of being falsely alleged of being an Al Qaeda terrorist, even by those who knew him the most and lived with him, only because he is a Muslim is certainly eye-opener for those whose perception are mostly colour-blinded by religious stereotypes. How dangerous can be the psychic damage caused by these stereotypes can be seen in self-reflexive recollection of the unnamed narrator who recounts his reasons for thinking of Karim as a terrorist:

> I am not saying I was uninfluenced by the atmosphere: "the Islamist Axe Plo", as it was being called, was at its height then, with adjectives being flexed and postures struck on all sides. But still I do not think I was paranoid. I had reasons to be suspicious, cause for caution. If you have a Muslim name, you have to be vary in some contexts. Remember the Indian doctor who was arrested and accused of being a terrorist in Australia just because his sim-card ended up in the wrong hands? There are many other stories like that, in Asia, America, Europe. Ravi could afford to ignore them; I could not. (172-73)

Thus having a Muslim name, the unnamed narrator suggests, may be a potential reason for stereotyped prejudice. There have been several detentions of Muslims of this nature across the globe. Despite its melodramatic musical foray, a movie like *My Name is Khan* (and I am not a terrorist) similarly highlights, perhaps in a more emphatic form and medium, and interrogates the stereotyped representation of Muslims in America.

Now the question is what has led to such prejudiced stereotyping of Muslims across the world. There are instances of Hindu Fundamentalism, Christian Fundamentalism and even Buddhist Fundamentalism apart from Islamic Fundamentalism, then why only Muslims are stereotyped as fundamentalists and terrorists? The current challenge to secularism in Western Europe is being debated, not just in terms of the wider issues of integration and multiculturalism, but also in terms of hostility to Muslims and Islam based on stereotypes and scare stories in the media best understood as that has come to be called *Islamophobia*, i.e. a specific form of cultural racism perpetuated against Islam through free floating images. It can never be denied that the mass media does impact the way we define the world around ourselves and also the way we define who we are. The media continually normalizes and reinforces stereotypes and creates myths of who we are as individuals. Images circulated via print and electronic media constantly reinforce our notions of cultural stereotypes. It fictively constructs and perpetuates certain stereotypes about groups and communities on the lines of race, gender, class and so on which is often hegemonic and manipulative and acts as persuasively indoctrinating an ideology to control people. It can easily be perceived that several forms of media such as movies, documentaries, magazines, music, TV programmes manipulate and manufacture 'the ways of seeing' and through repetitive reproductions of stereotypes may reinforce negative opinions about others, especially those who are powerless, weak or minority. There can be seen several instances of such biased, stereotypical reinforcements. Apart from the Danish cartoon controversy around which the plot of this novel has been woven, there has been another small Prophet Muhammad Cartoon crisis two years back, when Lars Vilks sketched a dog with the face of the Prophet. In Netherlands, Geert Wilders, a politician and best known for his criticism of Islam commissioned a short film, *Fitana* in 2008 which was dubbed blasphemous and he was summoned to the court for inciting hatred. Before all this could subside there was another row of violence due to the circulation of infamous video of *Innocence of Muslims* on YouTube. In view of this, there was an attack on U.S. consulate in Benghazi, killing U.S. Ambassador Chris Stevens and three other Americans by Libyan Islamist extremists. In Egypt too, a group of Egyptians angry over the same movie tried to storm into the U.S. Embassy in Cairo and burnt the American flag. After September 1, 2001 and the American invasion of Iraq, these images have been intensified through a well-structured network of television and film depictions. If the case of *Innocence of Muslims* is taken for study, it clearly reveals that images can be used as ideological weapon to articulate and transmit ideological propaganda and warfare within a particular historical and political context. These political cartoons and films certainly act as a cultural and ideological bomb discursively used to perpetuate negative images about Islam and thus are/may be used as a ploy by sectarian people and politicians to politicize Muslim immigration in European countries. It cannot be denied that such images create conflict between cultures, and mostly they are stereotypical. These images are constantly damaging the image of all Muslims across Europe and America. Although overt expressions of prejudiced stereotypes may be less prevalent in these multicultural, democratic, and secular societies, stereotypes do have a more subtle and, perhaps, more pernicious consequence which often leads to discrimination and stigma.

This novel too foregrounds one such damaging effect of repetitively manufactured and telecasted images when Karim's religiosity becomes a cause of stereotyping him as a terrorist. The panel over TV to discuss the attack on the cartoonist also shows a stereotypical way of 'guessing' the facts of the event:

> This sharpening of the weapons of assault was widely discussed in the media, especially on TV. I remember one such discussion. First (male) panelist: It proves that he had intended to murder Herr Hansen. Why else should he sharpen the weapons? Second (male) panelist: It definitely indicates a degree of premeditation. Third (male) panelist: But does one need to sharpen a knife or an axe in order to kill a man? I mean, it is not as if flesh is that resistant or... Hostess (interrupting): Barr, that's gory...(and turning to the 'expert on terrorism'): What would you say, Colonel? Expert (male) on terrorism: there is a chance that the accused was specifically influenced by the Taliban brand of Islamism. In all known cases of Islamist assault, axes and ceremonial beheadings have been employed by Taliban-influenced militants four

> times more often than by other jihadists groups.... (166-67)

What are the issues or problems that such representations create? In what ways does media coverage affect the popular mindset? One major challenge is that such kind of oversimplified and generalized 'guessing' of facts in the name of 'news' create a destructive and dormant ideology of hate in the minds of masses which leads to comparisons between "Judaism and Islam and judged the former to be the better religion" (170). Therefore, all such stereotypical representations must be challenged at the very outset as they function as dormant volcanoes which may erupt at any moment of history.

The other point which is also highlighted in the novel is the biased media coverage around the world which is mostly Eurocentric. There is silencing and restrain with regard to coverage of Christian fundamentalism but an equally powerful sensationalism towards Islamic terrorism. Foregrounding this point, the narrator recounts:

> Do you remember that in April last year a Christian preacher in USA had 'tried', condemned and burned a copy of Quran, after a year of infantile posturing back and forth? The news had been covered with surprising restraint by the international media but somehow it had reached fundamentalist Islamic preachers in Afghanistan, who had then led a mob attack on some UN workers, resulting in a number of shocking execution-like deaths. (132)

Common Citizenship and Cultural Difference

Then, which stance can be an appropriate with regard to secularism in the present multicultural world? The answer is never obvious and not one. One form of multiculturalism which can be an alternative is to develop the idea of secular tolerance. Tolerance here does not connote any kind of negative disapproval rather it emphasizes a positive acceptance of one in what one does not believe. This kind of tolerance is not imposed through state or majority community rather it is intrinsically structural and mutual. It is not a religious majority that forcibly imposes its will on the other in the name of secularization but a process of informed individual choice of tolerance of other religious communities as Habermas states:

> "Tolerance" is of course not only a question of enacting and applying laws; it must be practiced in everyday life. Tolerance means that believers of one faith, of a different faith and non-believers must mutually concede one another the right to those convictions, practices and ways of living that they themselves reject. This concession must be supported by a shared basis of mutual recognition from which repugnant dissonances can be overcome. This recognition should not be confused with an appreciation of an alien culture and way of living, or of rejected convictions and practices. We need tolerance only vis-a-vis worldviews that we consider wrong and vis-a-vis habits that we do not like. Therefore, the basis of recognition is not the esteem for this or that characteristic or achievement, but the awareness of the fact that the other is a member of an inclusive community of citizens with equal rights, in which each individual is accountable to the others for his political contributions. (*Notes*)

What Habermas suggests here is to develop a kind of public reason which is more positive and exhibits an attitude of *respect* rather than disapproval. In this light, the relationship between Karim and Clauses is of an importance to understand the true meaning of multiculturalism. Karim and Clauses share the same apartment. Great Clause and his friend were a regular visitor at Karim's place. When Karim is imprisoned for being a terrorist, it was only Great Clause who visited him in the jail. Although Karim had avoided meeting them after he had revealed his homosexuality to him, Great Clause's visit moved him so much. He had asked for his prayer beads which Great Clause provided him in the jail. It is obvious that Karim can never approve of his homosexuality because of the obvious cultural differences, but nevertheless learns to acknowledge what Habermas would call "shared citizenship with the cultural difference" (*Notes*). His act of asking Great Clause for his holy prayer beads symbolizes his first step towards a 'complementary learning processes' which is "certainly necessary on the secular side unless we confuse the neutrality of a secular state in view of competing religious world views with the purging of the political public sphere of all religious contributions" (*Notes*). It can be convincingly argued that Karim and Great Clause have reached an 'understanding' by the end of the novel which another very prominent political philosopher Rawls has called "overlapping consensus"—a consensus of the people with very different moral, religious and political positioning, and with complete awareness of their differing viewpoints as well as denial of the logic of cultural sameness for political/public consensus. With all their cultural differences, Karim and Great Clause have reconciled to their common citizenship and evolved an overlapping consensus.

Before I conclude, I would like to mention that there are other dimensions for reception of this novel. These aspects include a debate on the boundary between 'free speech' and 'hate speech', 'modernity' and Islam, contextualization of terrorism/fundamentalism with Islam in public debates and some other serious concerns. However, I need to add here that the novel is not a defensive discourse on Islam or a commentary on *Islamophobia* rather it is an artistically told tale of friendship, betrayal and post-realization of the politics of betrayal. It is thoughtfully emotive, humorously painfully story. The novel is never justificatory as the narrator himself remarks: "There are other answers too. But no, they are not answers. Who am I to answer for Karim Bhai? Who are you to demand answers from him?" (184). Instead it raises a pertinent issue that if we cannot understand one individual, the claim to understand a whole culture may produce a new set of 'oriental narratives,' essentialised, stereotyped and prejudiced misrepresentation. Therefore, this project should be left unfinished. The novel is more a story of resistance challenging dominant (mis)representations of Muslims across the globe by a group of population of the multicultural societies of the west/world who understand Muslims and Islam through narratives of *Islamophobia*, militant secularism and Eurocentric stereotyping of mass media, and this universalism this novel critiques. It is this remarkable interrogation that makes *How to Fight Islamist Terror from the Missionary Position* an important narrative of our times.

WORKS CITED

Habermas, J. "Notes on Post-Secular Society: New Perspectives". *Quarterly*, 25: 2008: 17–29. Web. 30 May 2012. http://www.signandsight.com/features/1714.html.

Khair, Tabish. *Filming*. London: Picador, 2007.

——. *How to Fight Islamist Terror from the Missionary Position.* New Delhi: Harper Collins, 2012.

CHAPTER

16

Shashi Deshpande's Moral Vision in *Ships That Pass*

Sunita Rai

As it is explained in the Author's Note, stories of crime and mystery have always had special appeal for Shashi Deshpande. She has always been keen to revisit a murder mystery that she serialized four decades ago for eve's Weekly. *Ships That Pass* as Deshpande would like it to be, is "a complete story of love and mystery." The immediate reactions of the scholars and reviewers to the new book have not been very positive as it has been in respect of her other novels. Reviewing the novel for *The Hindu* Vaishna Roy observes: "It is rather that the book fails to decide quite what it wants to be. It commits cardinal sin of faltering in its loyalties—whether to Tara's death and its mystery, to the death of Tara's marriage and its tragedy, or to the birth of Radhika's love. This irresoluteness is all pervasive and sets the book adrift." Agnibesh is of the view that the narrative of the book "weakens' at points and the characters do not leave desirable impact." It is certainly not one of the best works of Shashi Deshpande but it is very readable. As always with Deshpande, the novella deals with personal relationship and female friendship. It is a piece of literature which communicates Deshpande's moral vision.

Shashi Deshpande is a conscious artist with a moral vision. Form and vision, for her, are equally valuable in a work of literature. Much of the creative writings are inspired by the artist's desire for social reform. Aesthetics is also an important part of literature. In an essay entitled "Literature and Morality" Deshpande has made an important observation:

> Undoubtedly, the core of all great literature is a moral vision. But this moral vision has to be conveyed in the

> right form and every serious artist is conscious of this, no artist ever disdains the form. (109)

Deshpande's new novella has an underlying moral purpose. It portrays a world of moral and ethical values in which the central character is required to make a choice between right and wrong. In *Ships That Pass* the novelist is concerned with the exploration of human psyche. All her novels portray what happens in the psyche of her heroines as they pass through the process of self-realization. The portrayal of the mystery of mind helps readers to visualize the frailties and possibilities of human life. The novel presents the theme of a girl's journey of self-discovery. It also deals with the theme of love and goodness. Marriage is a public institution as well as an intensely private affair. Married couples live together and build a family. Family is the value-base of Indian society. It is the cradle for inculcation of values of sharing and caring. It is easy to see that society is an extension of family. Family is essential for social living. Relationship between husband and wife based on reciprocal love and friendship is necessary for successful social living.

Ships That Pass meanders round three centres of attraction—collapse of conjugal life of a married couple Tara and Shantanu, mysterious death of the married woman Tara and birth of love in the narrator for an older man. The novel is by no means an uncommon family drama which begins with a happy marriage, a union of true love between the partners. Tara is beautiful and wise who marries young after a fairy tale romance. She has poetic talent and her poems have appeared in magazines. The narrator gives an interesting account of her sister's marriage:

> In any case, everyone cannot have Akka and Shaan's luck, to fall in love the way they had done and to be sure of each other, to know with absolute certainty that this was the person with whom you wanted to live the rest of your life. (24)

Shaan has also been enamoured of Tara since their teenage. The day he gets a job, Tara gives up everything—her family, her studies, her friends. Harriage with Shaan, a chemical engineer, who works in a government concern, is her own decision. The couple has a happy married life out of which two children—a boy and a girl are born. They have excellent relationship and their conjugal life is absolutely free from disturbance. But as ill luck would have it the husband is awfully busy with his work and has little time to spare for the family.

> Shaan was rarely at home. He left early in the morning and returned late at night. His excuse of too much work...looked suspiciously like indifference. Well, in a couple married for fourteen years some indifference is to be accepted.... (42)

The death of five-year-old daughter Geetu is a severe blow to the family. Tara falls victim to some mysterious illness. Her arthritis gets worse. But she patiently bears her suffering as just punishment for her daughter's death:

> Her painful spells are getting more frequent. And worse. She suffers. And refuses to admit she's suffering. She won't see a doctor, she drugs herself instead.... (3)

Her husband summons Radhika with the request to stay with them for some time and hopes that "it would be some diversion" (3). The narrator is shocked at the plight of her sister: "She looked ravaged, no bruised is the right word" (31). Having lost all interests in the affairs of life, she is vaguely adrift. The fact of "devoted lovers being estranged from each other" (26) is extremely outrageous. Tara, who is now no more than a shadow of her former self, is constantly disturbed by her painful psychic problems. "In order to escape the ordeal of life she even tries to commit suicide twice by overdozing sleeping pills" (59). She blames her husband for her daughter's death of luckemia: "...she thought he had n't taken Geetu's illness seriously at first. She thought that if he had the child could have been saved" (112). Shaan's infidelity further aggravates the situation. The gossip regarding his extra-marital affair with a widow is now well-known:

> The names of Shaan and the woman, Rohini were publicly linked. They had been seen together. She was

> his mistress. She had insisted that Shaan marry her because she had become pregnant. (100)

Tara no longer trusts her husband. It is evident from one of the entries in her diary:

> I know things about Shaan, I've been afraid for some time now. A kind of sixth sense has warned me at times, like the time I didn't drink the tea he had brought me. Now I take my medicine myself. (102)

She begins to write poetry to "cope with her sorrow" (116). In the last months of the life, her friendship with a neighbour who happens to be the chief medical officer, is a great relief for her. Dr. Ram Mohan who quite often calls on her as a friend not as a doctor, happens to be a very good man. He is—"Tara's confidant, the man she turned to for comfort and companionship." Thus, the marriage of Tara and Shaan has failed. The partners have fallen apart. Tara seeks to drown her sorrow in drugs and the husband develops extra marital relationship. The wife is fully aware of her husband's infidelity. However, the marriage appears to be in perfect harmony and peace with each other. Life, for Tara has lost all its charm, however she strives to get over her daughter's death "for Abhi's sake" (114). Shaan feels a similar concern for his son. Being accused of murdering his wife he retreats into silence. He has become an enigma. He is neither angry nor frightened. He wants to leave his son to the care of Dr. Ram Mohan, the only confidant of his wife. "I want you to look after him" he said finally, abruptly, "I don't mean just for now. I mean for always" (1).

Ships That Pass is a very well written book that deals with the collapse of family relationship. As it is usual, human life is quite often painful, ugly and unsatisfying. Normal human life is upset, as is the case with the present couple, by disease, death or accident which stay beyond human control. The excellent relationship of Tara and Shaan based on genuine love and mutual trust is eventually upset. The wife dies in mysterious circumstances and the husband is arrested for murder.

Tara's tragic death takes place on a dark night when she is all alone at home and the power fails. A mysterious gasleak in the kitchen is detected and is repaired subsequently. But in the morning, Tara is found dead on account of an overdose of pills and Shaan is arrested. The death is a consequence of murder or suicide, it remains a mystery. In the introductory note of the novel, Deshpande clarifies that "the logistics of murder and detecting were not my forte" she is more interested "in the people and the great mystery of the human mind" (6). The novelist briefly sums up the crime. It is suggested that Tara does not and cannot commit suicide as it is obvious from her conduct a day before her death. She feels very happy advising her sister to marry a right man. She is also planning to help her the next day: "Would some one planning suicide speak of her plans for the next day?" (114). Despite his love affair with Rohini, it is not convincing that Shaan killed his wife to marry Rohini. He always feels care and concern for his wife and that is why he has summoned Radhika to help her. Moreover, he never felt hostile to her: "Does that make any sense at all? It doesn't. And whatever anyone may say, I don't think Shaan was hostile to Tara." It is suggested that Tara's death is an accident: "She swallowed a whole bottle of pills by mistake?" "Maybe she took one, became groggy, forgot that she'd already taken the pill and then..." (120).

At this critical juncture the action takes a sudden turn. It moves to explore the complexity and impossibility of human relationship. Usha K.R. aptly remarks: "Shashi Deshpande's *Ships That Pass* beautifully alternates between a crime novel and a piece of literature" (*Deccan Herald*, 22.8.2012). Human beings are like ships that pass at night and our deepest communication is "only a signal shown and a distant voice in the darkness" (86). Life may seldom turn out as expected. The only hope lies in finding the courage to take one's chances. The married life of Tara and Shaan begins with perfect trust and openness. The ideal relationship is eventually clouded and love and hate lose distinction.

The novella has a main plot and a sub-plot. The main plot deals with a crime and stresses the impossibility of perfect love.

The sub-plot deals with a romance between the narrator and the elderly Dr. Ram Mohan, a family friend who frequently visits the household. It suggests that the hope of perfect love makes life worth living. Radhika is a stupid young graduate who seeks escape from the problems of life through an arranged marriage. The girls of her age group are chalking out plans for the future, Radhika is not clear about her expectations from life. As marriage is an unavoidable certainty she decides on a whim to marry Ghanshyam, a man from a good settled family. She is quite hopeful that as a responsible husband and wife "they would lead a good life" (21). In course of time, she comes to understand the sombreness of such a decision. The disappointment, disillusionment and disenchantment in the family life of her sister bring about a remarkable change in her attitude. She comes to the conclusion that marriage is not the solution to the problems, "it is only the beginning of problems" (68).

Gender discrimination is a significant perspective of Indian reality. Every aspect of Indian society is gendered conferring specific advantages to men and disadvantages to women. Women are relegated to a subordinate status in family and society. They are expected to be dutiful daughters, loving mothers, submissive daughters-in-law and faithful wives. But now the time has changed. With the expansion of education and spread of democratic ideas people's attitude towards women is also changing. Radhika and her sister in the present novella are middle-class educated women who are not prepared to sacrifice their lives for others. They move away from patriarchal values to the values of self-discovery and self-assertion. Tara rightly advises her sister not to follow the example of their mother:

> 'Rubbish', she said, Don't listen to her. Things were different in Aai's days. They did not want anything of their own. To be married was their final goal of their lives. To have children and look after your husband and kids, may be even your in-laws—that was all there was to life. (90)

Women are also human beings endowed with inherent potentialities. They cannot ignore their household duties and responsibilities. But they must also strive for self-realization. Tara must do what she can for the sake of self-satisfaction: "It seems to me that there is so much of me. I have never used, never tried to use. I want to find out what there is that I can do" (90). Her advice to her sister also is to marry the right person and keep her inner self intact: "Keep yourself alive. When you marry—or is it whomever keep yourself intact. There's always a real you inside. Don't drown that real you in a man in the family" (91).

The death of her sister brings Radhika closer to the doctor. Like the doctor, she also feels worried about Abhi, her sister's growing son. It is necessary to prove Shaan innocent for the future of Abhi: "In any case, Shaan matters more now. Abhi needs him, Abhi doesn't need to have a dead mother and a father who killed her as his parents" (121). It is therefore she agrees to become "an accomplice in his charade of making a suicide note of Akka's scribbles" (118). Personally, she does not believe that the note that is produced to convince the police, is actually a suicide note. In course of their struggle to prove that Shaan is innocent, the narrator and the doctor develop deep intimacy and form close relations based on reciprocal trust and understanding. There is no scope for any doubt or misunderstanding between them. Radhika seeks her brother's permission to let her stay with the doctor for a week before marriage. She does not care what people think about it: "What do these things matter, Dada? I asked him. Who cares what people will say? Look at what we're struggling with. Akka dead. Shaan in jail and Abhi.... Does it matter what people say?" (111).

As Radhika feels genuine love for the doctor she can set off on the adventure of life with the person she loves. She calls to mind the words of her sister: "Never, never marry a man who doesn't seem right to you. And when you find the right man, never let him go" (123). She finds it hard to give a proposal of marriage. Her gender, upbringing, conventions and her own-cowardice stand as obstacle in her way. But she is aware if she fails now, she will have to repent throughout her life. She is bold enough to take initiative and without inhibition she speaks to the doctor:

> 'Do't you want to get married? Ever?
>
> 'Who would have me? he asked lightly.
>
> 'Me. I mean, I would'. (124)

The marriage takes place in a government office. It is a simple registered marriage without lights and decoration. Radhika is quite sure to be her true self with this man. Her loss of faith in love after Shaan and Tara returns. She observes: "I believe in love—if friendship is part of it.... Why didn't anyone tell me marriage could be like this" (136). The new novel thus captures the intricacies and intrigues of family relationships. The novelist has used murder or likely murder just to write about how life is mysterious and unknowable. Failure of marriage, the search for self-knowledge, grief over dead parents and dead children, all these occur in the new novel. We come across a very important statement on the significance of marriage:

> Marriage is a very strange thing. It's a very public institution, it's meant to tell the world that two people are going to live together, to declare that their children will be legal, that these children will inherit their property. It's meant for social living, to ensure that some rules are observed so that men and women don't cross the lines drawn for them. At the same time, marriage is an intensely private affair. No outsider will ever know what goes on in a marriage. It is a closed room, a locked room.... (60-61)

Mystery is an important part of human life. Human mind is also mysterious and unpredictable. Like a consummate artist, Deshpande digs too deep into the inner recesses of the mind which only a bold author chooses to explore. This crime thriller centres round a mind game played out between Tara and her husband Shaan. The surface shimmers with what lurks beneath. Happy relationship degenerating into a tortuous blame game, Tara's marriage to sweetheart Shaan shattered by their daughter's death, Tara's relationship to Dr. Ram Mohan and Shaan's with the young widow Rohini, Tara's assumed suicide and Shaan's imprisonment for murder, all these show how life seldom turns out as expected. In conversation with Deepa Ganesh, Deshpande aptly remarks:

> Human emotion is something you cannot discount. I am not ruling out any possibilities, but love according to me, is not calculated. It's hard to say why certain relationships happen and others, even with the right partners fail. A similar situation arises in my novel *In the Country of Deceit* as well; it's hard to unravel the mystery of relationships. (*The Hindu* 28.7.2012)

Man has emotional freedom. But he has no social freedom to act on these emotions. Family forms the basis of Indian society. It is a kind of laboratory where we learn the lessons of self-control and compassion for others. Deshpande has stressed the importance of these attributes which are necessary to protect the interests of the family as well as society.

Here one remembers Deshpande's earlier novel *In the Country of Deceit*, which explores the theme of a woman's journey of self-discovery. The protagonist is assertive and has the courage to make her own decisions. As a 'new woman' Devayani shows patience and courage to face life as it comes on her way. *Moving on*, this novel also shows, how to move on, how to make the most of one's life. One must understand the meaning of life and learn how to face it. In her *Afterward* to Shakti, the novelist states:

> What women need is the strength to deal with the problems of quotidian life, a sense of having the power to deal with everyday problems, as well as large ones. The power to take their own decisions, without being constrained by traditional ideas of honour or sacrifice, an ability to see beyond these ideas, to see things with their own eyes with their own minds.

Deshpande is of the opinion that the female of the species has the same right to be born and survive and to fulfil herself and shape her life according to her needs as the male has. It is not necessary that a woman may give up family life or hate men. The greatest revolutions can take place in the mind. It is not necessary to walk out, to commit adultery to divorce, to defy and reject traditions. Devayani, too, has the supreme joy out of her moment of self-realization.

A woman's self-assertion and self-realization which is the major concern of Deshpande as a novelist reappears in her new novel *Ships That Pass*. Tara and her sister Radhika are new, educated and independent women who do not play the roles enjoined on them by the society. They are capable of taking their own decisions which are not affected by the ideas of honour or sacrifice. They move away from patriarchal values to the values of self-identity and assertion of women's rights. Even in a disturbed state of mind Tara displays courage and spirit to face the horror of her family life on her own. She is fully aware of her duty and responsibility towards her husband and son. But she cannot sacrifice her own interest for others. Conscious of her inherent abilities she is very keen to "find out what there is that I can do" (90). That is what she expects from her sister: "There's always a real you inside. Don't drown that real you in a man, in the family" (91). From her friendship with her sister and Dr. Ram Mohan, Radhika comes to understand the meaning of life and the significance of self-assertion and self-realization. She has the courage to defy convention and overcome cowardice. Her marriage with the doctor is her own decision. He is the right person with whom she is sure to be her true self. Her faith in love that disappeared with the estrangement of Tara and her husband is restored—"I believe in love—if friendship is part of it" (136). Her love for the doctor contributes to her moral growth. She comes to possess two laudable attributes self-realization and compassion for others.

The situation portrayed here reminds us of Jane Austen with whom Deshpande has close similarity despite the fact that the two novelists come from different space and time. Like Jane Austen, Deshpande is a conscious artist with a commitment to humanitarian concern. She portrays a limited world which she knows best. Deshpande's novels are about the lives of ordinary women. She creates a familiar world in which authentic experiences of Indian women are effectively projected. In an interview she admits: "...my books go into the female and the psychology of the human female which a textbook may tell you about but a living human being you create in a book can tell you much better" (Kuortti Joel). Like Jane Austen, Deshpande chooses her own literary limitations. Her world is self-contained but the larger context is supplied by the values that govern the one she creates. Her moral message insists on the merits of good conduct, good manners, sound reason and marriage as an admirable social institution. She never scorns love but she balances its often disruptive nature with complementary qualities of self-knowledge and self-discipline. The attainment of self-realization on the part of the heroine is Deshpande's favourite theme, indeed goodness in her would almost be equated with the capacity for self-knowledge.

WORKS CITED

Das, Agnibesh. *Book Reivew*. New Delhi: July 17, 2012.

Deshpande, Shashi. *Ships That Pass*. New Delhi: Rupa Publications India Pvt. Ltd., 2012. Author's Note. All subsequent references to this edition are indicated by page no. in parenthesis.

——. *Writing From the Margin and Other Essays*. Delhi: Penguin, 2003, p. 109.

——. "Afterward", *Shakti: Multidisciplinary Perspectives on Women's Empowerment in India*. Jaipur and New Delhi: Rawat Publications, 2003, p. 319.

Joel, Kuortti. ed. *Tense Past, Tense Present: Women Writing in English*. Kolkata: Street, 2003, p. 34.

Quoted in *Deccan Herald*, Wednesday 22 August, 2012.

Roy, Vaishna. "Not Convincing" in *The Hindu Sunday*, July 1, 2012, p. 6.

"Writing is Catharsis" in *The Hindu*, 28 July, 2012.

CHAPTER

17

Image of Madhu as a Rebellious Character in Shashi Deshpande's Novel *Small Remedies*

Sanjay Prasad Sharma

Woman has been undoubtedly integral to the study of literature all over the world. She has inspired literature and has been its pivotal theme too. She herself is also a creator of literature and therefore a woman's presence in literature is all pervading. This is true of Indian English Literature as well. Ever since the dawn of civilization woman has been a myth, a metaphor, a symbol, a deity or a devil. But what is the real image of woman? What is her real character? What is her real nature? What is her real entity? Has she any identity of her own? Several such questions have to be asked and answered? As a matter of fact, there are several images of woman painted by novelists in Indian English novels—woman as a wife, a submissive creature, a fierce rebel, a mother, a sister, a beloved, a friend, a mistress, a floozy etc.

In *Small Remedies* (2000), Shashi Deshpande seems to be at her best. In this novel her protagonist is an urban, educated middle-aged woman. Y.S. Sunita Reddy aptly remarks: "Her protagonist is still the urban, middle-aged and educated woman, but her canvas has broadened to encompass a cross section of people who belongs to different communities, professions and levels of society. Madhu Saptarishi is not much different from her counterparts Indu, Sarita, Jaya, Urmi, Sumi, in age, education and family background." Reddy also says, "All of them in some measure or the other face upheavals in their marriages—upheavals which are inevitable when a woman refuses to conform to her accepted role as wife, mother or sister. But moving away from her near perfect portrayal of a traditional Kanadiga-Maharashtrian Brahmin family, Deshpande ventures to write about a *Goan Christian* family and also mentions a *Muslim Tabla* player and briefly touches upon his life and the people surrounding him, notably his grand daughter, Hashina."

The novel opens with Madhu, the narrator of the tale, travels to small town Bhavanipur from big time Mumbai to write the biography of Savitribai Indorekar, doyen of the *Gwalior Gharana.* She arrives in the wake of her adolescent son Aditya's death carrying with her the bleeding wound of that loss. In a sense, she is escaping, trying to get away to piece together her shattered life, "moving through the rubble of (our) devastated lives, searching for something, for any bits and pieces (our) past."

This search leads her to Bhavanipur and Savitribai—whose daughter was once Madhu's childhood friend—and to a young couple who open home to her. This couple Lata and Hari, as well as Savitribai and her student Hashina, become the counterpoint to the past that Madhu tries to escape.

In a review, Meenakshi Mukherjee briefly sums up Deshpande's works and observes the noticeable change: "In *Small Remedies*, Deshpande is attempting much more than she did in her earlier novels—all fives of them different from each other but smaller than this in scope.... But none of them gathered up as this new novel does, in one large sweep, the plurality, diversity and contradictions of our composite culture where an Anthony Gonsalves (the reference to *Amar Akbar Anthony* is deliberate), a Hamidabai and Joe can all be part of Madhu's extended family, and the daughter of *Ghulam Saab* can opt, though not very easily to get accepted as Shailja Joshi."

Madhu, the narrator of the tale is writing the biography of a famous classical singer, Savitribai Indorekar, doyen of the *Gwalior Gharana.* She plays with classical music. Of the four remarkable novels as I have read in recent times that deal with music—Vikram Seth's *An Equal Music*, Salman Rushdie's *The Ground Beneath Her feet*, Bani Babu's Bangla novel

Gandharvi and now *Small Remedies*, Shashi Deshpande, I think faces the toughest challenge. They have to do with incompatibility between the discourse of Hindustani Music and the English Language.

In her biography Madhu writes, Savitribai as a small-sized woman. Physically she appears to be a frail woman. Looking back, Madhu remembers her as:

> Savitribai as a small-sized woman. Even from my child's perspective she had seemed petite. Age and illness have so shrunk her that she's a doll-sized woman now. She was also, in my eyes, a very beautiful woman, but my standards had not been very high.... Savitribai with her fair complexion, her gold-bordered sarees and pearls had stood out among the tired, shabby women I saw around me. Now I realize that she must indeed have been very attractive. (14)

There are different yardsticks for men and women in our society are obvious to Madhu who, in her childhood, was a witness to the rejection of Savitribai by a conventional society. She remembers how in Neemgaon "each family had its place marked out for it according to religion, caste, money, family background, etc." (138).

Madhu is aware that her father with his unorthodox ways was an oddity. Being a widower and bringing up a daughter on his own with only a male servant at home, observing no rituals or religious customs and openly indulging in a drink or two every evening, he obviously stood out in a conservative place like Neemgaon. But, looking back, Madhu realizes that while people were willing to overlook her father's eccentricities and his foibles they were not so generous when it came to accepting Savitribai. He was a popular and trusted doctor. "Being a man he could get away with much. He could live way he wanted without open censure or disapproval" (139). It is only when a woman dares to defy conventions that people are shocked. As Madhu observes, "In a sense neither of us belonged. Muni's family, with her singer mother, absent father and another man—a Muslim sharing the home, was of course radically, shockingly different" (139).

For a man to indulge in his love of music and even to have a singer for a mistress was alright. But, for a daughter-in-law to be learning music seriously, as if she was going to be a professional, was scandalous and unmistakable. Though Bai and father-in-law supported and encouraged her, Madhu could imagine the anger, contempt and ridicule she had to face from the other women when she returned to her life among the women after her music classes. She could imagine the jibes and the way she would have been cast aside like an untouchable. She says:

> To be set apart from your own kind, not to be able to conform, to flood the rules laid down, is to lay yourself open to cruelty. Animals know this, they do it more openly their cruelty towards the deviant is never concealed. But the subtle cruelty of persistent hostility leaves deeper wounds. There is always the temptation to succumb, to go back to the normal path and be accepted. To resist the temptation speaks of great courage. (220-21)

Madhu also remembers the gossip surrounding Bai in Neemgaon. There was a Station Director who frequented Bai's house and got her many contracts with the radio and was generally believed to be her lover. Madhu remembers the children teasing Munni and calling him her *Mama,* a kind of euphemism for a mother's lover. Bai denies the existence of any lover while recounting her story to Madhu. But to the town, in Madhu's childhood, it was very simple why would a man go out of his way to do so many favours for a woman, only would he visit her so often? All such assumptions ending finally in the conclusion: "A woman who had left her husband's home—What moral would she have, anyway!" (222).

Madhu left quiet confused at times about Bai's courage or lack of it. She had, undoubtedly, led the most unconventional life anyone in her society would ever imagine. But behind these acts of bravado was a woman who wanted to conform, to be accepted by society. Savitribai was not to stereotypical feminist with a devil-may-care attitude. This is evident in her blanking out *Ghulam Saab's* name while relating a story of her life to Madhu, her biographer. This reveals her anxiety to cover up her youthful indiscretion in order to present a picture of respectability. She even goes to the extent of hiding the details of her daughter born through her association with *Ghulam Saab*. Madhu who is aware of Savitribai's past and her daughter Munni, is unable to digest her indifference to her daughter, more so, because Madhu herself is a doting mother, grieving over the death of her son.

Madhu feels that she can give Bai the immortality she desires only if she is willing to pay the price of revealing her daughter to the world—a daughter where existences she had successfully obliterated until then. She cannot understand why, when she had the courage to walk out on her marriage and family, she was so frightened to reveal the existence of her child. She wonders how "She gave that child the name 'Indorekar'—the name she adopted as a singer (from her mother's home town Indore)—not compromising either her maiden name or her married one, Meenakshi Indorekar. Marking her out as her child alone, not the child of her marriage, not the child of her lover. This surely is a statement I cannot ignore" (169).

Munni, however, desperately hankered after the name her mother had left behind and went to great lengths to dissociate herself from her father and after a while, her mother, Bai had found conventional life stultifying, but Munni yearned for it all her life. As a child Madhu recollected how Munni refused to accept *Ghulam Saab* as her father and instead concocted stories about a lawyer father who lived in Pune. She also remembers how the girls in their neighbourhood tormented her with questions:

> What is your name?
>
> What is your father's name?
>
> Where is your father?
>
> Who is the man who lives with your mother? (77)

Years later when Madhu met Munni in a bus and recognized her, the later refused to answer to the name of 'Munni' or even acknowledge her childhood friend. She declared that her name was 'Shailaja Joshi', trying as it were, to desperately wipe out any connection with her past.

Apart from Savitribai, Madhu's narrative also includes another character or perhaps more remarkable woman, her aunt Leela who was "a head not only of her generation, but the next one as well" (94). She was a fiercely independent woman and was strongly committed to the communist ideology. She had participated in the *Quit India Movement*, but was critical of Gandhi Ji's principles of *Ahimsa* and *Satyagrah* and thought that it was ridiculous to allow oneself to be beaten up. As she grew older, however, she mellowed down and regretted some of her actions. It was evident that she was no run-of-the will activist, but a woman who had the courage of her convictions. She resigned from her party when she felt that the party's reaction to a political situation was not appropriate.

Though Leela was a generation older than Madhu, she was financially independent and supported herself. When her first husband, Vasanth, died, she took up a job and educated her brother-in-law. She lived in the crowded *Chawls* among the cotton mills and worked for the welfare of the women, afflicted with T.B. It was this which first brought her into contact with her second husband, Joe, a doctor who had established a clinic especially for T.B. patients.

Leela and Joe were poles apart and Madhu exclaims at the strangeness of Joe falling madly in love with her. He was a widower with two children, spoke impeccable English and was very widely read, quoting from his favourite writers at the drop of a hat. Literature and music were the two great forces of his life, in addition to medicine, Leela on the other hand, were 'Ayahsaries', according to Phillo, Joe's housekeeper. She spoke no English and knew nothing of literature or music. She had no sense of humour. But there was a wonderful companionship and a beautiful relationship, according to Madhu.

Leela disliked the superior status her family gave itself and wondered what made them so special. She did not find anything even remotely worthy in their holding on to the lands which they had inherited. She did not believe in the caste system and was the only one among Madhu's relatives, who accepted Madhu's parents' marriage and invited them to stay with her when they had no place of their own.

Leela was a passionate believer in the communist ideology but did not hesitate to speak up against the party when the need arose. After putting in years of hard work, she was sidelined by the party bosses and never reached the top of the hierarchy while men who worked under her reached there easily enough. Once a widow of a sitting member, who was killed, was given a ticket to stand for elections. This provoked Leela, who had never earlier complained, to comment, "It seems you've go got to become a widow for them to remember that you exist" (224).

Savitribai too understood how much difficult it was for women to rise to the top when compared to men. Madhu wondered if she had ever heard the phrase gender discrimination but she had certainly experienced and accepted it as the normal course of things. Madhu remembers how she had once commented caustically speaking of a young instrumentalist who had reached the pinnacle in no time: "Now-a-day they become *Ustads* and *Pandits* even before they have proper moustaches".

At the final stage of the novel we notice that Madhu the narrator of the story is in the foreground of the novel. She is commissioned to write the biography of Savitribai. She has always been intrigued, even as a child by Bai's relationship with Ghulam Saab and Munni, their daughter. The novel covers that period of her life when she is grieving over the death of her only child Aditya. In remembering and retelling the stories of Leela, Savitribai and Munni, she presents the glaring inequalities in gender in society. The pity of it is that some of the victims are not even aware of the injustices heaped on them. Madhu herself is a victim of sorts of which the reader is aware only towards the end of the novel. She had been brought up as a child by two men—her father and Babu, a male servant, but she had no complaints. On the other hand, she felt pity for the children who seemed to be constantly harrassed by their mothers. She says:

> Motherless child that I am, motherhood is an unknown world to me. The mothers I see in my childhood are drab creatures, forever working, forever scolding their children; certainly they are not the women to arouse a sense of deprivation in me. (182)

But Madhu herself, turned out to be a doting mother and ever perceptive of her son's every need. Therefore, it was all the more tragic when Aditya, her son died in a bomb blast.

Our society has been so conditioned as to categorize women as immoral on the slightest deviation on their part from the normal course of behaviour. Madhu observed how Hari and Lata looked at her when she returned after inadvertently spending a night in a hotel room with Chandru. She thinks:

> It does not matter that Chandru is Som's friend and Chandru and I had been friends as well for nearly 25 years.... Men and women can never be friends. Men can be brothers, fathers, lovers, husbands, but never friends—is that how it is? (254)

The novel ends with the death of Savitribai whose death was not an ordinary one but very heartaching. At the time of death "Bai has gone into a *coma.* She has been cheated of the 'beg one'. Which, it now seems, will no longer come to her? She is crawling to her death" (321). Lying in bed and waiting for the day to break she says, "This is my last day in Bhavanipur. I remember my first morning here when I woke up in a strange house to the thought of living with two absolute strangers. I think of the voices I heard that morning. Voices raised in a choric harmony that woke me out of my uneasy troubled sleep. I never heard them again" (321).

In this novel, Shashi Deshpande has repeatedly expressed her displeasure at being considered the champion of oppressed women. It is indeed a tribute to her that some of the reviewers recognize her for what she is. Malati Mathur writes: "In portraying struggles of these women for identity, Shashi Deshpande waves no feminist banners, launches into no rabid diatribes. She drives her point home with great subtlety and delicacy."

Thus, in this novel Madhu projects the image of a rebellious woman—the woman who rebels against the norms and tradition of the society in a silent and subtle manner, trying to search for her own identity. Madhu's image as a woman is quite outstanding as she endeavours to time on quietly the kind of the life, she wants to live, silently and boldly transgressing the norms of the society. Thus, Madhu projects the image of woman subtly different from those of Deshpande's other protagonist.

WORKS CITED

Deshpande, Shashi. *Small Remedies*, New Delhi: Viking Penguin, India, 2000.

Mathur, Malati. "Rebels in the Household", *India Today*, April, 3, 2000.

Mukherjee, Meenakshi. "On Her Own Terms", *The Hindu*, 7th May 2000.

Reddy, Y.S. Sunita. "*Fractured Memories": Small Remedies*; A Feminist Perspective on the Novels of Shashi Deshpande, New Delhi: Prestige Books, 2001, p. 123.

CHAPTER 18

Aravind Adiga's *Last Man in Tower*: A Saga of Social Righteousness

Satendra Kumar

Last Man in Tower is the third novel of Aravind Adiga. A suspense-filled story of money and power, luxury and deprivation, a rich tapestry peopled by unforgettable characters, not least of which is Bombay itself. *Last Man in Tower* opens up the hearts and minds of the inhabitants of a great city-ordinary people pushed to their limits in a place that knows none. Ask any Bombaywallah about Tower A of the Vishram Co-operative Housing Society and you will be told that it is unimpeachably *pucca*. Despite its location close to the airport and bordered by slums, it has been *pucca* for some fifty years. But then Bombay has changed in half a century—not least its name—and the world in which Tower A was first built is giving way to a new city and a Mumbai of new development and new money, of wealthy Indians returning with fortunes made abroad.

When real estate developer Dharmen Shah offers to buy out the residents of Vishram Society, planning to use the site to build a luxury apartment complex, his offer is more than generous. Yet not everyone wants to leave, many of them have lived in Vishram for years, many of them are no longer young. But none can benefit from the offer unless all agree to sell. As tension rise, one by one those who oppose the offer give into the pressure of majority, until only one man stands in the way of Shah's luxury high rise: Masterji, a retired schoolteacher, once the most respected man in the building. Shah is a dangerous man to refuse, but as the demolition deadline looms, Masterji's neighbours—friends who have become enemies, acquaintances turned co-conspirators—may stop at nothing to score their payday.

As the novel opens we get the introduction of Ram Khare, the guard, who is enchanting the *sloka* of *the Bhagavad Gita.* Then one man comes who meets Mr. Kothari, Secretary of the Tower for getting the room on rent but he makes full enquiry. Tower A is what neighbours think of as 'Vishram Society'. It stands in the centre of the compound, six storeys tall, a marble block set into the gate-post says in weathered lettering:

> The face of this Tower once pink is now a rainwater-strained, fungus-licked grey, although veins of primordial pink show wherever the roofing has protected the walls from the monsoon rains.... Luxuriant ferns, green and reddish green, blur the corners of some windows, making them look like entrances to small caves. (5)

There is paucity of water found everyone being the first problem and the second one is the railway line full of noise.

Mary was the maid who used to map the tower. Mrs. Puri was also one of the residents of the tower who had her eighteen-year-old son Ramu, who kept turning to a stray dog that had followed them from the fruit and vegetable market (19). The novelist makes us acquainted with the lively messages coming from the mouth of the Secretary, "Men with gold rings are the biggest thieves in the world" (20). "Among young people today, it is a common thing for boy and girl to live without marriage. At the end, one says to the other, you go your way, I go my way. There is no sense of shame in the modern way of life" (22).

Mrs. Pinto was the oldest woman in the society who was blind by sight. Mr. Hirannadani, the owner and original resident of 3B, a shrewd importer-exporter of obscure goods, known for his guile in slipping phosphates and peroxides through customs, had moved to a better neighboured (Khar West) where he contacts with an unmarried woman (journalist) and became the cause of dispute when the neighbours found condom tumbling to the doorstep (23).

One of the most important characters of the novel is Masterji known as Yogesh Murthy who used to teach tuition to the children of colonizers. Masterji is of modern view, he is a widower. *A widower without a TV will go made*, revealed Mrs. Puri. His wife Purnima died of cancer and daughter Sandhya had fallen from train. Now he is survived by only son Gaurav, resides in South Mumbai. Masterji was "lean, moustached and of medium height, in physical terms, a typical representative of the earlier generations. Good with language, generous with books, passionate about education, an adorant to his society" (30). Purnima's favourite dialogue is, "Man is like a goat tied to a pole" (44).

Two characters namely Dr. Nayak and Dharmen Shah are found discussing the current theme of the society being the burning issue. "Look at the trains in this city. Look at the roads. The law courts. Nothing works, nothing moves; it takes ten years to build a bridge" (55). Mr. Shah is always in a mood to purchase property cheaply in order to build the modern posh building but a few people opposed him although his right hand Mr. Shanmugam tries his best to convince the people.

The author did not miss to draw the picture of the Indian philosophy of *Jeevo Jeevashay Bhojnam* when he narrates the lines, "The water buffalo moved near the sand, turning its long curved horns from side to side; a crow glided to the earth in between the buffalo's horn, and sucked a worm raw out of the hole" (65). He further provides the universal truth, "a man cannot punish himself for his desires, which are sent to him from another world..." (77) besides this image, "Instead of the image of his wife's soul, Masterji saw himself with the body of an eagle, flying over an ocean, as if his own death..." (78).

Once Masterji was also recapitulating the past incident of his daughter Sandhya who got a train accident, while observing her album:

> She had been on her way to college when someone had pushed her out of the train. A packed compartment in the woman's first class in the morning-someone had elbowed her out. She had fallen head first on to the tracks and lain there like that. Not one of her fellow passengers stopped the train. They didn't want to be late for their work. All of them women, good women. Secretaries. Bank

> clerks. Sales managers. She had bled to death. The very child that he had made, the tracks had unmade.... Surely in the men's compartment someone would have pulled the emergency chain, jumped out, surely someone would have.... (103-04)

Many months Masterji did not travel in train owing to this tragedy. He was Mr. Trivedi who performed rites for both—his wife and daughter and now Trivedi wants to do on the anniversary of his wife, "When Purnima died, it was Trivedi who had performed last rites, with coconuts and incense, at a temple in Bandra" (125).

Masterji revealed that "A man's past keeps growing even when his future has come to a full stop...the more he looked at his daughter's sketches, the more certain places within Vishram—the stairwell where she ran up, the garden that she walked around, the gate that she liked to swing on-became more beautiful and intimate" (150). Masterji used to read religious books regularly and his philosophy of life is to live, "like a lotus in a dirty pond, be in the world but not of it" (160). He never took napping or siesta in his life nor he allowed his family at all, "Not once in his adult, not even when sick, had he allowed himself this luxury, he had scolded his wife and daughter if he caught them napping in the afternoon, and punishment, by a stroke of a steel foot-ruler applied to the knuckles, his son" (161).

The novelist also snatches the picture of knotting in the *sari* as a reminder of modern clock watch through the character of Mrs. Puri who "tied a knot into her sari to remind herself...to be settled after Ramu went to sleep with his Friendly Duck" (157). Dharmen Shah, whose wife died just month before, being one of the spokesman and mouthpiece of the novelist, unveils his painful past with Rosie, who is like Nabbu or Smita, the story of his childhood in his village Krishnapur,

> I was four years old. She (my mother) jumped into the well in our house in Krishnapur.... A year later I had a stepmother. She had four sons. They got all my father's love. He would not even look at me with

> kindness. The worst part was this: he made me feel ashamed, Rosie. It was as if my mother's suicide were my fault. He would glare at me if anyone ever mentioned it. (86)

Dharmen Shah who is the big contractor of Tower A, distributes sweets of bride to make them agree in order to start construction but 3-4 people said no but he told his PA Mr. Sanmugham "to spend another lakh or two lakhs, if you have to. Spend even more than that, if absolutely necessary" (146). By his crooked trick he could get the permission of renovation in Tower B and the foundation was celebrated with crackers and lightening while he was in search of Tower A. As a result of that he sent his assistant to Mrs. Rego for convincing her but she flatly refused to say yes. Although he waited for her in nearby *dhaba* where she ultimately turned but she ate nothing of Shah's food yet she brought for her two children. It was a sort of bribe to them which they unwillingly accepted. Mrs. Rego unveiled, "An old woman's night is so small: a young woman's night is the whole sky" (175). Finally, Mrs. Rego was procured by Mr. Shah. Now three persons were left alone. But of three Masterji was firm to stay there till death as he unlocks,

> I do not want to take Mr Shah's offer. I have lived in Vishram Society with my friends and I wish to die here with them.... I have memories here Mrs Puri. My late daughter, my late wife. Shall I show you Sandhya's sketchbook? It is full of drawing of the garden. Every tree and plant and spider's web and stone and.... (184-85)

Meeting after meeting was held some in the presence of all and some in the absence of Masterji. One day a meeting was held in absence of Masterji and even notice was prepared in which each one showed his/her consent for the demolition of society with the forgery signature of Masterji. But as he approached and came to know he tore the notice into pieces and scolded each one for mustering such illegal courage.

Ram Khare, the security guard of the society, who used to read the *Gita* and the preaching of Lord Krishna to Arjun about the soul. He narrates his memories:

> When he was in his teens he had had hopes of playing cricket for Bombay in the Ranji Trophy; when he was in his twenties he dreamed of buying a home of his own; when he was in his thirties of taking his old parents on a pilgrimage to the city of Benaras. At the age of fifty-six he found his life had contracted to three things—his daughter Lalitha, ... his rum and his releigion. (205)

Mr. Shah did his best to convince Masterji by hook or by crook but he was as firm as stone. He invited him in a private parlour to give bribe, "There is a term we use in the business. A sweetener. Another thousand rupees per square foot? We don't reward teachers enough in this country" (224). But Masterji turned down his scheme like a house of castle and returned to his Vishram, "...man being like a goat ties to a pole. There is a radius of freedom but the circumstances of our actions is set" (228). After this face to face meeting Mr. Shah played another trick of threatening on phone to seduce Masterji, "Old man, is that you.... I have a lesson for you, old man; if you do not leave the flat, there will be trouble for you.... Act your age, old man. Grow up. Take money and leave before something bad happens" (233). Later on Masterji lodged unknown FIR and the police gave him consolation, "This is not a neighbourhood where a teacher can be threatened" (243).

Masterji also wrote letters to almost all national papers to open the *maurcha* against Mr. Shah, the so-called confident Builder, "So I am the last man in the building now, he thought" (261) as the rest of the residents wanted to vacate Vishram. Lastly, he faced a bolt not from the blue but from the black people living in Vishram Society who expelled Masterji from this Society and cut the light and water of him, "He lay in the dark, feeling the weight of two floors of people above and three below who had expelled him from his home of thirty-two years; who do not even consider him a human any longer-one that needs light and water" (276). Masterji took the help of advocate Mr. Parekh and replied the notice and proved his right to live there.

But with the changing passage of time Mr. Shah also purchased the lawyer of Masterji who also gave the advice to vacate the society and revealed "Politicians and police are in their pay, you must know that. They shot an elected member of the city corporation dead the other day. In broad day light. Did not you see it in the papers. Old men must stick together in this new world" (284). But Masterji replied, "You are threatening me now...my own lawyer" (284). "I am threatening you sir, with the facts of human nature" (284). Finally, he left his chamber and once again remembered his dead wife, "Poornima, swoop down and lift me from the land of the living" (286).

Masterji now accessed to his son Mr. Gaurav who works in a private bank afar from Bandra and shared all what happened with this advocate, "Corruption has become physics; its precise frequency had been discovered by Mr Shah. If he engaged another lawyer, that thick tongue would fine tune him too. My last hope is Noronha. At the *Times*" (286). His son strives to contact Noronha but meanwhile, Shanmugham again warns him of, "Old man we have given you every chance, and now we are left with no..." (288). Finally, the newspaper had the nose for Masterji, "Last Man in Tower Fights Builder" (296).

It is universal truth when misfortunes come, they come not alone but in battalion. Likewise when a person falls in misfortunes, even his shadow starts leaving him in the lurch. His only and solely son also strives his best to persuade his father for the sake of his wife and son—Ronak but he too got disappointment in the end and he burst out,

> Every other parent in Vishram Society has thought of their children. But you not. It's always been this way. When I was in your physics class in school you punished me more than others...all my life I've been frightened of you. You and that steel foot-ruler with which you hit my knuckles. For sleeping in the afternoon. It that a crime. You made my mother's life a living hell. Fighting with her over every five rupees she spent. Don't you remember what she said on her

> deathbed, when I asked if she had had a good life? She said, I had a happy childhood, Gaurav. A happy childhood, Father—and nothing after that.... Your students always came first after you. Always. Not that they had any love for you.... They used to give you nicknames in class. Dirty nicknames. (298)

Mr. Shah distributed sweets to each one of the members of which some accepted and some turned down and he also invited many people face to face, "Mrs Rego had been to some restaurant in Juhu, Masterji had been asked to his palace in Malabar Hill; she (Mrs Puri) thought the minimum for her would be a five star" (316). Of course Mrs. Rego and Masterji had been brought to see him in the Mercedes but she, to her surprise, on bike. After her meeting with him she called Gaurav finally to leave the society for the welfare of all. The result was that Gaurav did for what every father to be ashamed of, in black and white a notice to the residents of Vishram Society Tower A:

> I, Gaurav Murthy, son of Y.A. Murthy, am putting this notice up to say I have no father. I am shamed by the actions of the present occupant of flat 3A, Vishram. After promising my wife and me that he would sign the proposal, he has not signed, this is not the first time he has lied us. Many jewels in my mother's possession and also bank certificates in her name meant for me and my son Ronak, have never been transferred to us. My son Ronak, my wife and I will perform the one-year Samskara rites of my mother on our own. We request all of you not to associate us with the actions of the present occupant of 3A, Vishram Society. (320)

This was the bolt from the blood of his own colour but Masterji did not lose his heart and continued on the path of fight remembering , "Mr Shah came to Bombay on barefoot" (323) and now he is Bombay millionaire. The same idea came in the mind of Ajwani who

> thought about the details of Mr Shah's story. Now it seemed to him that something was wrong with the

> information. If Shah had come to Mumbai with only twelve rupees and eight paise and no shoes on his feet, how did he manage to open grocery store in Kalbadevi. (379)

"All of Vishram Society is helpless before a bird," revealed Mrs. Puri (356). Finally all the residents of Society—Mr. & Mrs. Kudwa, Mr. & Mrs. Kothari, Mr. & Mrs. Puri took the final step of murdering Masterji and throwing from the roof to prove that he committed suicide. Kothari brought the Scotch tape and also inserted the spare key to 3A into the hole and struggled with it:

> The door opened. Masterji had gone to sleep in his living room, his feet on the teakwood table, the Rubik's Cube by his chair. Kudwa came in behind the others and closed the door. The secretary moving to the chair, cut a piece of Scotch tape and pressed it over Masterji's mouth. That awoke the sleeping man.
>
> He ripped the Scotch tape off his mouth.
>
> 'Kothari? How did you get in?'
>
> 'You have to agree now, Masterji. Right now.'
>
> 'Think of Gaurav,' Mrs Puri asked. 'Think of Ronak. Say "Yes." Now.'
>
> 'Get out,' the old man said. 'All of you get out of my—'

The secretary moved before he could finish the sentence: he cut another slice of Scotch tape and tried to stick it over the old man's mouth. Masterji pushed the secretary back. Mr. Puri stood stiff near the door.

> 'Kothari, do not touch him,' Ibrahim Kudwa warned.
>
> Masterji, recognizing the voice of his protector, got up and began to turn in his direction.
>
> 'Ibby,' Mrs Kudwa said. 'Ibby.'

At once, Ibrahim Kudwa lifted the hammer he had brought from the Secretary's office, lunged forward, and hit Masterji on the crown of his head, who, more from surprise than anything else, fell back into his chair with such force that it toppled over and his head landed hard on the floor. Masterji lay there like that, unable to move, though he saw things with clarity.

Kudwa stared with an open mouth, the hammer dropped from his head. He tried to shout but he heard only a groan from his mouth. Kothari thought of a line from the *Mahabharata*: "...King Dhritharashtra's heart was like a forest lake, warm on the surface but icy at the bottom" (389).

Kothari hit his forehead again. Now Sanjiv Puri came from the bedroom with a large dark thing, which he lowered on to Masterji's face. His legs thrashed, not to free themselves, but to take him down to the bottom of the lake faster. Two men lifted Masterji's body and moved towards the door, two men staggered with the body which had begun to squirm, to the edge of the terrace, on a count of three, they heaved it up and pushed:

> And this was because he was neither good nor bad enough and neither strong nor weak enough. He had lost his hands; he had lost his legs; he could not speak. Yet everything he had to do was right here, in his head. He thought of Gaurav, his son, his living flesh. 'Help me,' he said. Then he realized that the thing that was blocking his passage was clear, and he was falling; his body had begun its short earthly flight—which it completed almost instantaneously—before Yogesh Murthy's soul was released for its much longer flight over the oceans of the other world. (391)

Down on the ground it lay, sprawled, in perfect imitation of a suicide's corpse. It was the mystery whether Masterji was murdered or suicide for the Inspector yet he quizzed each resident one by one but got no conclusion.

"If you enjoy fish, you have to swallow a few bones," unraveled Mr. Shah (288). After the Masterji's soul went to heaven he demolished the Vishram Society and constructed a new villa of his dream. Mr. Shah added with Rosie, "Teachers are the worst kind of people, Rosie. All that time they spend beating children, it makes them cruel. Twisted on the inside" (304). When Shah was hospitalized she was with him with the desire to love and marriage.

> He could feel Rosie's fingers still warm on his own. He could smell her legs on his trousers. He thought again of the abandoned old mansion that he passed everyday on his way down Malabar Hill, the green saplings breaking through the stone foliage. It was as if each green sapling were a message: *Leave Mumbai with Rosie, find a city with clean air, have another son, a better one—you still have time, you still have...* (408).

Shah took a deep breath and closed his eyes. On any evening Juhu beach is overwhelmed with cricket matches of poor style and great vigour; on a Sunday, perhaps a hundred matches are in progress along with the length of the sand. After match Mrs. Rego invited all for the speech on late Masterji which was delivered by all one by one.

> 'I once saw Masterji sitting under a tree near the temple. He was eating all the fruit...' spoke Timothy. (415)

> '...late Mr Yogesh Murhty, was my neighbor, but I do not have much information about his life...', spoke Ajwani. (416)

And finally Mrs. Rego unlocked,

> Boys, where Masterji was born, where he studied—these things don't matter now. What matters is this. He did what he believed to be right. He had a conscious. No matter what people said to him or did he never changed his mind, and never betrayed his conscious. He was free to the end.... All we need are a few more good men like Masterji and this island, this Mumbai of ours, it will be a paradise on earth. As it used to be, when I was a girl in Bandra. When I see you boys sitting here before me, I know that there are future Masterjis among you and this city will again be what it was, the greatest on earth. And so gentlemen of the cricket team, so as not to keep this speech going on any longer, let us all stand up and put our hands together, and give a hip-hip hooray in

memory of our late Masterji, whom we promise to remember and honor. (416)

As long as Masterji lived in Vishram Society he did not allow Mr. Shah to enter in the Tower A, though his wife and daughter left him in the lurch of the journey of life. Though Masterji is no more in this world, yet his soul is immortal and becomes the subject of debate and discussion for the future generation for the years to come for Mumbaiwashi. The novelist put the full stop to his novel with these lines, '*Nothing can stop a living thing that wants to be free*' (419).

Adiga also used the Hindi vernacular words in the novel to create the interest of Hindi people, *sansad* (21), *channa* (22, 23, 336, 337), *amaltas* (51), *gutka* (57, 62, 99, 107, 203, 229), *chai* (59, 242, 313, 403), *sahib* (62), *baniyan & dhoti* (63), *biryani* (67, 68, 182, 375), *paani-puri bhelpuri, gulab jamuns* (70, 174, 354, 355, 409, 410), *sari* (71, 76, 109, 117, 127, 159, 187, 258, 272, 286, 322, 327, 354, 360, 366, 369, 386), *almirahs* (76), *aa chalk e tujhe* (91), *dhaba* (92), *chappals* (98), *dhobi-ghat* (102, 174, 187), *kebabs* (109, 110, 111), *petticoat* (174), *pucca* (182, 312, 412, 418), *gulmohar* (191), *mantras* (191), *barfi* (192), *baksheesh* (215), *khachada-wali* (216), *idli* (227), *dhanush asana, yoga* (235), *goondas* (238, 243, 313, 347), *saarey jahan se accha* (251), *kala paani* (270, 374, 380), *khaki* (280, 313, 316), *dharma* (283), *vada pav* (285), *dhoti* (286), *pappad* (287), *lungi* (293, 337), *salaam* (297), *mafia, kebab* (300), *geet amar kar do* (311), *moosambi* (316), *burqa* (322, 415), *ishwar allah tero naam* (326), *salwar kameez* (360), *namaaz* (367), *basmati* (369), *kumkum* (370), *banians* (375), *chow mein* (392), *gutka, ek aise gagan ke tale* (394), *lungi* (404), *salaam* (406), *allah* (418), *dabba-wallahs* (419).

WORK CITED

Adiga, Aravind. *Last Man in Tower*. Noida: Harper Collins Publishers, 2011.

(All the references are quoted to the same edition.)

CHAPTER 19

Githa Hariharan's *Fugitive Histories*: A Tale of Trauma and Catastrophe

Deepak Kumar Singh and *R.P. Pradhan*

It is absolutely not an easy task to situate a writer who is still living and writing with vigour and skill. This is more so in the context of Githa Hariharan who believes in plurality. Hariharan's corpus may not be sizeable still she has managed to represent her views with fidelity to character and situation. Her commitment to the representation of the human condition in her novels remains the matter of utmost significance. She realizes her responsibility as a writer and exhibits her social and political consciousness. This is evident in her concern about women's question, gender, communalism, prejudice, etc. As a writer she accords greatest value to human life and never lags behind in attacking the enemies of human kind. Life for women even in contemporary times offers very limited choices. Moreover, women are constrained by the prescriptive as well as proscriptive norms of the patriarchal society. These limitations further constrict their lives but Hariharan argues for the equality of both genders. Notwithstanding the centrality of gender and women's question in some of her novels, there are other issues of prime importance which are thematized in her novels. The novel *Fugitive Histories* (2009) reveal the ugly face of fundamentalism and communal prejudice leading to riots. Although each of her novels embodies an idea of seminal importance, it would be far from truth to assume that she is acting as an ideologue. Besides, she has repeatedly asserted that she writes fiction which may not be mistaken for political tracts. Similarly, she advocates activism but shuns being politicized because she is not publicity-crazy.

Githa Hariharan's novel *Fugitive Histories* (2009) is divided into three sections—Missing Persons, Crossing Borders and Funeral Rites—the novel recounts the pathetic but traumatic tale of 2002 Gujarat riots. Hariharan invested a lot of energy and time studying the documents and holding personal interviews with some of the riot-affected individuals. This book is definitely a vigorous attack on the most dreaded enemies of a healthy democracy—prejudice against a community and its ultimate expression as communal riots leading to a massive loss of property and life. There is a specific focus on the theme of loss in human lives. Mala has lost her husband Asad and though theirs was an inter-religious marriage, it was a model of understanding and love. Yasmin who figures prominently in the second section becomes a highly significant metaphor for the pain of loss as she has experienced the fear, pain and loss which accompany as well as follow a communal riot. Hariharan seems to condemn such riots as anti-human and conveys the message of amity, peace and understanding. The last chapter 'Conclusion' briefly sums up the observations made in the preceding chapters. It tries to situate Hariharan as a writer in the canon of English writing in India.

Fugitive Histories charts out the crisis which comes into force because of the walls which the forces of power in society erect not just to divide the people, but to keep some people in and some out. In an interview with S. Bageshree, Hariharan responded to her question regarding the central concern of *Fugitive Histories*. Asked whether this novel concerns itself with liberal spaces being under attack, Hariharan replied:

> Yes, but *Fugitive Histories* looks at these familiar ideas in a more personal, private way. It presents a mosaic of lives that collide in unhappy ways, but also in ways that produce love, passion and tenderness. After all, shrinking of public spaces also shrinks private spaces. The novel says that we can no longer be satisfied with overused rhetoric. A lot of people with liberal ideas would not hesitate to formally condemn prejudice against a community. But what

> happens to that same middle class person in day-to-day life when he or she is continuously exposed to the profiling of a community? There is a need to not just define prejudice, but also fears in our individual lives. Prejudice is not something that comes up only when we are in public meetings. (*The Hindu*, 4.8.2009)

The novel is divided into three parts: 'Missing Persons', 'Crossing Borders', and 'Funeral Rites'. The first introduces us to Mala and Sara and their loss of Asad. Sara, needless to say, goes to Ahmedabad and meets Yasmin in the second part of the book. Though the exact starting point of the third part is open to speculation and debate, one might assume, for purposes of convenience that it forms the part of Yasmin's present fears induced by the trauma of her past experiences. It is in this part that Yasmin gets her point of view. Yasmin emerges as an archetype of the victims of 2002 Gujarat riots. Even a walk to her school becomes a harrowing traumatic experience and comes up as a sad but bitter indictment of government's rehabilitation efforts directed to improve the plight of the riot-affected people. Hariharan's description of the time of riots and of the period preceding and following them is highly graphic, imaginative and appealing.

The first section of the novel is entitled 'Missing Persons'. It connotes a profound sense of loss on Mala's part that has lost her husband Asad. The novel opens a note of loss which begins with a picture of Mala's empty home in Delhi. Her children, Sara and Samar are settled in cities far from Delhi. The only companions left with Mala are a lifetime of sketches left behind by her late husband Asad and the memories they conjure. Sifting through them on restless afternoons and sleepless nights, Mala summons ghosts from childhood, relives the heady days of love and optimism when Asad and she robustly defied social conventions (because theirs was an inter-religious marriage Mala being a Hindu and Asad a Muslim) to build a life together—and struggles to understand how events far removed could so easily snatch away the certainties they had taken for granted.

The novel opens with Mala's attempts at digging her memories of her husband. The immediate object is the tin trunk containing Asad's sketches and papers. The box "was recognizable and unfamiliar, as if she had come face to face with someone she knew well but hadn't met for years" (*Fugitive Histories*, 1). The memory of her past life induces her to reflect on her present for which "she had to fine-tune her memory to set right the difference between what she remembered and what she actually saw" (1).

Mala derives both solace and sustenance from the thought that with old friends the years in between can collapse. Although she suffers the loss of her husband which is further intensified by her staying alone as both her children are away from her. As a mother and a single guardian, Mala puts more value on the individuality and independence of her children: "Go back to you work. I can manage. Get on with your lives" (3). Mala does this for the betterment of children though she also feels the pang of separation from them. She thinks as if her children teach her the art of survival or reconciliation. But she is keenly aware of the fact that this art of living is the real thing which means learning to live all over again.

Sara is more attached to Mala as she takes pains to visit her at Delhi at least once a month. Samar, being far away, keeps himself connected to his mother through cellphone, willing her to get on with life. To some extent, Mala's loss of Asad seems to be attenuated by the emotional sharing of her children. Mala shares her time between her job as a librarian at a school located on the outer fringe of Delhi and sorting out the relics (the belongings) of Asad and putting them in order. As part of this venture, she first cleaned Asad's cupboards, sorted out his clothing's, files and etc. While doing all this, Mala had to exercise lots of restraints, because she decided she had to learn to resist anything familiar which could emotionally unsettle or destabilize her.

The opening of Asad's trunk, more than that of cupboards, proves an altogether different experience which sweeps out her restraint and she is caught unawares in the vortex of memories of her husband and their past life together: "There are sketchbooks inside, what at first looks like dozens of them, packed tightly, row after neat row. Rows, piles encompass a lifetime" (5).

The first part of the novel called 'Missing Persons' covers nearly half the space of the entire book. Further subdivided into five chapters, this section brings to life Mala's memory of Asad, his creative life as an artist, the several displacements which they underwent before they finally settled at Delhi. In the opening chapter of the first section, Mala comes across a sketch-painting by Asad which, though being her husband's cheerleader, she had never seen. The description of this sketch is highly poetic and seems to give Mala a lesson to live and move on:

> The figures don't look at each other, but it's impossible to look at one without seeing the other. Their limbs are entangled though they don't touch. It is this strong sense of coupling that gives the image, and what the image stands for, meaning. But something more than the obvious sexual spark between them makes them throw their arms and legs in the air with abandon. (7)

The image seems to give a message loud and clear: I am alive! We are alive! The implications of this message for Mala are two-fold; she receives an impetus to live but she is, at the same time transported into her past life when she enjoyed the essence of togetherness with Asad—a sort of coupling as suggested by the image of the sketch. Mala discovers or rather imagines she has discovered a sketch of young girl standing on a stool. This too makes her recall her own childhood. In addition to these two sketches, Mala recalls with passionate intensity what Asad's life was like. This retrospective memory recasts Asad in a better and more appealing light than he might have been in his real life with Mala. However, the recollection is teasing when she thinks: "He's gone—or an uncharacteristically still and silent Asad was carried out of this flat. But he has left behind these, what she can only think of as an artist's diaries" (7). Mala wades through the diaries and sketches of Asad. She does all the things that stimulate (or help restore) normalcy. For her, normalcy really means returning to the school where she works as a librarian, including whatever mess the assistant librarian may have made in her absence. Her journey to school is not easy one. She has to go driving past the Delhi-Gurgaon border, doing battle with bigger and speedier cars and vehicles. She reflects that her routine work may help to be normal again but "she can't go back to being herself again, at least not yet" (10).

However, Mala is strong enough to admit defeat so easily. There are other possibilities of her staying normal because the loss of her husband Asad is beyond repair. She can keep herself busy in domestic chores and divide the rest of her time in communicating with her children and friends. Nevertheless, she is invariably put down with a sense of guilt that she is staying and living alone without Asad. A nagging fear haunts her:

> ...she is afraid of what she'll find in Asad's sketch-books, especially in the newer ones. She's afraid of the stories she may find there, stories that may collide. And once such a collision takes place, it's going to be hard to pretend ignorance of other lives, other people's stories. This may be why Mala is sitting in the terrace smoking a cigarette instead of going through the sketch books, or deciding whether she should share them with Sara and Samar. (11)

Mala takes recourse to going back to stories which have layers to be peeled off. These stories of her past life seem to form a kind of chain and Mala has to unravel them if she has to reconcile herself with the loss of Asad. This may lead to a beginning, an altogether different life without Asad. In the long chain of stories which are real and have affected her life positively, Mala recalls her parental household. As a child Mala (Malathi) wanted to find a place to be in or a thing to do that would set her free from her family, her home and school in the city, her annual summer home in the village. What she wanted was to be set free from herself. "What she really wanted was to be someone else" (15).

Mala distinctly recalls the moment when she arrived at this realization. When she was about ten years old, she visited her grandparental home in the village. The house was crowded and Mala had to spend her summer holidays there. Her memories of her grandfather and grandmother are crystal clear. Her mother equated living at the village home with "prison conditions." Her grandfather was a bully. Never lovable but sometimes human, he was the undisputed warden. The real inmate, a prisoner for her own good was Bala, her grandmother. Bala suffered from hysteria which shows that she was psychologically and emotionally repressed and deprived. She was strange, and ignored everyone most of the time except Mala. Mala knew that Bala ignored the running of the household as if it had nothing to do with her. Neverthless, Bala's choice territory was the house: "But it was impossible to imagine Bala anywhere but in that house. She was married to the house even more than she was married to Mala's grandfather" (15).

Bala's story highlights the constraints which were imposed on women. First, it was child-marriage because she was married at the age of twelve, a week after she began menstruating. Her husband was only seventeen but he was well-versed in putting his household and life in the strict order of patriarchal rules. Giving little attention and regard to his girl-wife, he made rules which Bala was to follow. The "law of the threshold literally and categorically applied to Bala because she was never allowed to step out of the house, not even to visit her parents. She belonged to the house" (15).

As the above statement suggests, the house was ruled by the grandfather who rigorously and despotically turned it into a prison house. The others, like Mala and her parents, turned into inmates of a prison the moment they arrived in the village. They became a family by the sheer fact of numbers, and of course, obedience. Thus, there was no room or scope for the slightest independence or the assertion of individuality under the despotic rule of the grandfather. Even Mala's father was more or less reduced to an overgrown child. As for Mala and other children of the house, they were taken as a lot, a cluster of squirmy appendages.

Mala is transported back to the memory of her grandmother, Bala and she recalls how she had evolved a tie with her grandmother. She also remembers how her despotic (and rather cruel) grandfather had confined Bala to storeroom because he had seen her sitting on the roof of the house. This memory of grandmother's unwarranted punishment is interspersed with Mala's memory of her life at Delhi with Asad and her children, Samar and Sara. Bala's last days were marked by disease and pain as the following excerpt makes clear:

> When Asad finally met Bala, she lay on her filthy deathbed. They had shaved her head when her husband died, but now that she belonged to no one, Bala had grown her hair into long, stringy rat-tails. She refused sponge-baths most days and her sari was a shameful rag just like her choli on the days she agreed to wear it. But she insisted on her being combed twice a day, oiled with a stinky hair-oil and plaited. She then arranged the oiled-tails on her body in loving display, one for each side so she had parallel hairy tracks running from neck to waist. (25)

Thus Bala's behaviour may be seen as a reaction against her husband's cruelty who imposed ruthless instructions on her. Interestingly, it was Bala who informed Mala that she had a twin brother who died soon after birth. From the bits of Mala's memory of her grandmother Bala, we gather that Bala was a miserable poor woman who suffered immensely at the hands of her 'dangerous' husband. Intermixed with her recollection of Bala's pain, is the memory of her own adult life when her first child Samar was born. It was only then that Mala realized the import of her grandmother's words spoken to her. While thus invoking her past, Mala recalls that Asad came into her life when she was twenty-one.

In the third chapter of the first section of *Fugitive Histories*, Hariharan brings into focus the life of Sara living in Bombay (Mumbai) with her room partner Nina who is planning a documentary on the riot-affected people of 2002 Gujarat riots. Hariharan makes the best use of authorial skill in depicting the minute details of the city called Mumbai—its crowded railway stations, busy traffic, posh and no-so-posh (ordinary) localities. In her description, the city comes alive:

> But as she gets nearer the area where she has a room as a paying guest, the breeze seems to recognize this is not an up market place: it goes still. The sea too is not far away. The roads get narrower: the traffic is even slower than before. There is not a single glass building, only stunted old structures stuck to each other on both sides. They sit frozen in bewildered dementia, forced to hear blaring horns all day long and to stare at shops, too many shops, and pavement hawkers. (37)

Thus the city where Sara lives in a building is a patchwork of buildings and slums, unfolding both its beauty and ugliness at the same time. She stays with her landlady Rosy. Sara's roommate is Nina. Hariharan creates a unique sense of humour when she draws an analogy between the windows of the buildings and TV screens. Sara checks out the reality shows being played out in the buildings across. This is how Hariharan puts it:

> The windows of these buildings are like innumerable TV screens, except the actors here are live ones, not images on a screen. If there is something promising going on, the kind that long shots can't do justice to, Rosy uses a pair of binoculars. (38)

Sara's roommate, Nina, is planning a documentary on the riot-affected people of 2002 Gujarat riots. Incidentally, this touches upon the central focus of the novel. Nina's brief write up of what she plans to do is clear from the first paragraph of her document:

> On 27 February 2002 the Sabarmati Express was attacked in Godhra Station in Gujarat and two of its carriages set on fire. The train was carrying Hindu activities on their way back from Ayodhya. Godhra is a 'Muslim locality'. In the days and weeks that followed, the Muslims of Gujarat became the target of brutal violence. The statements of survivors, eye-witnesses and relief workers suggest that state

> officials and the police connived with the attackers. (42)

While reading this paragraph on the screen of her laptop, Nina modifies the last phrase 'in their own city' and changes it to 'in their own country'. This phrase clinches the central theme of the novel and also explains its title *Fugitive Histories*. Her documentary aims at narrating the stories of some of these people in their own voices. What happened to them in 2002, what the state government did (or didn't do) to rehabilitate them and how these people are now trying to rebuild their lives.

This recollection of Laila's sad plight shakes Sara to the roots. She feels the shock of Laila coming back to the present, even if it is only by proxy. It is a shock in which disbelief takes charge, keeps Sara from coming face to face with unknown sources of terror. Sara distinctly recalls Laila's second marriage and then feels the void left by Laila's tragic end. The news reached Sara quite late that Laila and her husband were burnt to death when Mumbai erupted. In that sense, Sara's memory of Laila places the communal violence in perspective.

However, it would be worth its while to briefly consider the situation and reactions which Mala's inter-religious marriage with Asad caused, since it has a bearing on the second section of the novel which concerns the miserable plight of the victims of 2002 Gujarat riot. When Mala married Asad, there were angry reactions from all quarters of Hindu community in Madras. This storm of communal prejudice blew over after a while. Both Mala and Asad held tenaciously to their 'love marriage' which continued through to the end of Asad's life. Thus, the first section of *Fugitive Histories* is marked by a sense of loss which ramifies into Mala's unbearable loss of her husband, and then into Sara's painful memory of what happened to Laila. Laila had to suffer two tragedies: divorce and her brutal death by being burnt alive alongwith her husband in the flare up of 2002 Gujarat riots whose murderous tongue reached far and wide including Mumbai.

Space figures as a prominent trope of loss in *Fugitive Histories*. Dilkush mansion which is referred to at the end of the first section prefigures the change and an acute sense of loss brought about by the riots in the lives of Muslim populace in Gujarat, especially the city of Ahmedabad that unfolds the story of Yasmin who remains at the centre of narrative in the second section of the novel.

Hariharan has discreetly chosen the title of the second section: 'Crossing Borders' which embodies discrete meanings in varying contexts. Crossing of borders has been inevitable and integral part of human civilization. Places are circumscribed, bearing a nomenclature and a line that identifies its autonomy as well as its interconnectedness with other places (spaces). Thus borders demarcate one place from another. In Sara's case, the city of Ahmedabad which she purposely visits is an appropriate example. After arriving there, she finds that Ahmedabad is as real as Mumbai and Delhi. But she feels oppressed with an unfamiliar fear of losing her carefully collected data and documents about the Gujarat riots of 2002. She tries to remain cautious and alert lest she should lose her documents which are the potent tools of her research through fieldwork. Her notebook and files are packed with solid facts which are supposed to facilitate her task. But Sara does not believe in the authenticity of the documents which she has assiduously and painfully collected. Her mind acts like that of a surgeon who makes marks on a specific part of the body, reaches inside and performs the surgery. She feels intrigued by the situation which has appeared to her only as an overview. So she gets caught up in the dilemma of what is real and what is unreal. She is anxious about two things: the right questions to ask and the courage to broach those questions.

Hariharan places the riot-torn city of Ahmedabad in perspective. It seems as if "it has been reduced to its recent history, as if the city itself dates from 2002" (107). The city configures as a living being. It doesn't care what they (Sara and Nina) see, whether it's ancient clothes drying sadly on wires outside windows or in mock-balconies, a range of hillocks made of hardening garbage, or autos pretending to be buses, packing any number of live bodies into its stomach so it can expel them like pellets at work and the school and the market.

Obviously, this is a scathing comment on modern civilization, especially the city which is bereft of sanity, compassion. It is likened to a mob which is solely guided and motivated by the heat of passions and reduces human populace to head-hunting, hating devils. Both Nina and Sara intend to excavate the story of human suffering caught in the strangle-hold of communal violence. While venturing to document the human condition of the dislocated but temporarily relocated Muslim population of the city, Nina advises Sara to keep up appearances lest their slightest mistake should hurt the sentiments of riot-victims. This is why she warns Sara to carry no equipments, cameras, tapes or notebooks. As they are going to meet some of the dislocated families in their relocated colony, Nina says: "We'll listen to them, let them decide what they want to talk about. Let's go to the Alis first you remember those photos you saw? And the girl Yasmin?" (109)

As they cross a highway, Nina takes a cue and tells Sara that the locality beyond it is sometimes called mini Pakistan for the simple reason that it is largely inhabited by muslims. The area is a bizarre mix of bungalows, short and tall buildings, many hovels, too many hovels. This area is ironically known as 'safe for muslims zone'.

Interspersed with the account of this area specified for the rehabilitation of the riot-affected, displaced muslims is a poetic description of the road which outlines the trajectory of Sara and Nina's targeted place of visit:

> Despite the people, the open shops, the stalls, the noise, all the breathing, throbbing signs of, the road is somehow cheerless, as if it has assessed the whole business of living and knows it's pointless. (110)

Nina has taken care to carry 'some vegetables and fruits from Mumbai' in a plastic bag and hands it over to the mother in the family, who comes back with glasses of water and a bowl with a few powdery biscuits. The mother is very alert, careful and attentive. She does everything quietly as if the last thing she wants is to draw attention to herself. What follows this is an account of Yasmin whose personality and figure loom large in the second part of the novel:

> The daughter, Yasmin, has a thin, watchful face. She lets her mother do the talking but she doesn't leave the room. .... When Nina talks to her, all she does is nod or shake her head. Her eyes are on the sewing, she's silent, but Sara thinks she can sense the girl letting her guard down despite herself. (111)

Yasmin is a shy girl. She is interested in Bollywood films. She asks Sara if she is in films. When Sara tells her that she is helping Nina, Yasmin's initial enthusiasm seems to cool down a bit and she says 'Then you don't know Shabana Azmi?' In fact, Yasmin is a committed fan of Shabana Azmi and her mother tells Sara that Yasmin has 'seen all her pictures, she thinks Shabana Azmi will come and save her from here'. This fantasy of Yasmin embodies the harsh reality of riot-affected people. The more striking aspect of Yasmin's family is evident in their fugitive status which is borne out by a detailed description of the room in which they live. Yasmin's mother does tailoring along with training a few girls in the art. The details about the room are minute but graphic:

> What she [Sara] has to see is a room that appears to be more walls than room, walls reluctant to let in too much sun or fresh air. Walls painted a long time ago, a blue-green colour that darkens the room to a deeper shade. There's a battered old wooden cupboard against one of the walls, it has a broken glass front that has been taped with newspaper. There are also three chairs and a small table.... The room is neat, but it's full of plastic bags with cloth, skirts, thread, mirrors and sequins, paper patterns. It looks like luggage on a train platform. Someone has just arrived or someone is about to leave. (112)

Apparently, the details of the room may not appeal to one who takes them casually but when we connect the antecedents of Yasmin's family with their present condition, the room virtually becomes a metaphor of their lives. That is, before the riots erupted, Yasmin's family had a good living with a house of their own having enough space for them. A house of one's own also stands for social and economic status and security. Unfortunately, the riots have pushed lots of respectable families into a state of disgrace. Furthermore, the trauma of loss—both of lives and property—haunts the psyche of the rehabilitated people. The new accommodation loudly announces the sad stories of their forced displacement, reminding them harshly that they are fugitives in their own country. All these facts come to light when the story of Yasmin's and others' unfolds. Sara's cryptic documentation of Yasmin's story reads as follows:

> Yasmin, seventeen years old. Yasmin's father had a shop downstairs in the house where they used to live. Yasmin's mother used to be a housewife, now an NGO helps her and other women in the area sell the skirts they stitch and embroider. Yasmin's brother was in college when the trouble started, he did not come back home. He's still missing. Her father was forced to sell the house for whatever he could get and move to a safe area. He's trying to set up a small business, but is often sick. Yasmin is in the last year of school. She wants to go to college, but she failed her boards last year. (114)

Having written the above on the monitor of her laptop, Sara speculates whether it will help her particularize the general or generalize the particular. She imagines that Yasmin is lying alone on a mattress on the floor of the front room, waiting to fall asleep. There is a poetic line loaded with beauty, meaning and poignancy: "Across the city, across the border, Yasmin lies in bed, waiting for sleep to find her" (114).

Evidently, the life in this 'safe-for-muslims' zone is hard. She has suffered considerable loss-especially her brother Akbar and her home—which persists in her psyche. Besides, the memories of the riot haunt her mind as a traumatic experience. Being ill, her father is mostly confined to the house provided to them by the government as a temporary relief. Yasmin, her mother and her father are intensely aware of their fugitive status. Still, the desire to survive makes them somehow carry on. Yasmin is particularly scared of darkness which may not be seen as a common childhood trait as children usually fear darkness. Her mother also has a sense of fear because she persistently warns Yasmin to go straight to her school and return in the same way. Their trauma and suffering have been caused not by fate or unexpected turn of events but by fanatics infected with communal frenzy. Yasmin's fear of darkness is succinctly expressed in a single line: "But, like Yasmin; sleep too is afraid of the dark" (115).

Yasmin is now in the XIIth class, the final year of her school. This time she has to really study history and geography. She had failed in three subjects including geography and history last year. She has to pass this time because she is already seventeen and a half, almost eighteen. Hariharan highlights Yasmin's loss:

> She has lost two years, once when she couldn't do the tenth boards because of what happened, once last year when she failed the twelfth boards. Two years lost. Lost is a better word than gone, what is lost may be found. There are still stronger reasons for her to pass the examination this time. She has to pass because her mother is working too hard and her father is getting sick too often. It doesn't matter how much housework Yasmin does, they still have a hard time earning enough, sending her to school. If she passes, she can go to college, her mother has already agreed. Then may be she can get a job. (116)

The family is really hard-pressed and Yasmin is both aware of the difficulties and her sense of responsibility. However, the greatest loss for her as well as for her family is her brother Akbar. He is not lost, but finally gone. Earlier she used to think it was only till he came back from wherever he was hiding that she had to be Abba and Ammi's daughter and son. Now she knows he will not come back, she has to be their daughter and son forever.

Adversity is sometimes a good teacher. Yasmin has learnt from the difficulties how to act responsible. She has to play the dual role of a daughter and son but in the absence of her brother she has to do it all alone somehow. If she gets a job, the conservative elements in her community would find it better not to advise her parents against her further education. It's better she does some work right now. She is resolved to help her parents and is unwilling to be a burden on them.

Yasmin's mother also appears as an individual who is strongly determined not to admit defeat in the midst of adverse circumstances. She has a firm will to survive and sustain and maintain her family at all costs. This is why she works harder on the sewing machine than her physique might allow her. Yasmin as a grown-up child realizes as well as recognizes the value of her mother's toil and sacrifice. Though they are the worst-affected victims of the communal riots in 2002, they gather up their scattered energies which is fortified by their strong desire for survival. However, it would be naive and puerile to assume that their past is absolutely forgotten or consigned to the recycle-bin of memory. The memory of trauma—a consequence of the riots—persists, haunting the psychic terrain of the family now reduced to a trio (Abba, Ammi and Yasmin) because Akbar, the son and the brother is lost forever.

Staying in a poorly lit and almost dark place as they do, they feel not because of inconvenience but because darkness conjures up the ghost of already traumatized memory. Thanks to Sultana, another young girl affected by riots, who accompanies Yasmin for quite some distance on her way to school. Unsurprisingly, Yasmin is perhaps the only Muslim girl among the rehabilitated Muslims who attends school at the 12th standard level. This is definitely and indisputably a solid proof of Yasmin's courage and resolve to steer ahead in studies. Notwithstanding the obstacles and difficulties, Yasmin aspires to get higher education and a respectable job which might enable her to stay independent and help her parents. Yasmin has made many promises to Ammi, to Abba, to herself, to Akbar, though he is no longer with them. She is sometimes invaded by the apprehension lest she should fail in keeping her promises. This fills her with insecurity and fear but she seldom loses her self-confidence and conviction that she must win in the end.

A walk in the open day-light comes as a big relief to both Yasmin and Sultana though it may not be a free-walk but a short trip to school for Yasmin. On her way to the school, Yasmin accompanied by Sultana passes by a lane which bears a muddy, morose look. Hariharan's description of this make-shift settlement for the victims of 2002 communal riots exposes the pathetic condition to which these poor riot-affected Muslims are doomed:

> As always it's boxed in by the one-room and two-room tenements standing about like orphans. No wonder its lost hope that someone will save it from being suffocated by the smell of its drains, or by the big black plastic water tank sitting heavily on its stomach. (120)

In the close vicinity of these pitiable tenements is Rahim Park Society. Ironically enough, it has no semblance to any park Sultana and Yasmin have ever seen. The cramped nature of its space, garbage piled here and there obviously explain the inhuman condition of its inhabitants:

> Everyone in this society lives practically in the open. It's as if life itself has taken a look at the shelter the society people have been given, screwed up its nose and moved out in the open with its bundle of possessions. The society people scrub the pots and pans around them on the ground, they soap clothes under a tap and dry them, and they roll agarbattis and sort out rags and waste. People fill water at the pump. Some sit on the saggy ropey cots to recover from what they have already done, others catch their breath because there's still so much to do. (120)

The foregoing picture of the Rahim Park Society and its inhabitants amply explains the fugitive and uncertain nature of their lives. They have no security, no facilities and lack even the bare minimum of life to subsist on. Moreover, the poverty is further intensified by the filth and dirt all around the Rahim Park Society. Hariharan's realistic observation of the surroundings comes as a sharp attack on the way things are there: Yasmin and Sultana can only helplessly and dolefully watch the miserable plight of the inhabitants while walking past the makeshift structures ironically called abode. Of the fugitives, a place full of tents and jhuggis pretending to be houses, a park, a society:

> Pretending to be *rahim,* merciful. Any one can see that real houses would not have half their insides spilling out or the toilets outside in a row like a goods train, or the garbage mounting and toppling over so it can get swallowed by the open mouth of the train. The swampy drain itself runs down the middle of what should be the road, except this road hasn't had the time or heart to become one. The houses like they've been built by children or by crazy adults. Or by people desperate enough to hope that scraps of tarpaulin and canvas or sheets of plastic and filthy cloth will make a roof over their heads, and a few poles, bricks and stones, even some stray crates and old tyres, will keep the roof standing in place. (120-21)

The sight of the slum area compels Yasmin to compare her plight with that of jhuggi-dwellers. On her way to school, Yasmin is thinking too hard. She thinks that she is lucky enough to have two rooms even if they are dark and small. She enjoys a greater security because her dwelling is in a safe area. There is a water tap in the bathroom. She realizes that her family has the facility of electricity. She is lucky that she can go to school. She feels lucky because her father got some money at least for the old house. But her feeling of being more fortunate than the denizens of Rahim Park Society gives way to a sense of insecurity when Sultana leaves her company to meet her sewing classes. Now she has to walk alone on the longer road but she has to be very careful at the same time. Being careful means avoiding an empty road but also a crowd. It also means not going to shady or dark places or where there may be policemen. Yasmin is once again reminded of the communal violence, and the fleeting image of the perpetrators emerges distinctly in the guise of the instruments of violence "Trishuls, or swords, pipes, rods, hockey sticks" (125).

Violence subsumes arson, looting, killing, sabotage and other means of creating terror. In Yasmin's case, the fear of violence means being shied, watchful and alert against men. But most of all, being careful means choosing to live. She finds it very hard to forget being careful. To her, safety and life go together. And this growing sense of insecurity equips her with a tenacity to hold on to life with greater hope and energy. This is why the words 'careful, alert, guarding against, taking care, anything can happen' continue to make their sustained presence on the screen of her memory. However, Yasmin does seldom gain any relief in so far as the persistent feeling of being careful is quite exhausting.

Sara's surprise-visit to Yasmin's school during the lunch-recess temporarily relieves Yasmin of her persistent sense of insecurity. For purposes of privacy, Sara persuades Yasmin to move to a lonely place where Yasmin might eat her tiffin and unravel some knots which have stuck deep into her consciousness. And, unsurprisingly Yasmin is carried away by nostalgia and the pain of displacement from her parental house. Though her house came to be an offering in the inhuman communal violence and besides which her abba (father) was put under immense pressure to sell the house at a very nominal cost. The memory of her parental house evokes other memories, inextricably linked to it. She remembers the Muslim and Hindu houses of her locality. She distinctly recalls the each and every item in the household. Her father's shop on the ground floor, his bookshelf bequeathed to him as a legacy from his grandfather and the most painful memory of her brother Akbar missing during the riots all appear vividly on the screen of her mind. She remembers how her parents suffered agony and humiliation at the police station which they frequented for days together to lodge a missing persons report for their son Akbar. The way in which her parents were treated by inhuman and callous policemen exposes the corrupt and communal nature of the police force in our country. Yasmin wistfully remembers her old parental house, her friend Saba who lived in the neighbourhood but the memory of her forever-missing brother, Akbar haunts her mind. Thus, the loss of home and of her brother in the wake of communal riots persists in her psyche as a traumatic experience. There are, however, other related memories of her mother, grandmother which appear as a silver-lining in the gloom of the painful sense of loss.

Suddenly, Sara's journey down the memory-lane is disrupted when she becomes conscious of the real and hard world around her. At this moment she is engrossed in the memory of her brother, Akbar. She recalls that she was waiting for him because he promised to be home earlier than usual that day. However, she knows it for certain that "Akbar is not coming back unless Allah is saving him for a miracle" (135). Later on, she curses herself for unfolding this personal and sad narrative to Sara. It is often seen that sharing the grief with a friend or sympathizer reduces the intensity of pain but in Yasmin's case it is not so: "Not only has Sara made Yasmin go back home, she has made her dream pointless dreams about her old house and old life. Akbar is gone; she's finished with waiting for him" (135).

However, when Sara and Yasmin part, Yasmin once again finds herself alone, and being alone implies being insecure with a staring or strange look at her from around the nearest corner. She feels disoriented even while she meets her classes. Now she remembers only one thing her missing brother—and the words spoken by the not—so unkind police sub-inspector, "Missing is not so bad, it's better than dead" (136). She is filled with a mixed sense of guilt and remorse at having failed to recount the remaining part of the narrative about Akbar. She gloomily reflects that both the missing and the dead can be found in hospitals and morgues. Her memory of what her abba had seen while searching for Akbar lays bare the ugly fangs of communal violence and the ravages perpetrated on innocent and helpless victims. Nowhere can we find such a heart-rending description of communal violence evoked through the metaphor of body by Hariharan:

> Abba spent all his time visiting the places where the corpses were piling up. He had never seen something like it before, the parade of body after body that bore so little resemblance to a real body. To a human being, even a dead one. It's the first time Abba saw that being dead meant being cut. It meant missing a body part—an arm, a leg, even a head. It's the first time Abba saw that being dead could also mean a new body part had grown overnight to stick out of the old body: an iron rod, a hammer or a wooden stump or a screwdriver. There was one body with its belly torn open: a spear stuck out of it like a sharp-edged hand calling for help. Another body was just burnt coal. If you touched it, it would fall apart; crumble into a small heap of grimy black powder. Abba didn't know how the others managed to recognize fathers, mothers, sisters and brothers, people, in these monstrous discoloured lumps of flesh, bloated, burnt or cut to pieces. (137)

This ghastly sight of the dead bodies testifies to the ravages and inhuman cruelty performed on innocent people who were victimized on account of communal hatred. Yasmin's father continued to visit morgues and hospitals in the hope of tracing his missing son, Akbar. But he was being consumed from within everyday as his hope turned to dismay. The continued failures almost filled him with a profound sense of loss and left him a broken person:

> Every night he came back home looking a little more lost. He was losing bits of himself, the bits that made him human like everyone else. At this rate he would lose himself entirely, he would grow lighter and quieter till he was only a nameless shadow. (137)

Although the pain of losing Akbar hung too heavy on Yasmin's family, the loss of their parental house together with the looting and burning of their shop was no mean loss to them. The rioters had left a message which amounted to a very real and grave threat to their lives. Incidentally, the message was written on the charred wall outside the shop. In such a difficult situation, Yasmin's father was left with no choice except selling the house for almost nothing. They found themselves homeless fugitives in their own country, accepting their helpless lot with a sense of resignation:

> They had to quit their neighbourhood, their India. They found a safe house in a Muslim neighbourhood, but in return the safe house made them give up their house, their old life. It made them gives up on Akbar; shift him secretly in their heads from the missing lot to the declared dead list. (138)

In fact, Yasmin is haunted by a terrible sense of insecurity and fear especially when she is alone on her way back home from schools. Even the looks of some stranger apparently staring at her scare her beyond measure. The rehabilitation home provided as an accommodation by the government always seems unfamiliar and she feels certain that she can never belong to this new dwelling even though her family has been staying there for five years:

> She doesn't want to see it because when she finally gets out of here she doesn't want to remember this building's face. They have lived here solely for almost five years, but it's still a pretend home. It will remain that no matter how long they live here, no matter how hard they try to make its mean rooms theirs. The only way to bear it is to see it as a temporary arrangement, to hope she is here on the way to somewhere else. (150)

Nasreen's narrative is supplemented by the sad tales recounted by other women. Sara along with Nina carefully recorded the splintered bits of their tragic experience in order that all this exercise might help them to piece together the facts for their proposed documentary on Gujarat riots of 2002. The injuries, insults and inhuman cruelty exercised on Muslims shows the ugliest face of communalism in India. No doubt, Sara and Nina had neither witnessed nor heard such awful and terrifying accounts of the first-hand experience of inhuman cruelty in the name of communal hatred. But both of them are surprised by the resilience shown by a host of Muslim women.

Despite the ravages and ruins caused by the communalist forces, they have a strong desire to live—to survive even in the midst of the boring, dull and joyless circumstances. They don't want revenge, they want to live again.

This documentation of the broken lives of the fugitives—especially Muslims—is placed in contrast with a description of the Sabarmati Ashram. Hariharan makes an ironic dig at the title 'the abode of peace' which stands as a counterpoint to the city of Ahmedabad torn apart by both visible and invisible borders. The author recreates a situation in which an angry mob of communal fanatics storms the Ashram, violently subverting the ideal of non-violence preached and practiced by Mahatma Gandhi. The following extract aptly brings out the extent of cruelty perpetrated on Muslims:

> It's a diverse crowd. It's brought together doctors, goondas, housewives, looking for God, policemen, real estate agents in search of a killing, priests in search of new converts and ministers in search of votes. But they must have something in common. They have worked hard together; they have just finished with Nasreen's dargah. They have just lit the match-stick in Zakia's little neighbour's mouth. So he burst like a firecracker. They have just shot Sabiya's sister as she was drying clothes in her courtyard. They have just finished gang-raping Zainab's sister as her little son cried. They have just left Zuleikha's girls with stumps of wood in their vaginas. They have just given Abeda all those bodies to wash, some of them burnt, others split down the middle.... They have just burnt Noorjehan's husband and father and son. They have just converted Mahrukh's neighbor's corpse with kerosene and cremated it. (175)

After having witnessed the trauma and tragedy of communal riots in Ahmedabad, Sara leaves for Delhi to meet her mother Mala who now lives alone in her DDA flat. Sara is intrigued by a casual question about her 'native' or 'identity' by a co-travelling elderly couple. They shrink from her when she tells that her father was a Muslim and mother a Hindu. She is, in fact, in a fix to decide whether she is a Muslim Indian or Indian Muslim.

The third section of the novel is titled 'Funeral Rites'. Once again the reader is drawn, perforce, into the lives and memories of Asad, Mala, Samar and Sara. The memory of Asad, who is dead and gone forever, haunts not only the minds of Sara and Mala but the house itself also seems to be trying to adjust with the empty space caused by Asad's departure. It is through memory that Sara can recall as well perform in her imagination the funeral rites of her father. There are several snatches of memory concerning Asad, his life and his paintings. Back home, Sara feels disoriented in her own room. ".... The room no longer holds her like a cradle. She is too restless to sleep. She would like to go out somewhere, but if she does, she'll feel guilty about leaving Mala alone" (187).

In fact, Sara is intent on dissipating her boredom and restlessness for which she searches for some old but solid tokens of memory. By sheer stroke of her luck she comes by an old photograph—black and white—in which she stands with Samar flying a kite. She is drawn to her past—her childhood and its memories. Her attention veers to another photograph which brings to life the memories of Laila who lives in Sara's neighbourhood during her childhood. The photo was taken the last time Sara met Laila, the day before she was married. Not for the first time but the second, the time Laila married for love. She, however, feels sure that the Laila of this photograph is not her usual self, but a self-conscious pose offered for the sake of decency and etiquette.

It is difficult to say that Sara deliberately or purposely strains her memories, trying to seek refuge from the pain of boredom. In her busy schedule as also in her personal life, Sara keeps old memories and things at bay, but the moment she is in the dark, they're back, the tenacious intruders she has known for little more than a week. This obviously relates to Yasmin. She has already lost Laila, the shocking news of Laila and her husband burnt to death in Mumbai riots reached her only through newspapers. She is afraid of losing Yasmin because Sara is not fortunate enough having many friends. She is, no doubt, keen on helping Yasmin but the very idea of documenting her story into a script comes up as something awful to her.

In addition to the unhappy memories of Laila and Yasmin, Sara is drawn to retrospective memories of the time and space which formed the last days of her father Asad's life. Asad lived and died as an embodiment of the ideal of freedom and communal harmony. While recalling the moments when Asad died and the way his furneral rites were performed. Sara feels the pain of loss as well as the helplessness of her mother and that of her own. Sara wished that her father Asad should be cremated after Hindu rituals but her brother Samar decided otherwise, ignoring what Sara and Mala thought or felt about the final rites:

> Though he knew how Sara felt about it, Samar decided that everything must be done as it should be done. Asad had never said anything about what he wanted done with his body, so in his heart of hearts he must have wanted to do the right thing. He must have wanted to go back to his ancestral home, its airless waiting room, till his maker was ready to see him. Mala was silent through it all. She let Samar do what he wanted. Actually she didn't seem to notice what Samar was doing. Sara doesn't know if it was shock or complete defeat, but Mala was tearless, withdrawn, as if Asad's body had nothing to do with her. (195)

Both Sara and Mala engage in what may be called the imaginative journey into the world of loss. While Sara visits Asad's grave both in person and in dream, Mala seeks psychic comfort through the memories of Asad by looking into his past sketchbooks and even visits Asad's studio to find an unfinished painting. There is a aweful intensity about the way she remembers Asad but the pain of loss makes her more lonely, sad and desolate. However, Sara has other props to hold on and she decides to help Yasmin as she is not prepared to suffer another loss. Yasmin was both a discovery and an opportunity for her to prove her worth, to make her life meaningful. As a step in this direction, Sara has written to Yasmin, promising her to help with the admission and the college fees.

Sadly enough, any hope of future in Yasmin's family is tainted with fear for the precise reason that they are still under the pernicious impact of the trauma that uprooted them and devastated their lives to the extent that they can never be or feel the same (as they were before riots). In a stern response to Ferozakhala's objection (It's dangerous for our girls to travel, anything can happen) against Yasmin's going to Mumbai for education, Yasmin's mother explains the cruelty directed against Muslim women: "The angry ones on both sides want to put our daughters in burqas so they can prove their point. Did their burqas keep our women safe five years ago?" (227).

Yasmin's mother means that Muslim women are under attack from two sides: conservative Muslims and communalist Hindus. No doubt, Yasmin feels brave and admires the courage of her mother who notwithstanding the trauma of past and the fear of present stands resolute to educate her daughter further. As a fitting link to this resolution, we come across Sara's reflections on her plan to help Yasmin. This can give a positive and fruitful direction to Sara's life, something she may realize as worth doing: "The difference she [Sara] can make in Yasmin's life is nothing compared to the difference Yasmin can make in Sara's life. The thought comes to her whole and indisputable..." (235).

The foregoing analysis of the novel reveals that there is an intense feeling of loss which envelops the lives of Yasmin and other victims of the riots. At the other end, though interlinked with the narrative of Yasmin, there are Mala and Sara trying to get over the feelings of pain, defeat, and loss and, of course, reparation. Hariharan's creative vigour comes to its fullest growth as she documents the contours and maps of human feeling of loss, be it Asad's death or Akbar as forever missing. The writer has forcefully celebrated the value of human life and cast aspersions on anti-human forces of communal violence and riots.

WORK CITED

Hariharan, Githa. *Fugitive Histories*, New Delhi: Penguin Books, 2009.

List of Contributors

Amod Kumar Rai, Assistant Professor, Deptt. of English, BPG College, Kushinagar.

Deepak Kumar Singh, Head, Deptt. of English, D.A.V.(P.G.) College, Lucknow.

Deepak Upadhyay, Assistant Professor, Deptt. of English, Agra College, Agra.

Gourhari Behera, Associate Professor, Deptt. of English, D.D.U. Gorakhpur University.

Jaya Kapoor, Associate Professor, Deptt. of English and Modern European Languages, University of Allahabad.

Nazneen Khan, Assistant Professor, Deptt. of English and Modern European Languages, University of Lucknow, Lucknow.

Neeru Tandon, Associate Professor, Deptt. of English, V.S.S.D. College, Kanpur.

Prakash Chandra Pradhan, Associate Professor, Deptt. of English, BHU, Varanasi.

Prabin Sinha, Head, Deptt. of English, D.A.V. College, Gorakhpur.

R.P. Pradhan, Assistant Professor, Deptt. of English, V.S.S.D. College, Kanpur.

R.P. Singh, Associate Professor, Deptt. of English, Lucknow University.

Rahul Chaturvedi, Assistant Professor, Centre for English Language, Central University of Jharkhand, Ranchi.

Sanjay Kumar Swarnkar, Associate Professor, Deptt. of English, CSJM University, Kanpur.

Sanjay Prasad Sharma, Assistant Professor, Govt. P.G. College, Agra.

Sarvajit Mukerji, Associate Professor, Deptt. of English, University of Allahabad.

Satendra Kumar, Head, Dept. of English, Govt. P.G. College, Lansdowne, Pauri Garhwal.

Shikha Singh, Associate Professor, Deptt. of English, Gorakhpur University.

Sudhir Kumar Arora, Assistant Professor, Deptt. of English, M.H. P.G. College, Moradabad.

Sunita Rai, Assistant Professor, Deptt. of English, K.N.I. Sultanpur.